Creating a
"Win-Win IEP"
for
Students with Autism

2nd Edition

Beth Fouse, Ph.D.

Future Horizons, Inc.

Future Horizons, Inc.
721 W. Abram Street
Arlington, TX 76013

800-489-0727; 817-277-0727
817-277-2270 Fax

Website: www.FutureHorizons-autism.com
E-mail: edfuture@onramp.net

This book is for information purposes only.
Contact your attorney for legal representation.

ISBN #1-885477-52-X

About This Book

This book has been written to provide parents and families of students with autism necessary information and skills to meet the challenges of the Individualized Educational Program (IEP) process. Although it should be especially helpful to parents of children who have been recently diagnosed as having autism or other pervasive developmental disorders, it also contains useful information for parents and educators who have more experience dealing with the IEP process. The book takes readers through the child-centered educational process from the stages of initial diagnosis to implementation and of students' individualized educational programs. The book provides practical suggestions for parents and school districts based on federal and state legislative requirements, case law, and the many years of experience the author has in working with the IEP process as a teacher, special education administrator, regional special education consultant, and a university instructor.

This second edition of the book includes relevant information from the *IDEA Amendments of 1997* and the final regulations published on March 12, 1999. Although further interpretations and clarifications may come out later, this book reflects the current status of the requirements.

Chapter One establishes the need for this type of book. Chapter Two addresses the definitions of autism and discusses the basic components of the IEP. This chapter also includes information about state and federal regulations impacting the field of autism. Chapter Three addresses other legislation, such as *Section 504, ADA,* and *FERPA* which relates to the education of students with autism.

Chapter Four begins the child-centered process with a discussion of appropriate assessment necessary to guide the development of IEPs. Chapter Five addresses the actual mechanics of the IEP Committee meeting and is followed by a discussion in Chapter Six about goals and objectives. Chapter Seven discusses the provision of related services with recommendations related to students with autism. Chapter Eight looks at the special issues related to development of behavioral goals and objectives versus development of behavioral or discipline management plans. Chapter Nine addresses issues and concerns about placement of students with autism. Chapter Ten discusses the IEP process related to students with high- and low-functioning autism and Asperger's syndrome.

Chapter Eleven discusses common mistakes made by personnel in school districts while Chapter Twelve discusses common mistakes made by parents. Both chapters provide suggestions for facilitating the IEP process. Chapter Thirteen, which is co-authored by Dr. Jane Ann Morrison, provides suggestions for resolving conflicts. The final chapter presents reflections on the IEP process and comments on future trends as they relate to students with autism. Chapter Fourteen also presents *Educator's ABCs for IEPs* and *ABCs of Parent Empowerment for IEP Meetings.*

About the Author

Beth Fouse, Ph.D. recently retired as an Associate Professor in the Department of Special Services, School of Education and Psychology, at The University of Texas at Tyler. She taught courses in special education and gifted education. Special education courses covered various disability areas including autism, communication disorders, behavior disorders, and mainstreaming/inclusion. She has over twenty years experience in the public schools as a classroom teacher and school administrator.

She works as an educational consultant providing family/parent training, school/home liaison services, on-site classroom consultation, and in-service training for school districts and educational agencies. She has Texas teacher certificates/endorsements in elementary education, serious emotional disturbance and autism, learning disabilities, mental retardation, early childhood handicapped, deficient vision, gifted education, educational diagnostician, school counselor, supervision, special education supervisor, and mid-management. She has been a certified instructor in Nonviolent Crisis Intervention through the Crisis Prevention Institute and was certified by Dr. Guy Berard as an auditory integration practitioner. She has published several articles in special education and gifted education publications. She is also co-author of a Phi Delta Kappa Fastback and FastTrack, *A Primer on Attention Deficit Disorder* and *A Treasure Chest of Behavioral Strategies for Individuals with Autism.*

Also contributing to this book:

Jane Ann Morrison, Ed.D., co-authored the chapter on conflict resolution and provided assistance in editing. She is currently Assistant Superintendent with the Lindale Independent School District. She has experience teaching regular education and special education and was a special education director for more than ten years. Her Texas teacher certifications include generic special education, high school english, gifted education, educational diagnostician, mid-management, and superintendent. She has co-authored several articles related to special education and gifted education with Beth Fouse.

Dedication

I dedicate this book to my husband, William D. Fouse, and my father, Wilfred D. (Chris) Chrisner. They have provided financial, emotional, and moral support for many years. Their encouragement has been the stimulus for many endeavors in my professional career. For this, I give them my love and appreciation.

Acknowledgments

I want to thank the students with autism and their parents with whom I have worked, for expanding my knowledge about autism They have taught me as much or more than I have taught them. For that, I give them my special thanks and admiration.

I wish to express my appreciation to my friend and colleague, Dr. Jane Ann Morrison, for her generous assistance in helping me edit the first edition of this book and co-writing Chapter Thirteen, *Resolving Differences*.

Additionally, I wish to express appreciation to Wayne Gilpin, President of Future Horizons, Inc. for having faith in my ability to write the first edition of this book I would also like to thank Polly McGlew for her assistance in editing the second edition of this book.

Beth Fouse, Ph.D.

Author Note

The names of individuals have been changed to protect their confidentiality.

Table of Contents

Figures

Tables

Chapter One
The Battle Rages On

When I reflect on my professional experiences with individuals who have autism, I see how many changes have occurred. Although there is still much progress to make, the field has progressed a great deal since Kanner (1943) first described children with autism. One memorable personal experience related to autism occurred many years ago when I was a public school special education director. Although I had a doctorate in special education with certification in several areas, including mental retardation and emotional disturbance, my knowledge of autism was limited. Autism had been discussed briefly in some courses about emotional disturbance.

Matthew <u>Can</u> Read!

A surprising experience occurred near Christmas one year. My office was on the same campus with special education self-contained classes for early childhood and older students with severe to profound disabilities.

Miss Davis, an early childhood teacher, came flying into the office. "Beth, Beth, Matthew can read!" She exclaimed. "Are you sure," I queried? I was shocked since four-year old Matthew could not even say his name when you asked him.

"Yes, yes!" She exclaimed. "He was straightening the books on the bookshelf like he usually does, when suddenly he opened a book and started reading! I couldn't believe it, so I had him read from another book. He reads about second grade level. Come see for yourself."

My innate curiosity spurred me to go see this remarkable happening. Just as Miss Davis said, Matthew could read. Of course, he still didn't communicate through oral language. When I asked him his name, he wouldn't respond. If you showed him a picture of a Christmas tree, Matthew could not say "tree." However, this young child sang the whole song, "Oh, Christmas Tree." This was a puzzling occurrence since we had not encountered children who could sing whole songs, but could not use oral language for communication.

At the 1996 Autism Society of America conference in Milwaukee, Wisconsin, Julie Donnelly described her son, Jean-Paul Bovee. He could sing songs at the age of two, but he did

not use oral language for communication. His first oral communication used a phrase from a song. He wanted to get on a large tractor and looked at his mother and sang, "with a little help from my friends." After using phrases from songs for communication, he expanded his language with more appropriate forms of communication (Donnelly, Grandin, Bovee, Miller, & McKean, 1996b).

Since school district personnel tried to do things the "right way," the teacher began to experiment with Matthew to find out more about his "hidden skills." Could he read numbers? Just exactly what could he read? Miss Davis found that Matthew could read most numbers and many words. She was astounded when he read from the blackboard, "one thousand, three hundred and eighty three." He was very interested in comic books and could identify and write the names of comic heroes like "Superman" and "Batman."

Miss Davis called his mother, assuming she would be thrilled. When the teacher talked with her, she was not surprised. His mother responded without surprise, "Oh, he reads the Sears catalogs all the time." We were astonished that his mother had withheld such significant information. However, to her, it was insignificant since Matthew still did not interact in socially acceptable ways or communicate through oral language.

Our thoughts then turned to "labeling." According to federal law, school districts must assess and identify students prior to provision of special education services. Matthew's school assessment indicated mental retardation because he responded to very little during the comprehensive evaluation. I reasoned, he must not have mental retardation since this four year old child could read at the second grade level - an activity most four year olds rarely accomplish. I contracted with a school psychologist to reevaluate this child. From my limited knowledge of autism, I surmised that Matthew might be autistic.

Matthew's evaluation was conducted at school because the psychologist believed he would get a more valid perspective of Matthew in his classroom environment instead of a new, strange setting at the psychologist's office. I accompanied him to the classroom for the observation because this child's unusual behavior had aroused my curiosity and interest.

As we stood in the classroom observing Matthew, the psychologist questioned the teacher about his behaviors at school. Miss Davis said, "Matthew has to have everything in its place in the classroom. If books and toys aren't put up where they belong, he straightens everything when he comes into the room each morning."

Timidly, I asked the psychologist, "do you think he's autistic?" His response surprised me. "No, he's not autistic, I'll probably label him PDD."

"PDD? What is that?" I questioned. He explained that PDD stood for pervasive developmental delay. I again questioned, "What is that?" Although I prided myself on my knowledge of special education, I really didn't have any concept of the term, PDD. I certainly didn't know how it differed from autism, so I again questioned the psychologist.

I was not satisfied with his answer, **"Pervasive developmental delay is the label psychologists use when they really don't know what is wrong with the child."**

 Psychologists referencing the *Diagnostic and Statistical Manual of Mental Disorders (DSM-IV)* recommend that terminology such as "Pervasive Developmental Delay-Not Otherwise Specified (PDD-NOS)" be used when individuals don't meet specific criteria for autism or other conditions in the pervasive developmental disorders category. According to the psychological report, Matthew had a Pervasive Developmental Delay. Matthew retained the label of mental retardation since "pervasive developmental delay" and "autism" were not identified as disability categories under the *1975 Education of the Handicapped Act (EHA)*, landmark legislation which provides students with disabilities a free appropriate public education (FAPE).

School personnel must rely on their best judgment and the professional judgment of individuals with whom they contract or employ. When assessments are inadequate, appropriate programming decisions are not always made. Another student, now in his thirties, that I sometimes wonder about was identified as having autism after becoming an adult. As educators, we knew he was different, but we didn't know how to provide the best possible programming without an appropriate diagnosis.

CASE EXAMPLE

The school's assessment staff evaluated Dustin. Even though the special education staff agreed he had definite needs for special education, Dustin did not fit any of the typical profiles for learning disabilities or mental retardation. Although federal law required a comprehensive evaluation only once every three years, I requested evaluations from three different psychologists for this puzzling young man in the same year. Each psychologist evaluating him provided the school district with a different diagnosis. Now, with "hindsight and additional knowledge about autism," I clearly see that he exhibited characteristics of autism.

Dustin's intelligence quotient differed on each of the evaluations—not surprising when you realize that individuals with autism typically perform inconsistently in different places and with different people. His performance on standardized achievement tests was puzzling to school staff because Dustin scored much higher than expected for his assessed intellectual level. A ninth grader, he scored at grade level in reading recognition and twelfth-grade level in spelling. This high academic functioning was inconsistent with his social and functional life behaviors. He did not function well in class or with his school peers. Dustin appeared to have no friends. I frequently observed him at the local little league ballpark watching his brother play ball. This young man was subjected to frequent teasing and bullying from other children because he was so different from his same-age peers.

The results of the psychological assessments left his parents and school staff confused. One psychologist labeled Dustin with "mental retardation." Another psychologist labeled him as having "schizophrenia," a form of emotional disturbance. The last said he had a "learning disability." The Individualized Educational Program (IEP) team, totally confused by these reports, finally made the decision to label him with mental retardation, which was more consistent with Dustin's functional daily living skills. Without the mental retardation label, there were virtually no resources for young adults with disabilities in the community where he lived.

Autism Becomes a Category

This confusing state of affairs continued for students with autism for several more years because Congress did not include autism as a legal disability under federal law until *Public Law 94-142* was reauthorized in 1990 under the name, *Individuals with Disabilities Education Act (IDEA)*. At that time autism and traumatic brain injury (TBI) were added as  additional disability categories. Students like Matthew and Dustin could then be identified with a diagnosis of autism for school eligibility purposes, which is a more accurate reflection of their disability. Since that time, the number of students identified as having autism has continued to increase. According to the Autism Society of America (ASA, 1996), the current incidence rate is approximately 15 out of every 10,000 births. In the January 20, 1999, issue of *USA Today*, the incidence rate for autism was reported as 1 in 500 by L. A. Johnson, Associated Press reporter.

The IEP Process: An Intimidating Experience

With inclusion of autism as a disability condition in 1990 (and reauthorized as a disability in 1997), and the explosion of knowledge about autism during the last decade, it would seem that development of the IEP is an easy process. However, as a professional working with many school personnel and parents of students with autism, I know that the IEP process is not much easier. "Currently, there is reason to believe that the IEP is most often viewed by professionals as an isolated document far removed from the provision of educational services." (Smith, 1990, p. 3). The Individualized Educational Program tends to be viewed by some professionals as paperwork to be completed instead of an ongoing, developmental process critical to the development of appropriate educational programming for students with disabilities (Banbury, 1987; Morgan & Rhode, 1983; Nadler & Shore, 1980; cited in Smith, Slattery, and Knopp, 1993). However, the intent of *Public Law 105-17*, the *IDEA Amendments*, is to use the IEP to improve the quality of education to all students with disabilities by providing for more parental input, greater access to the general education curriculum, and better accountability for students and educational programs.

One professional advocate, a friend and parent of a student with a disability, reports "the IEP process is very intimidating for most parents." Another parent, also a professional special educator, relates that it takes him a week to get "psyched" up for the IEP meeting. Even though he is knowledgeable and mentally prepares for the annual IEP meeting, he still gets unnerved when he walks into the room and the school district has a large group of people sitting at the table to discuss his child. A song by Denzil Edge, *The Exceptional Parent Blues*, says, "How could it possibly take so many people to talk about Billy to his mother and me?" This probably echoes the sentiments of many parents who attend IEP meetings.

For many parents, just the mention of IEP meetings invokes thoughts of "I Expect Problems." Dixon (1991, p. 19) described her feelings for many years as she attended IEP meetings for her son.

> As the date of my son's IEP meeting drew near, knots would form in my stomach. I knew several things would characterize the meeting. The room would be filled with too many people, sometimes as many as 21, all eager to push their own agendas. The meeting would begin with evaluations, present levels of performance, and a list of things that Andrew could NOT do.

Her description of these meetings ended with, "By the time the meeting ended, my husband and I were so drained and depressed it was hard to function."

Many school personnel, when preparing for IEP meetings for students with autism, approach the IEP meeting with feelings of anxiety. The needs of some children with autism are so great that families experience extreme amounts of stress, and many school districts are frequently unprepared to deal with such great needs. Families may request relief through respite, residential placement, or additional instruction and related services. School districts trying to meet these children's needs with currently available resources often put the family and school in conflict.

IDEA (*Federal Register*, 1992 & 1999) mandates that the Individualized Educational Program be tailored to meet the individual needs of each child. The student's chronological age; the needs of the family; medical, social interaction, and functional skills development needs; as well as generalization and maintenance needs (Smith, Slattery, & Knopp, 1993, p. 1) should be considered. Ideally, development of the IEP should be a fluid, formative procedure providing the structure to guide the student's ongoing educational program through longitudinal planning to meet the diverse needs of students with autism.

Consequently, the purpose of this book is to help parents and school personnel jointly meet the challenges of the child-centered process for students with autism, from initial referral to program implementation. Although the emphasis is on development of appropriate individualized educational programs, referral and assessment are necessary prerequisites to the development of appropriate individual educational programs and will be addressed.

Suggestions will be provided for collaborative planning between parents and school staff because the best educational programs for students with autism are generally developed when the IEP is viewed as a *process* fostered by joint ownership and shared development responsibilities. School staff and parents must work as a team to fully maximize the potential of each child with autism. The changes mandated by the *IDEA Amendments of 1997* and the final regulations for the *IDEA Amendments* that were published on March 12, 1999, are included and discussed as the law and the regulations apply to each section of this book.

Chapter Two
Laying Foundations

For six years of my career, I worked as a special education consultant at a regional education service center serving 99 school districts in 17 counties. I had the opportunity to observe many programs with varying degrees of quality. In most programs, special educational professionals do as much as they can in spite of financial limitations and attitudes of other educators and community members. The quality of programs varies greatly from district to district and even from campus to campus in large school districts. Factors such as personality, philosophy, and administrator's attitudes can influence the quality of school programs at the local level.

Although state and federal laws set forth minimum standards, personnel in local education agencies (LEAs [commonly known as public school districts]) may interpret federal and state standards in very different ways. Additionally, some programs look good on paper, but the actual day to day operations don't live up to the written program descriptions. Federal law gives parents the right to question the appropriateness of school programs when they do not agree with the proposed or current educational program developed for their child. The final regulations for the *Individuals with Disabilities Education Act (IDEA) Amendments* which were published on March 12, 1999 have placed greater emphasis on ensuring that students with disabilities show educational progress. The new *IDEA* places greater emphasis on parental involvement and access to general education. It is designed to improve educational results for students with disabilities. According to U. S. Secretary of Education Richard W. Riley, "the thrust of *IDEA* has changed from one that merely provides disabled children access to an education to one that improves quality for all children in our schools." (NASDE, 1999).

In addition to state and federal regulations, school districts are guided by case law which develops from rulings in due process hearings and state and federal court cases. Rulings from precedent setting cases in federal district level courts apply to all schools within the area of the federal district. Rulings from the Supreme Court apply to all schools in the nation. One precedent setting case, *Rowley* (1982), set forth standards for examining the appropriateness of educational programs in terms of meeting minimum standards, not in terms of providing the best or quality programs. Therefore, parents must question programs in terms of "appropriateness," not in terms of "quality".

Even with the new focus from *IDEA* on improved educational results, schools are required to provide an appropriate program, not a quality program. However, many appropriate programs are also quality programs. Consequently, it is imperative for parents to know minimal standards established by *Public Law 94-142* and reauthorized most recently by *Public Law 105-17*, the *IDEA Amendments*. State regulations are also important because some states have additional requirements related to autism which are not included in the federal guidelines. When the educational program developed is appropriate in terms of these minimum standards, it is all that a school district must provide.

In order to learn the basics of developing appropriate individualized educational programs (IEPs), we must lay the foundation. In this instance, the foundation consists of:

- learning the basic terminology related to the field of autism and education;
- becoming familiar with the characteristics of autism; and
- acquiring knowledge about legislation that impacts students with autism and their families.

Therefore, this chapter will include: various definitions of autism and other pervasive developmental delays; a discussion of the *Individuals with Disabilities Education Act* and the *IDEA Amendments* including basic components of the individualized educational program (IEP); and information describing specific state regulations.

Definitions of Autism

Autism Society of America Definition

Although definitions of autism vary to some degree, there are basic commonalities because each addresses difficulties in communication, social relationships, and a narrow range of interests. The Autism Society of America (1998, p. 3) defines autism as "a developmental disability that typically appears during the first three years of life. The result of a neurological disorder that affects functioning of the brain, autism and its associated behaviors occur in approximately 15 of every 10,000 individuals." According to this definition, "autism interferes with the normal development of the brain in the areas of reasoning, social interaction and communication skills. Children and adults with autism typically have deficiencies in verbal and non-verbal communication, social interactions, and leisure of play activities. The disorder makes it hard for them to communicate with others and relate to the outside world. They may exhibit repeated body movements (hand flapping, rocking), unusual responses to people or attachments to objects and resist any changes in routines. In some cases, aggressive and/or self-injurious behavior may be present." According to the Autism Society of America, it is conservatively estimated that nearly 400,000 people in the U. S. have some form of autism, and it occurs four times more frequently in boys than in girls. This prevalence rate makes it the third most common developmental disability–more common than Down syndrome.

No known factors in the psychological environment of a child have been shown to cause autism. A critical element of this definition is that *autism is a neurobiological disorder, not caused by the environment.* A once widely accepted theory proposed by Bettleheim (1967), theorized that autism was caused by "cold, unfeeling and unresponsive mothers." The acceptance of this theory by many psychologists and educators caused guilt and anguish to countless families of individuals with autism. Parents of children born during the Bettleheim era still sometimes fight feelings of guilt or anger caused by this erroneous theory even though, intellectually, they know autism is a neurobiological disorder, not caused by the environment (Stehli, 1991, p. 27-37). At the first national ASA conference which I attended, I was surprised at the strength of feelings that continue to be exhibited by parents of adult individuals with autism toward Bettleheim.

Autism and Mental Retardation

As parents and professionals have learned more about autism, the spectrum of this disability has broadened. A problem associated with appropriate identification of Dustin was professionals' typical assumption that individuals with autism generally function in the intellectual range of mental retardation. Although the *Diagnostic and Statistical Manual of Mental Disorders (DSM-IV)* (American Psychological Association [APA], 1994, p. 67) states that "approximately 75 percent of children with Autistic Disorder function at a retarded level,"

11

we now know that individuals with autism may function from severe mental retardation to levels in the superior range of intelligence. Temple Grandin and Donna Williams, excellent examples of individuals with autism functioning in the intellectually superior range, report that they must still cope with the sensory manifestations and dysfunctions of autism (Grandin,1995; Grandin & Scariano, 1986; Williams, 1992, 1994, 1996).

Mental retardation is not a characteristic of autism. Individuals may have autism and mental retardation, but their mental retardation is not caused by the autism. It must be noted that the 75 percent figure quoted from the *DSM-IV* relating to coexisting conditions of autism and mental retardation included only Autistic Disorder, not other pervasive developmental disorders such as Asperger's syndrome which is generally characterized by higher intellectual functioning. Additionally, some persons with autism who function like individuals with mental retardation may not actually have mental retardation. Their inability to communicate and perform specific tasks on demand affects their assessed intellectual functioning. Fullerton (1996, p. 1) states that autism is sometimes misdiagnosed as mental retardation resulting in inappropriate and ineffective treatment. When autism coexists with conditions such as fragile x syndrome, tuberous sclerosis, or Down syndrome, autism may not be recognized as a co-occurring condition. It is frequently assumed that all inappropriate behaviors are related to the specific condition or syndrome generally associated with mental retardation.

John, another young boy with whom I have worked, was diagnosed with Down syndrome at an early age. His mother and the school system diligently worked with him trying many methods commonly recommended for students with mental retardation. In the last couple of years, even with an excellent teacher and a supportive home situation, he regressed. In a recent conversation, his mother expressed her remorse and frustration as she listed the things that John used to do, but cannot or won't do now. Concerned about his obvious regression in many areas and frequent withdrawal or shutting down in the classroom, the school district contracted to have a neuropsychological evaluation performed as part of his three year comprehensive individual assessment (CIA) that was required by federal law for continued eligibility for special education services.

At the age of 14, he was also diagnosed with autism. The diagnosis has answered some of the questions concerning withdrawal and shut down periods. His parents and school personnel are now contending with new concerns centering around best practices for individuals with mental retardation which are not appropriate for individuals with autism. In fact, some of the techniques commonly used for stimulating individuals with mental retardation may have contributed to his shutdown and withdrawal periods due to overstimulation problems. An appropriate IEP, the foundation and framework for special education programming, must now be developed for John which meets his specific, individual needs based on a functional assessment of his skills and takes into account his characteristics of autism and mental retardation.

I would like to report that John is the only child in this situation. However, I recently met a mother who related a very similar scenario except that her child received a diagnosis of autism at the age of 12. She reported contacting the Down Syndrome Congress to determine whether other children with Down syndrome also had autism. Despite the fact that they had no such reported instances, this mother had already located another parent of a child with Down's syndrome and autism in a town about 40 miles away. Three children, including John, within a 40 mile radius have been identified as having Down syndrome and autism. Additionally, a significant percentage of individuals with Tuberous Sclerosis and Fetal Alcohol Syndrome also have autism as a coexisting condition.

Autism and Sensory Impairments

As the spectrum of autism has broadened, there has been recognition that students with vision impairments and/or hearing impairments may also   have a coexisting condition of autism. This may account for the individual differences sometimes found within the population of students with vision or hearing impairments. It was always puzzling why some students with vision or hearing impairments failed to progress like their peers with the same type of disability. Gense & Gense (1995) noted that many individuals with blindness exhibit behaviors similar to those seen in students with autism.

The relevant literature in the field of visual impairments identified these problems as "blindisms." The lack of literature associating blindness with autism indicates the newness of this concept of coexisting autism and blindness. Autism was not mentioned in the courses that I took for certification in deficient vision in the early 1980s, although "blindisms" were discussed. I have chosen to include a table (*I'm Okay, You Have a Mannerism* [Moss & Blaha, 1993]) in this book. The table was initially published in *P.S. News!!!*, a newsletter of the Texas School for the Blind and Visually Impaired Outreach Department. The information which describes self-stimulation behaviors of individuals with blindness or deaf/blindness, is also very appropriate for individuals with autism. Individuals interested in more information about persons with a dual diagnosis of autism and deafness or blindness may contact the Autism & Sensory Impairment Network associated with ASA by writing to Dolores and Alan Bartel, 7510 Oceanfront Ave., Virginia Beach, VA 23451 (Phone: 757-428-9036; Fax: 757-428-0019).

Individuals with Disabilities Education Act Definition

The Individuals with Disabilities Education Act (IDEA) (*Federal Register*, 1992, 1999) defines autism as "a developmental disability significantly affecting verbal and nonverbal communication and social interaction, generally evident before the age of 3, that adversely affects a child's educational performance." (*Federal Register*, 1999, p. 12421). Other characteristics often associated with autism include engagement in repetitive activities and stereotyped movements, resistance to environmental change, changes in daily routines, and unusual responses to sensory experiences. *IDEA* regulations note that a child exhibiting all other characteristics of autism can still be labeled with autism, even if characteristics are manifested after the age of three.

For special education eligibility purposes, disability labels including autism cannot be applied if the child's educational performance is not adversely affected. An educational need must be exhibited in developmental, academic, behavioral, or social areas. The federal definition also excludes any child from identification with autism if the disorder results primarily from a serious emotional disturbance. Autism is a *neurobiological* disorder, not an emotional disturbance.

 CASE EXAMPLE

Jerry has been identified by a school psychologist as having high-functioning autism. When the IEP team met, everyone agreed that Jerry does have autism. However, Jerry is performing well in the regular classroom setting with no modifications or supports. Consequently, Jerry is not eligible for special education services as a student with a disability because he has no educational need.

A significant change made by the *IDEA Amendments* is discussed in Section 300.7. This section defines a child with a disability. According to this section in the final regulations, a child is not a child with a disability under *IDEA* if the child only needs a related service and not special education.

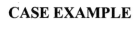

CASE EXAMPLE

Joey is in second grade. He has been identified as having autism. His parents and IEP team agree that the only service that he needs is occupational therapy. Since this is considered a related service and not special education, Joey would not be eligible as a child with a disability as defined in Section 300.7 of *IDEA*. This appears to indicate that Joey would not then be eligible to receive occupational therapy because he does not need any "special education services" and occupational therapy is a related service, not special education.

There is an important exception to the above *IDEA* regulation. If the related service that the child needs is considered to be special education (and not a related service) under state regulations, then the child is still considered to be a child with a disability.

CASE EXAMPLE

Sammy has autism, but the only service he needs is speech therapy for difficulties with communication. However, Sammy lives in Texas where speech therapy is considered to be special education, not a related service. Therefore, because of the *IDEA 1997* exception to the above regulation, Sammy is still considered to be a child with a disability.

The definition of autism in *IDEA* is important to school personnel and parents of students with autism because this definition is used to determine eligibility for services in public schools. Each state has flexibility to supplement federal criteria in the state regulations, as long as the standards specified with the *IDEA Amendments* are met.

Despite inclusion of autism in federal law in 1990 and reauthorized in 1997, much confusion still exists over labeling of individuals with autism. *IDEA's* definition does nothing to distinguish between different forms of autism such as low- and high-functioning autism, Asperger's syndrome, and other pervasive developmental disorders.

DSM-IV Definitions

Autistic Disorder

According to the *Diagnostic and Statistical Manual of Mental Disorders, Fourth Edition (DSM-IV)* (American Psychological Association [APA], 1994, p. 66), autistic disorder is a form of a pervasive developmental disorder. "Essential features of Autistic Disorder are the presence of markedly abnormal or impaired development in social interaction and communication, and a markedly restricted repertoire of activities and interests. Manifestations of the disorder vary greatly depending on the developmental level and chronological age of the individual." Onset prior to the age of three years is a critical element in the diagnostic criteria. The disturbance is not better accounted for by Rett's Disorder or Childhood Disintegrative Disorder (APA, p. 71). In John's case, onset was prior to the age of three, but it was not identified as part of his problem until he was fourteen. It seems his mental retardation commonly associated with Down syndrome caused significant people in his life to attribute his autistic characteristics to mental retardation, not autism.

Asperger's Syndrome

The *DSM-IV* does indicate that Autistic Disorder should be differentiated from other forms of pervasive developmental disorders. Asperger's syndrome, referred to as Asperger's Disorder in the *DSM-IV*, is differentiated from early infantile autism or Autistic Disorder by the lack of delayed language development in Asperger's syndrome. Characteristics of Asperger's syndrome include severe and sustained impairments in social interaction and the development of restricted, repetitive patterns of behavior, interests, and activities. Although the *DSM-IV* reports that individuals with Asperger's syndrome do not have clinically significant delays in language, cognitive development, self-help skills development, or adaptive behavior, some individuals are still misdiagnosed. One mother reports that her son was diagnosed with autism as a preschooler, but was recently reclassified as having Asperger's syndrome in his three-year reevaluation.

Although Asperger's syndrome is closely related to high-functioning autism, they are separate developmental disorders. In high-functioning autism, "the higher functioning refers to the cognitive ability of the individual which is usually in the average to above-average range" (Fullerton, 1996, p. 1). Individuals with Asperger's syndrome may exhibit learning disabilities in reading, writing, or mathematics. Individuals with high-functioning autism exhibit a wide range in the severity of autistic characteristics (Fullerton, p. 1); but most have continuing difficulty in understanding social situations. They frequently learn appropriate social responses by imitating responses of persons within their environment.

High-functioning Autism

Although high-functioning autism is not distinguished from autistic disorder in the *DSM-IV*; it should be mentioned here to differentiate it from Asperger's syndrome. Ruth Elaine Hane (1996) and Sara Miller (1993; 1996; Donnelly, et al, 1996) report being diagnosed as having high-functioning autism in their adult lives. Each experienced relief by the diagnosis because it answered many long-term questions related to their daily functioning. This was not an indication that the autistic disorder had just manifested itself. Autism was just not recognized as the cause of their different behaviors until they were adults.

Moreover, Hane and Miller describe behaviors characteristic of autism occurring from infancy on. They describe sensory dysfunctions similar to those of Grandin (1995; Grandin & Scariano, 1986), McKean (1994,1996), and Williams (1992, 1994, 1996). It is interesting to note that although many adult individuals with autism have provided much insight into the sensory dysfunctions related to autistic disorders (Grandin,1996, McKean, 1994, 1996; Miller, 1996; and Williams, 1992, 1994, 1996), the *DSM-IV* does not include sensory dysfunctions in the diagnostic criteria or characteristics associated with autistic disorder.

These adults have described their constant need to cope with problems associated with their responses to sensory stimuli. Grandin (Grandin & Scariano, 1986) developed *The Hug Machine*, also known as the "squeeze machine," to provide the deep pressure that she frequently needs for calming. McKean (1996) wears pressure bracelets and also describes his sound and tactile sensitivities. In a book by Donna Williams (1996), she describes her difficulty with various forms of sensory stimulation including visual and auditory stimuli. She discusses her difficulty in responding to more than one sensory modality at a time. Williams prefers visual input to auditory input. At the 1996 ASA Conference, Miller (Donnelly et al, 1996) discussed her need to wear ear plugs because of her hypersensitivity to sound.

One young boy I work with doesn't like bread. If the cafeteria worker places bread on top of his meat, he recognizes the bread smell and refuses to eat it. This hypersensitivity to smell is also noticed in the classroom. When working with tempera paint or colored markers, the smell of yellow in the paint or markers is irritating to him.

Rett's Disorder (RD)

Another disorder sometimes confused with autism is Rett's Disorder. This disorder has been identified only in girls with onset of symptoms beginning as early as five months old. Symptoms include "a characteristic pattern of head growth deceleration, loss of previously acquired purposeful hand skills, the appearance of poorly coordinated gait or trunk movements, and a severe impairment in expressive and receptive language development." (APA, 1994, p. 71).

Childhood Disintegrative Disorder (CDD)

Childhood Disintegrative Disorder is distinguished by a "marked regression in multiple areas of functioning following a period of at least two years of apparently normal development" (APA, p. 73). This disorder, more rare than autism, is characterized by normal development for at least two years; then a loss of the previously acquired skills in at least two of the following areas: expressive or receptive language, social skills or adaptive behavior, bowel or bladder control, play or motor skills. Childhood Disintegrative Disorder is usually associated with severe mental retardation.

Pervasive Developmental Disorder Not Otherwise Specified (PDD-NOS [Including Atypical Autism])

According to the *DSM-IV*, "this category should be used when there is a severe and pervasive impairment in the development of reciprocal social interaction or verbal and nonverbal communication skills; or when stereotyped behavior, interests, and activities are present" (APA, 1994, p. 77-78.), but specific criteria are not met for other pervasive developmental disorders. This category includes "atypical autism" when the individual exhibits atypical symptomatology or fewer criteria than necessary for a diagnosis of autistic disorder. It is also used when symptomatology of autism occurs after the age of three. Individuals must meet at least one of these conditions to be labeled as PDD-NOS. Dr. Luke Tsai suggested to families that in the event of a diagnosis of PDD-NOS, they "insist that atypical autism be noted so that services can be obtained." (Tsai, 1995). However, this need may vary from state to state. For example, the Texas Education Agency issued a clarification letter stating that all students identified as having a pervasive developmental delay qualify under the *IDEA* disability category of autism.

Basic IEP Components of the New *IDEA*

According to the *IDEA Amendments*, "the individualized educational program" is a written statement for each child with a disability that is developed, reviewed, and revised in a meeting by an IEP team. This team includes (*IDEA,1997, §*300.341; *Federal Register*, 1999):

- a representative of the public agency who is:
    * qualified to provide, or supervise the provision of, specially designed instruction to meet the unique needs of children with disabilities,
    * knowledgeable about the general curriculum, and
    * is knowledgeable about the availability of resources of the public agency.
- a regular education teacher of the child (if the child is, or may be, participating in the regular education environment);
- a special education teacher of the child, or, if appropriate, at least one special education provider of the child;
- other individuals (at the discretion of the parent or public agency) who have knowledge or special expertise regarding the child, including related service personnel as appropriate;
- an individual who can interpret the instructional implications of evaluation results, who may be a member of the team previously specified;
- the parents or guardian of such child; and
- whenever appropriate, the child.
- in IEP meetings that consider transition services, transition services participants should also attend the IEP meeting.

The federal definition in the *IDEA Amendments* describes the basic components of the IEP which are:

- A statement of the **present levels of educational performance** of the child, including
    * How the child's disability affects the child's involvement and progress in the general curriculum (i.e., the same curriculum as for nondisabled children), or
    * For preschool children, as appropriate, how the disability affects the child's participation in appropriate activities.
- A statement of **measurable annual goals**, including **benchmarks** or **short-term objectives**, related to:

* Meeting the child's needs that result from the child's disability to enable the child to be involved in and progress in the general curriculum, or for preschool children, as appropriate, to participate in the general curriculum, (i.e., the same curriculum as for nondisabled children), or for preschool children, as appropriate, to participate in appropriate activities; and

* Meeting each of the child's other educational needs that result for the child's disability;

- A statement of the **special education and related services and supplementary aids and services** to be provided to the child, or on behalf of the child, and a statement of the program modifications or supports for school personnel that will be provided for the child;

  * To advance appropriately toward attaining the annual goals;

  * To be involved and progress in the general curriculum, and to participate in extracurricular and other nonacademic activities; and

  * To be educated and participate with other children with disabilities and nondisabled children in the activities described;

- An explanation of the extent, if any, to which the child will not **participate with nondisabled children in the regular class** and in the activities described in this section.

- A statement of any individual **modifications in the administration of State or district-wide assessments** of student achievement that are needed in order for the child to participate in the assessment; and

  * If the IEP team determines that the child will not participate in a particular State or district-wide assessment of student achievement or part of an assessment), a statement of :

    - Why that assessment is not appropriate for the child; and

    - How the child will be assessed;

- The **projected date for the beginning of the services and modifications** described in the IEP and the **anticipated frequency, location, and duration of those servic**es and modifications; and

- A statement of:

* How the child's **progress toward the annual goals** described in the IEP **will be measured**; and

* How the child's **parents will be regularly informed** (through such means as periodic report cards), at least as often as parents are informed of their nondisabled children's progress, of:

  • Their child's progress toward the annual goals; and

  • The extent to which that progress is sufficient to enable the child to achieve the goals by the end of the year.

• When age-appropriate, **transition services.**

  * For each student with a disability beginning at age 14 (or younger, if determined appropriate by the IEP team), and updated annually, a statement of the transition service needs of the student under the applicable components of the student's IEP that focuses on the student's courses of study (such as participation in advanced placement courses or a vocational education program); and

  * For each student beginning at age 16 (or younger, if determined appropriate by the IEP team), a statement of needed transition services for the student, including, if appropriate, a statement of the interagency responsibilities or any needed linkages.

• In a State that **transfers rights at the age of majority**, beginning at least one year before a student reaches the age of majority under State law, the student's IEP must include a statement that the student has been informed of his or her rights under Part B of the Act, if any, that will transfer to the student on reaching the age of majority, consistent with Section 300.517.

Section 300.342 (*Federal Register*, 1999, p. 12440) specifies that an IEP must be in effect at the beginning of each school year for each child with a disability receiving special education services. **Schools cannot provide special education and related services until an IEP is in effect.** Moreover, the IEP should be implemented as soon as possible following the IEP meeting in which it was developed. Exceptions to immediate implementation might include school vacations or short delays necessary to work out special arrangements for services such as transportation or related services. However, undue delays in implementing the IEP constitute a violation of federal law and is considered a procedural error in due process hearings. This section also mandates that each "regular education teacher, special education teacher, related service provider, and other service provider who is responsible for its implementation' is informed of his or her specific responsibilities related to implementing the child's IEP. Additionally, parents must be given a copy of the IEP at no cost.

Although generally not relevant to students with autism, it should be noted that special rules concerning the content of IEPs for individuals with disabilities convicted as adults and incarcerated in adult prisons are contained in Section 300.311 (b) and (c).

Other Minimum Standards

Other minimum standards originally set forth in *Public Law 94-142, The Education for All Handicapped Children Act of 1975*, include a mandate for provision of a free appropriate public education for (FAPE) all children with disabilities. This provision affirmed rulings from two previous court decisions, *Pennsylvania Association for Retarded Citizens (PARC) v. Commonwealth of Pennsylvania, 1972,* and *Mills v. Board of Education, 1972.* The PARC case ended with a consent agreement that provided for a free appropriate public education for all students with mental retardation in Pennsylvania.

A court ruling in the *Mills* case extended the provision of services to include all students with disabilities, not just students with mental retardation. The court ordered the District of Columbia to provide all children with a disability, regardless of the severity of the disability, with a publicly-supported education. *Public Law 94-142* and the *Individuals with Disabilities Act (1990, 1997)* also ensures due process rights for students and parents. It mandates education in the least restrictive environment. This law is the core of federal funding for special education programs (NICHCY, 1991, p. 7).

Zero Reject

A key concept enacted by Public Law 94-142 was "zero reject." This means that public school districts cannot reject any student because of his or her handicap or characteristics of the disability. Every student must be accepted. In the late 1970s, I worked in developing an educational program for a ten-year-old boy who had never attended school. His mother had tried to enroll him in public school kindergarten prior to the passage of the *Education of the Handicapped Children Act of 1975.* School officials rejected him because he was not toilet trained. Almost 25 years later, that seems absurd because it is very common to encounter "untrained" students with autism or other disabilities enrolled in public school programs. For some special classrooms, diapers are the norm.

Individualized Instruction

What about individualized instruction? Does this mean that the school district has to provide one-on-one instruction? Individualized instruction does not refer to the delivery of instruction in a one-on-one setting. It means that the IEP team must review all data and develop an individualized program for the student based on the individual's needs. If the program meets the student's individualized needs, it doesn't matter if the services are delivered one-on-one or in a regular classroom. The important concept is that needs are determined and addressed on an individual basis. Goals and objectives are based on the needs of the individual student, not on a specific curriculum or program used in the classroom.

Stating that the school district does not have an appropriate program for a specific student does not relieve the district of its obligation to provide educational services for the student. If the IEP team agrees that specific services are needed and appropriate, the school district must develop those services. In situations where the school program is inappropriate, day placement or residential placement for educational reasons is an alternative way of providing educational services.

Person First Language

When *Public Law 94-142* was reauthorized in 1990 as *Public Law 101-476*, the name was changed to *Individuals with Disabilities Education Act (IDEA)*. The name change was a reflection of current trends in language usage. The field as a whole moved from terminology, such as the autistic child to person first language, which correctly puts the individual first. Examples of more appropriate and politically correct terminology are individuals with autism, child with autism, or student who has autism. Emotionally neutral expressions should also be used. Language that evokes connotations of pity should be avoided. For example, say the individual has autism instead of the individual is suffering from or inflicted with autism. The importance of person first language was illustrated when Jean-Paul Bovee ended his speech at the 1996 ASA conference with "I have autism, but I am not autism. We are people, we are not a label." (Donnelly, et al, 1996b). (See Appendix B for additional information on person first language.)

Other Requirements of *IDEA*

IDEA also mandates inclusion of transition services and assistive technology services in the student's IEP. In 1990, the categories of autism and traumatic brain injury (TBI) were added to the list of disabilities eligible for special education and related services. Rehabilitation counseling and social work services were added as related services under *IDEA*.

Although public schools and states must meet minimum requirements established by federal law, there is flexibility in the actual interpretation and implementation of the federal requirements at the state level. "State constitutions and laws may go beyond what is provided in federal law as long as there is no conflict between them, and as long as state laws do not address areas reserved to the federal government." (*NICHCY*, 1991, p. 13). Consequently, this book includes a comparison of state procedures for students with autism. Most states will take six months to two years to change state rules and regulations to reflect the changes that have been published in the final regulations for the *IDEA Amendments of 1997* in the *Federal Register*, March 12, 1999.

Although special education professionals are generally cognizant of federal and state special education rules and regulations, many general education professionals and parents are not always aware. Most special education professionals have a working knowledge of the special education regulations in their state, but may not be aware of specific regulations in other states. It is sometimes difficult to answer questions posed by parents from other states because of a lack of knowledge about the specific requirements for IEPs and special education programs in a particular state.

It Doesn't Apply to Me!

In some situations, I have encountered administrators who seem to believe that state and federal guidelines do not apply to them. At the 1996 ASA Conference in Milwaukee, a parent said that her district had violated many of the provisions of federal law. When she discussed the violations with the school administrator, his response was "Sue me!"

A special education director asked me to mediate a situation between a parent and school principal. The parent had taken her son (at her own expense) for an independent educational evaluation (IEE). His written psychological report presented to the IEP team specifically stated, "corporal punishment is not only nonproductive, it would be psychologically harmful for this student." With the report in hand, the principal still insisted that corporal punishment be written into the IEP as an appropriate method of discipline for this child.

Before going to the district, I consulted with several school law attorneys who agreed that the principal was putting herself and the district in a dangerous situation because corporal punishment is not protected by tort liability. If the principal spanked the child, the parents could sue the principal personally and receive damages if they prevailed. After a couple of hours of mediation, it was obvious that neither party was willing to negotiate.

I asked to speak with the principal privately. She responded with, "You come here, make recommendations, and then leave. I am the person at the campus on a day-to-day basis, and I will do what I believe is necessary." I left with the comment, "I hope that you have good liability insurance." Although school principals are the authority on school campuses, their power is not great enough to override decisions made by the IEP team documented in the IEP. However, an administrator's power probably does influence decisions made by campus staff during IEP meetings.

Thankfully, most school administrators are not so hard lined and do have students' best interests at heart. Even when their perspective differs from the parents' perspective, both are generally acting from their personal perspectives about what is best for the child.

Parents as Experts

I encourage parents to learn their legal rights and to become knowledgeable about the characteristics of autism and appropriate educational methods and materials. Parents frequently complain that they are tired of having to be the "expert." They would like the school to have knowledge and expertise about autism so that parents don't have to constantly be the "imparter of knowledge." Some parents dread each new school year because they must again begin educating school staff about autism.

If parents do not learn about appropriate programs and techniques, how can they evaluate the appropriateness of the school program? To feel comfortable participating as an equal partner on the IEP team, parents must become knowledgeable about their child, autism, and their parent and student rights under federal and state law. However, becoming an "expert" will not necessarily result in obtaining school implementation of a parental preference for a specific program. Selection of methodology is generally the decision of the school district. However, parents can be instrumental in developing goals and objectives that might be indicative of certain programs. For example, if the parent wants the North Carolina TEACCH program implemented, goals and objectives should target the use of schedules, visual cues, and supports in all areas. Although school district personnel might deny that parents are treated differently, my personal observations indicate that "the squeaky wheel gets the grease," and vocal, well-informed parents generally obtain better services for their children.

State Requirements

To assist parents in becoming aware of the requirements specific to their particular state, I examined the requirements for each state and summarized this information in *Table 2.1. State Regulations.* In analyzing the data from the state plan, it became clear that most states have just adopted the minimum requirements in federal law. Very few states have added additional requirements. Therefore, the areas of similarities are summarized below, and the areas containing differences will be presented in *Table 2.1.*

1. As required by *IDEA* (*Federal Register,* 1999), all states have a full continuum of services. This means that they have instructional arrangements including the least restrictive environment, the regular classroom, to residential placement, the most restrictive environment. Although the names of the classes vary from state to state, they are essentially the same categories as described in Chapter Nine: *Placements for Success.* Massachusetts used different terminology from the rest of the states. Different classes were referred to as prototypes in the Massachusetts regulations.

2. All states addressed surrogate parents. Although the appointment procedures and training differed from state to state, the basic process of identifying a surrogate parent for a student when the parent cannot be located is essentially the same.

3. Assistive technology was addressed in all of the state plans. Federal law requires that school districts address the need for assistive technology in the assessment process. Specifications must be provided for students in need of assistive technology devices or services.

4. All state guidelines addressed due process and complaint procedures.

5. Procedures for student confidentiality and access to student records were described in the state regulations for each state.

6. Each state plan also delineated procedures for obtaining an Independent Educational Evaluation at public expense.

7.   Each of the state plans required notice and consent for initial assessments and notice and consent for initial placements. However the specific days required for notice varied from state to state. Within some states, notice periods differed depending on the type of notice.

8.   All related service personnel must meet the highest standard as specified in *IDEA*. Consequently, all must be licensed or certified.

9.   Although all state regulations listed parent training and in-home training, only Texas required that both be addressed in the IEP meeting for students with autism. Guidelines effective in July, 1996, now allow Texas schools to address those areas when needed. Previously, in-home and parent training were addressed at the IEP meeting for all students with autism. Both services are still listed specifically under additional IEP requirements for students with autism.

10. All of the guidelines address extended year services for students who exhibit a need for services beyond the school year. Methods for identification of the need for extended year services may differ from state to state. However, all states require that extended year services must address objectives on the current year IEP.

11. Most states require certification in an area of special education. Few states offer a certification program for autism. For those that do, it is frequently combined with another disability such as serious emotional disturbance. Many states had provisions for persons with any kind of teacher certificate to be employed on a temporary or emergency permit because of critical shortages of qualified special education teachers.

12. Conderman and Katsiyannis (1996) identified nine states that required vision and hearing screening for students with autism. An examination of state guidelines indicates that states without screening requirements for vision and hearing include an assessment of vision and hearing at another stage of the process. For example, in Texas, a state listed as not having vision and hearing screening procedures, vision and hearing screening is performed on all kindergarten, first-grade, third-grade, junior high, and high school students. However, this is considered a function of general education, not a function of special education screening procedures. Additionally, every student suspected of having a disability referred for special education must have an assessment of vision and hearing before the referral may proceed to the individual assessment stage. Vision and hearing problems can affect performance on tests.

27

13.   All states included special education transportation regulations. Federal law requires that special transportation be provided as a related service when the IEP committee identifies a special need for this service.

Table 2.1 (pages 29-35) provides more specific information related to each state. The key for *Table 2.1* is on page 35.

Table 2.1 State Regulations
See Key for Abbreviations on Page 35

Item	AL	AK	AR	AZ	CA	CO	CT	DE
Date of Regulations	1993	1995	1993	1994	1996	1992	1996	1993
Definition	SC	F	SC	SC	SC	SC	SC	F
Eligibility Category	AU	AU	AU	AU	AU	PD	PD/NI	AU
Multidisciplinary Team								
Same as Federal Requirements	AdRq	F	F	F	F	F	F	F
Neurological Report	IN		IN	IN				
Physician Report	R		IN	R				R
Psychologist/Psychiatrist	R	R	IN	R				R
Behavioral Observations	BRS				FAB			
(Additional Assessment)	ABS	PI		SLE				
	SLE	ADL						
Notice of Assessment	F	F	7 CD	F	F	F	F	F
Consent for Assessment	F	F	F	F	F	F	F	F
Notice of IEP Meeting	F	F	7CD	F	F	F	F	F
IEP Meeting Committee	F	F	AdRq	F	F	F	F	F
Content of the IEP	F	LP	F	F	F	F	F	F
Behavioral Management Required				R				
Additional IEP Requirements	APE		LP	PreVoc/ Voc				
Timelines								
Ref to Evaluation								
Ref to Assessment Report								
AR. to IEP mtg.	60CD	45CD			30SD	45CD	30CD	
Ref. to Placement	90CD	45SD					45SD	30CD
AR. to Placement	30CD	30CD				30CD		
IEP mtg. to Placement				15 SD				
Age of Eligibility (pub. sch. prog.)	3-21	3-21	3-21	B to 21	3-21	3-21	B to 20	
Age for Transition Requirement	16	16	16	16 9th G	16	16	15(14) IN	15(14) IN,9t G
Prevoc./Voc. Assessment	16	16	16	16	16	16	15(14)	15(14)
Teacher Certification	SE			SE	SE			
Teacher/Student Ratio	1t:4s 1t,1a:5s 1 t,2a:7s					SLP: 55		
Special State Projects				A-6 hr. training			TF on AU	AUP MR

Table 2.1 *Continued*   **State Regulations**

Item	FL	GA	HI	ID	IL	IN	IA	KS
Date of Regulations	1995	1994	1995	1993 Rev. 95	1995	1995	1995	1996
Definition	EC	EC	SC	SC	F	DSM	F	F
Eligibility Category	AU	AU	AU	AU	AU	AU	AU.	PH/OHI
Multidisciplinary Team								
Same as Federal Requirements	F	F	F	F	F	F	F	F
Neurological Report	IN						IN	
Physician Report	R		IN	R	R			IN
Psychologist/Psychiatrist	R	R	IN	R	R			R
Behavioral Observations	Y		Y	Y		ABS		
(Additional Assessment)	SLE Sens. F.					SLE EC		
Notice of Assessment	F	F	F	10CD	F	F	F	F
Consent for Assessment	F	F	F	F	F	F	F	F
Notice of IEP Meeting	F	F	F	10CD	10CD	F	F	F
IEP Meeting Committee	F	F	F	F	F	F	F	F
Content of the IEP	F	F	F	F	F	F	F	F
Behavioral Management Required	R		R					
Additional IEP Requirements	ADL							
Timelines								
Ref to Evaluation			20CD		10CD		10CD	
Ref to Assessment Report				30CD		40SD	30CD	30CD
A. Rep to IEP mtg.		30CD	30CD					30CD
Ref. to Placement		100CD		60CD				
A. Rep. to Placement						15SD		
IEP mtg. to Placement			20CD		10CD		10CD	
Age of Eligibility (pub. sch. prog.)	3-21	3-21	3-20	3-21	3-21	3-22	3-21	3-21
Age for Transition Requirement	16	16	16	16	16	16	16	14
Prevoc./Voc. Assessment	16	16	16	14IN	14 1/2	16	YgIN	14
Teacher Certification	SE				IL & SE	I/ST		SE
Teacher/Student Ratio	1t,3s				age/dis 1t, 5s or 1t, 8s	age/dis		1t, 1s 1t, 1a,3s 1t,2a,6s
Special State Projects	4 Regional AU							Centers

Table 2.1 *Continued* State Regulations

Item	KY	LA	ME	MD	MA	MI	MN	MO
Date of Regulations	1994	1994	1995	1991	1994	1996	1995	1994
Definition	EC	F	F	SC	SC	SC/EC	DSM	SC
Eligibility Category	AU	AU	AU	OHI	AU	AU	AU	AU
Multidisciplinary Team								
Same as Federal Requirements	F	F	F	F	F	F	F	F
Neurological Report								
Physician Report	IN			R				
Psychologist/Psychiatrist	IN			R	IN			
Behavioral Observations	Y						ABS	
(Additional Assessment)	SLE						FAB	
	ScSk						AU √ list	
	Rec/Leis.							
Notice of Assessment	F	F	F	AdRq	F	10cd	F	F
Consent for Assessment	F	F	F	F	F	F	F	F
Notice of IEP Meeting	F	F	7CD	F	F	F	F	F
IEP Meeting Committee	F	F	F	F	F	F	AdRq	F
Content of the IEP	F	PE	F	F	F	F	F	F
Behavioral Management Required						R	R	
Additional IEP Requirements				address Grad.	address Grad.		AU √ list	
Timelines								
Ref to Evaluation		60CD	45SD		30SD		30CD	
Ref to Assessment Report								
A. Rep to IEP mtg.	30SD							
Ref. to Placement	60SD				45SD	30SC		
A. Rep. to placement								
IEP mtg. to placement								
Age of Eligibility (pub. sch. prog.)	3-20	3-21	5-20	3-21	3-21	under 26	3-21	3-20
Age for Transition Requirement	16	16	16	16	16	16	14 or 9th gr.	16
PreVoc./Voc. Assessment	16	16	16	16	16	12	14	16
Teacher Certification SE	PH,LBD		SE				SE	
	EMF					& AU Exp.		
Teacher/Student Ratio	By Ins. Argmt.	1t:4s Sp:1:30	1t, 6s st, 10s		1t,8s 1t,1a,12s		1t,2a,6s 1t,1a,4s	FTEs
Special State Projects						BI Stand.		ACCESS

Table 2.1 *Continued* **State Regulations**

Item	MS	MT	NE	NV	NH	NJ	NM	NY
Date of Regulations	1993	1995	1996	1994	1994	1994	1994	1993
Definition	SC	SC	EC	F	SC	SC	SC	SC
Eligibility Category	AU	AU	AU	AU	AU	AU	AU	AU
Multidisciplinary Team								
Same as Federal Requirements	F	AdRq	AdRq	F	F	F	F	AdRq
Neurological Report	IN	IN	IN					
Physician Report	IN	IN	IN		R	R		
Psychologist/Psychiatrist	IN		R	R	R	R		
Behavioral Observations				ABS		FAB		Y
(Additional Assessment)			SLE	SLE	SLE	Soc A.		VA
					VA			
Notice of Assessment	F	F	F	F	F	15CD	F	F
Consent for Assessment	F	F	F	F	F	F	F	F
Notice of IEP Meeting	F	F	F	F	10CD	F	F	F
IEP Meeting Committee	F	F	F	F	F	F	F	AdRq
Content of the IEP	F	F	F	F	F	F	F	F
Behavioral Management Required								
Additional IEP Requirements		PE						
Timelines								
Ref to Evaluation			30CD	45SD				
Ref to Assessment Report								
A. Rep to IEP mtg.								
Ref. to Placement					90CD		30SD	
A. Rep. to placement		15CD	5SD					
IEP mtg. to placement								
Age of Eligibility (pub. sch. prog.)	3-21	3-21	3-21	3-21	3-21	3-21	3-21	3-21
Age for Transition Requirement	16	16 14IN	16 14IN	16	16	14	16	16
Prevoc./Voc. Assessment	16	16	16/14IN	16/14IN	16	14	16	16
Teacher Certification	SE	SE	SE	SE		SE	SE	SE
Teacher/Student Ratio					1t.12s 1 period: 1t,6s EC, 1t,2s	1t,6s	1t,8s 1t,2a,9s	
Special State Projects								

Table 2.1 *Continued* **State Regulations**

Item	NC	ND	OH	OK	OR	PA	RI	SC
Date of Regulations	1996	1995	1994	1996	1995	1992	1992	1996
Definition	F	F	SC	F	SC	SC	F	SC
Eligibility Category	AU	AU	AU	AU	AU	AU	AU	AU
Multidisciplinary Team								
Same as Federal Requirements	F	F	AdRq	F	F	AdRq	F	AdRq
Neurological Report	Rec.		IN					
Physician Report	Rec.		IN	R	R	R		
Psychologist/Psychiatrist	R		IN	IN		R		R
Behavioral Observations	ABS			Soc. A.	R			R
(Additional Assessment)	SLE	TPL		SLE	SLE			SLE
								ARS
Notice of Assessment	F	F	F	F	F	F	F	F
Consent for Assessment	F	F	F	F	F	F	F	F
Notice of IEP Meeting	F	F	F	F	F	F	F	F
IEP Meeting Committee	AdRq	AdRq	F	F	F	AdRq	F	F
Content of the IEP	F	F	F	F	F	AdRq	F	F
Behavioral Management Required				Y				
Additional IEP Requirements					R	R		
Timelines								
Ref to Evaluation						45SD	45SD	
Ref To Assessment Report								
A. Rep to IEP mtg.	30CD			30CD		30CD		30CD
Ref. to Placement		120CD						
A. Rep. to placement								
IEP mtg. to placement						10SD		
Age of Eligibility (pub. sch. prog.)	3-20	3-21	3-21	3-21	3-21	3-21	3-21	3-21
Age for Transition Requirement	16	14	16	16	16	16/14IN	16/14IN	16
Prevoc./Voc. Assessment	16	14	16	16	16	16/14IN	16/14IN	16
Teacher Certification	SE	SE	SE	SE	SE	SE	SE	SE
Teacher/Student Ratio	2:6		6-12			1t,4s 1t,1a,8s		
Special State Projects	TEACCH							

Table 2.1 *Continued*   State Regulations

Item	SD	TN	TX	UT	VT	VA	WA	WI
Date of Regulations	1993	1994	1996	1993	1996	1994	1995	1993
Definition	SC	F	F	SC	SC	F	F	SC/EC
Eligibility Category	AU	AU	AU	AU	AU	AU	AU	AU
Multidisciplinary Team								
Same as Federal Requirements	F	F	F	F	F	F	F	F
Neurological Report		IN	IN	R	IN			
Physician Report	R	R	IN	R	R		IN	IN
Psychologist/Psychiatrist	IN	R	IN	IN				IN
Behavioral Observations	BRS		R				ABS	
(Additional Assessment)	SLE	Voc.A.		E-2			SLE	
Notice of Assessment	F	F	F	F	F	F	F	F
Consent for Assessment	F	F	F	F	F	F	F	F
Notice of IEP Meeting	F	10CD	5SD	F	F	F	F	F
IEP Meeting Committee	F	F	F	F	F	F	F	F
Content of the IEP	F	AdRq	AdRq	F	F	F	F	F
Behavioral Management Required			R	ABS			R	
Additional IEP Requirements		PE				A. Req.		
Timelines								
Ref to Evaluation		30CD	60CD	30CD	60CD		35SD	
Ref to Assessment Report								
A. Rep to IEP mtg.	30CD		30CD		30CD	30CD		
Ref. to Placement		90CD					90CD	
A. Rep. to placement								
IEP mtg. to placement		14CD						
Age of Eligibility (pub. sch. prog.)	3-21	3-21	3-21	3-21	3-21	2-21	3-21	3-21
Age for Transition Requirement	16		16	16	16	16	16	16
Prevoc./Voc. Assessment	16	16	12	26	YIN	16	16	YIN
Teacher Certification	SE	SE	SE	SE	SE	SE	SE	SE
Teacher/Student Ratio			Not specified					
Special State Projects					BI	Manual		

Table 2.1 *Continued* **State Regulation**

Item	WV	WY	Key for Table 2.1	
Date of Regulations	1995	1994	A	Aide (paraprofessional)
			ABS	Adaptive Behavior Scale
Definition	DSM	F/EC	ADL	Activities of Daily Living
			AdRq	Additional Requirements
Eligibility Category	AU	AU	APE	Adaptive Physical Education
			AR	Assessment Report
Multidisciplinary Team			ARS	Autism Rating Scale
Same as Federal Requirements	F	F	AU	Autistic/autism
Neurological Report			B	Birth
Physician Report			BI	Behavioral Intervention
Psychologist/Psychiatrist		R	BRS	Behavior Rating Scale
Behavioral Observations		R	CD	Calendar Day
(Additional Assessment)		ADL	√ list	Checklist
		.	Com.	Community
Notice of Assessment	F	F	D	Day
			DSM	Diagnostic & Statistical Manual
Consent for Assessment	F	F	EC	Evidence of Characteristics
			F	Same as Federal Criteria
Notice of IEP Meeting	F	F	FAB	Functional Analysis of Behavior
			G	Grade
IEP Meeting Committee	F	F	IEP mtg.	IEP meeting
			IN	If necessary (as needed)
Content of the IEP	F	F	IST	Inservice Training
			LP	Learning Processes
Behavioral Management Required			N	No
			NI	Neurologically Impaired
Additional IEP Requirements		PE	PH	Physical Handicap
			PI	Parental Input
Timelines			PMRB	Program Monitoring Review Board
Ref to Evaluation			R	Required
Ref to Assessment Report			Rec.	Recommended
A. Rep. to IEP mtg.			Rec. Ls.	Recreation/Leisure
Ref. to Placement			Ref	Referral
A. Rep. to Placement			s	Student
IEP mtg. to Placement			SC	State Criteria
			SD	School Da
Age of Eligibility (pub. sch. prog.)	3-21	3-21	SE	Special Education
			Sens. F.	Sensory Functioning
Age for Transition Requirement	14	16/YIN	SLE	Speech/language Evaluation
			Soc/ A.	Social Assessment
Prevoc./Voc. Assessment	14	16/YIN	Stand	Standards
			ScSk	Social Skills
Teacher Certification	SE	SE	t	Teacher
			TF	Task Force
Teacher/Student Ratio		1t,4s	TPL	Transition Performance Levels
		1t,1a,8s	Voc. A.	Vocational Assessment
			Yg	Younger
Special State Projects				

35

In areas not specified under a specific state, federal regulations are in place. Some interesting observations can be gleaned as they relate to autism. States have great variability in the specificities related to their guidelines. Texas has included the most additional areas to be addressed that include: daily schedules reflecting a minimum of unstructured time; the need for in-home and parent-training; needs for extended educational programming, prioritized behavioral objectives, prevocational and vocational needs of students 12 years of age of older, and suitable staff-to-students ratio.

An important change in Texas assessment rules is significant for students with autism. Prior to *IDEA*, a special multidisciplinary team including a psychologist, educational diagnostician, speech pathologist, administrator, and individuals knowledgeable in autism, was required to identify students with autism. As a result of the change, administrators may now decide the composition of the assessment team. The state regulations no longer require a psychologist and speech pathologist to be part of the team. Although the guidelines do indicate that school districts must be able to support placement decisions with quality assessments, there is concern that many school districts currently contracting with psychologists for this type of evaluation will use inadequately trained personnel to perform assessments for autism. However, this is a concern in many states which do not have requirements different from federal law. It will be up to the parents of students with autism to ensure that assessment personnel selected to work with their children have appropriate qualifications in the area of autism.

Colorado, Connecticut, Kansas, and Maryland still subsume autism under another major category even though it was identified as a separate category in *IDEA* in 1990. However, these states must still provide appropriate educational services to students with autism, regardless of the disability category. In 1996, Connecticut published a report of a task force on autism, which provides information for school districts and parents related to identification, placement, and programming for students with autism. Missouri, North Carolina, and Delaware have developed statewide programs that provide services for autism.

Parents must be actively involved and knowledgeable about state guidelines. If the guidelines of state are inadequate, use autism support groups to actively encourage more appropriate legislation. As always, parents, are the "watchdog" for their children.

Most states will work on revisions of state regulations to reflect the final regulations of *IDEA*. Schools, parents, and advocacy groups will carefully watch to see how each state interprets *IDEA* and the final regulations published on March 12, 1999. Regulations go into effect on May 11, 1999. However, for requirements that were not pre-existing regulations or statutory requirements, states have until the Fiscal Year 1998 funds become carryover funds for mandatory compliance with the final regulations. This will be either October 1, 1999 or July 1, 1999, depending upon when the funds become available for obligation to the specific state(s).

Chapter Three

Becoming a Legal Eagle

Parents of children with autism should become "legal eagles." They should not only know the major components of *IDEA* and the *IDEA Amendments*, but they should also be familiar with other laws that impact students with autism. The best way to ensure that your child is getting the kind of education to which he or she is entitled is to become aware of all pertinent information related to legislation for individuals with disabilities. *Public Law (PL) 457* applies to young children from birth to three years of age. *The Technology Assistance Act* and the *Assistive Technology Act of 1998 (S.2432),* passed and signed into law in late 1998, apply to students with disabilities of all ages. *Section 504* and *ADA* prohibit disability discrimination and require accessibility for individuals with disabilities. *ADA* applies to employment practices for individuals with disabilities, and the *Vocational Act of 1984* provides for equal access to vocational education. *The Family Education and Privacy Act (FERPA)* deals with confidentiality and parental and student rights to access information. The *Attorney's Fee Bill* is important to any parents contemplating a due process hearing. However, the *IDEA Amendments* placed certain limitations on attorney's fees. Although acquiring parental information has been stressed, it is just as important for special and regular educators to be aware of the legislation discussed in this chapter. The best method for developing good IEPs is to develop legally defensible IEPs—those that meet all the requirements of the law.

The Family Educational Rights and Privacy Act of 1974

The Family Educational Rights and Privacy Act of 1974 (FERPA), often called the *Buckley Amendment*, gives parents of students under the age of 18, and students age 18 and over, the right to examine records kept in the student's personal file (NICHCY, 1991). This prohibits the release of personally identifiable information to third parties without the consent of the student, if the student is 18 or is attending an institution of post-secondary education (or without the consent of his parents). Thus, we are looking at parental and student rights.

CASE EXAMPLE:

Mr. Smith, the school principal, wanted to ensure that all teachers were aware of the students in their classroom who had IEPs with modifications. He sent a list of all special education students in the school to the teachers and asked them to make sure that he or she was aware of each student's IEP. All though this was a well-intentioned act, it was also a violation of student confidentiality. School personnel should not distribute a list of students in special education to all teachers because that identifies students as having a disability. Only teachers working with the student have a legitimate educational need to know that a student has a disability. Additionally, special education teachers who display student work in the hallway should only use first names, or first names and last initials. Just the fact that a student is in a special education class reveals the student's disability, which is supposed to be confidential information.

CASE EXAMPLE:

One year, when working at an annual *Very Special Arts Festival,* I overheard a couple talking about a child enrolled in a special private school for students with disabilities. They saw his name and school on artwork displayed at the local mall. The woman said, "So that's what happened to him. He used to be in Joey's class." Although these students are proud to have their artwork displayed at the local mall, and their parents sign permission for display of their works, the organizers now only put the age, grade, and school name on the front of exhibited work to protect the confidentiality of participating students. Even though the purpose of *Very Special Arts* is to highlight the abilities of individuals with disabilities, confidentiality was being violated because only students with a disability could participate. This issue could be addressed by changing the permission form to include consent for display of student names with their works.

FERPA allows parents to access their children's educational records. They have the right to obtain copies, inspect, challenge, and, to a degree, control release of information in the student's educational record. *FERPA* regulations define a parent as a natural parent or a person acting as a parent or guardian in the absence of the child's natural parent. In the case of divorced or separated parents, both parents have equal rights of access to the child's records, unless there is a court order terminating or restricting the rights of one parent (*FERPA,* 1988).

Annual Notice

FERPA requires that school administrators adopt a written policy informing parents of their rights under this law. Administrators must inform parents and students over eighteen of their right to inspect the student's records. This notice must include the location of the records, procedures for gaining access to the records, and the cost for reproducing them. Some school districts do this by publishing an annual notice in a local newspaper or in the school handbook given to students at the beginning of each school year. Other school districts meet this requirement by posting the notice in a prominent place in each school or at the school administration building. This would probably be posted in the same place where notice of school board meetings are posted. Some special education programs print this notice on IEP forms.

Directory Information

Parents must also be notified as to which information is directory information. This information may include such items as:

- the student's name, address, and telephone number;
- date and place of birth;
- major field of study;
- participation in extracurricular activities;
- height and weight of members of athletic teams;
- dates of attendance at the school, and degrees and awards received; and
- the most recent previous school attended.

Although the exact items included may differ from school to school, directory information can be given to third parties unless parents make a timely objection; i.e., before the information is released.

Parental Access

Parents and school personnel sometimes disagree over which educational records can be accessed by parents. Anything in the student's special education records or permanent school file is open records and can be accessed by parents and students over the age of eighteen. Some advocates recommend that parents request access to all records with their child's name on it.

Records that schools do not have to release to parents are personal notes kept by teachers, related service personnel (such as a school counselor or occupational therapist), and administrators. Personal notes should not be placed in the student's permanent file or special education folder. Once the notes are placed in the student's records, they are no longer considered to be personal notes and are subject to access by parents. Notes are no longer considered "personal" if the teacher, counselor, etc., shows the notes to another person. School professionals desiring to keep personal notes may do so as long as the information does not go into school files and is not shown to other persons.

Confidential Information

Additionally, schools must ensure that files containing confidential information are secure. This generally means that the files must be kept in locked filing cabinets. A locked classroom is not sufficient because many people, including custodians, have master keys to school classrooms. Therefore, anyone gaining entrance to the room could have access to the information if it is not locked in a file cabinet or closet.

Schools may release confidential information to other school officials who have a "legitimate educational interest in the student." However, the annual notice must include the type of records and under what circumstances this information would be released. Typical situations include allowing state monitors and Office of Civil Rights (OCR) investigators access to student records when the school district is being monitored or investigated as the result of an official complaint to OCR. Other persons who actually work with the student, such as classroom teachers, related service personnel, or consultants specifically employed to provide services for the student, are considered to have a "legitimate educational interest in the student." Schools must keep a record of any people granted access to the student's records. This may be done by placing an access page in the front of the student eligibility folder. Individuals reviewing the folder contents must sign their names, the date, and the purpose for review of the student folder contents.

Transferring Educational Records

School districts transferring educational records of a student to another school system in which the student seeks, or intends, to enroll, should notify the parents by sending a notice to the last known address of the parent or eligible student except:

- if the parent or eligible student requests that the records be transferred, or

- if the agency or institution includes a notice in its policies and procedures that it forwards education records on request to a school in which a student seeks or intends to enroll. The agency or institution does not have to provide any further notice of the transfer.

Filing a Complaint

A parent wishing to file a complaint related to *FERPA* may write to the Family Policy and Regulations Office, U. S. Dept. of Education, Washington, D. C. 20202. The complaint must indicate the reasons why the individual believes that a *FERPA* violation has occurred. The specific factual allegations should be described.

IDEA Reinforces *FERPA*

The *IDEA Amendments* reinforce the concept of confidentiality that is guaranteed by *FERPA*. Section 300.127 requires that each state develop written policies and procedures to ensure that confidentiality of any personally identifiable information is protected when the state is collecting, using, or maintaining information related to Part B of *IDEA*. Section 300.562 also requires that each participating agency allow parents to inspect and review any education records relating to their children that was collected, maintained, or used by the state agency under *IDEA*. It also requires that the public agency comply with parent "requests for records without unnecessary delay and before any meeting regarding an IEP, or any hearing pursuant to Sections. 300.507 and 300.521-300.528, and in no case more than 45 days after the request has been made.

The *IDEA Amendments* also define the "right to inspect and review education records under this section" as:

- the right for parents to make reasonable requests for explanations and interpretations of the records, and to receive a response from the participating agency;

- the right to request copies of records containing information from agencies if failure to receive the copies would prevent the parent from inspecting and reviewing the records; and

- the right to have a parent representative inspect and review the records.

CASE EXAMPLE:

Johnny Green has an IEP meeting scheduled for two weeks from today. Mr. and Mrs. Green decide that they want to look at the assessment report and have the appraisal staff member explain the report to them prior to the IEP meeting. According to the guidelines, the school has to provide Mr. and Mrs. Green with access to Johnny's assessment report prior to the IEP meeting. A time should also be set for Mr. and Mrs. Green to meet with the school appraisal specialist to discuss the report. If Mr. Green is unable to inspect the records unless copies are provided, copies should be provided for him.

Personnel at the public agency may assume that the parent has the authority to inspect and review records relating to his or her child. This is correct unless the agency has been advised that the parent does not have the authority under applicable state law governing matters such as divorce, custody, and guardianship. The laws of the state and the specifics of the divorce and/or custody orders will determine whether one or both parents has the right of access to school records. The court decree should specify parental responsibilities and rights related to the educational process for the child.

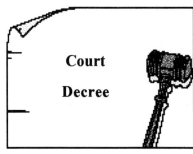

Court

Decree

Public Law 99-457

PL 99-457 (The Education of the Handicapped Act Amendments of 1986) extends the rights and protections of *Public Law 94-142* to children with disabilities, ages three to five years. It also provides funding for states wishing to implement programs for children with disabilities in this age bracket through the establishment of the Part H Program. *Part H - Handicapped Infants and Toddlers (Part C* in the *IDEA Amendments)* legislation was designed to assist states in the development of comprehensive, multidisciplinary, statewide systems of early intervention services for children with disabilities. Preschool children can begin receiving educational services at the age of three instead of waiting until they are of school age in their state.

Most states developed statewide systems of early intervention programs for children with disabilities from birth to three, which enables infants or toddlers and their families to access services as soon as the infant or toddler is identified as a "child with a disability." Some programs were developed as an extension of public school programs, while other states elected to have a different agency provide early intervention services. A key component of this legislation is the requirement for development of Individual Family Service Plans (IFSPs). IFSPs must be developed for students receiving services for children in the birth-to-three age range. The IFSP must consider the needs of the family, not just the individual needs of the child. Therefore, families may receive services that are needed to help them assist in the development of their young child. A case manager is appointed for each child to help the family identify and access needed services. Transition services were also expanded with a requirement of an Individual Transition Plan (ITP) for children transitioning from early childhood intervention programs into public school early childhood programs (NICHCY, p. 9).

The Technology-Related Assistance for Individuals with Disabilities Act of 1988

and

The Technology Act of 1998

P. L. 100-407, *The Technology-Related Assistance for Individuals with Disabilities Act of 1988*, extended the availability of assistive technology (AT) to individuals with disabilities and their families. The *Assistive Technology Act of 1998* (S. 2432) reaffirmed the federal role of promoting access to assistive technology devices and services for individuals with disabilities. The purposes of the *Assistive Technology Act of 1998* (*ATA*) are to:

- support states in sustaining and strengthening their capacity to address the assistive technology needs of individuals with disabilities;

- focus the investment in technology, across Federal agencies and departments, that could benefit individuals with disabilities; and

- support micro-loan programs to provide assistance to individuals who desire to purchase assistive technology devices or services.

The law defines an assistive technology device as "any item, piece of equipment, or product system whether acquired off the shelf, modified or customized that is used to increase, maintain, or improve functional capabilities of individuals with disabilities." *Title I* of the *ATA* provides states with funds to develop state systems of assistive technology services through multiple grant programs from fiscal years 1999 through 2004. This is an important law for students with autism because so many use various technology devices. Even something as simple as a calculator, a pencil holder, and pencil and paper communication boards, can be considered to be assistive technology. However, the more common forms of assistive technology include the computer and augmentative communication devices (equipment with special programming capabilities that allow voice output for nonverbal students).

School districts cannot deny assistive technology to individuals with autism before an evaluation has been made to determine whether the requested technology is an element of a free appropriate public education for the individual student. (Schrag letter dated Aug. 10, 1990 and 16

EHLR 1317 as cited by Carl & Zabala, 1994). The determination of the need for assistive technology must be made on an individual basis using *IDEA* regulations for assessment, IEPs, and placement. If the school district determines that the student has an educational need for assistive technology, the provision of assistive technology may be special education, related services, or supplementary aids and services necessary to support the student with disabilities in the regular educational classroom (34 CFR §300.308 and 16 EHLR 1317 as cited in Carl & Zabala, 1994). When the IEP team determines that assistive technology devices or services are required for individual students to receive a free appropriate public education, they must be provided at no cost to the parents. Section 300.308 specifically states "on a case-by case basis, the use of school-purchased assistive technology devices in a child's home or in other settings is required if the child's IEP team determines that the child needs access to those devices in order to receive a free appropriate education (FAPE).

Section 504

Section 504 is part of Public Law 93-112, *The Rehabilitation Act of 1973.* This law established a comprehensive plan for providing rehabilitation services to all individuals, regardless of age or severity of the disability. This law is broader than *IDEA* because it applies to a larger category of individuals. All students identified as having a disability under *IDEA* are covered under Section 504. However, some students who are not eligible under *IDEA* may be eligible under Section 504. For example, students with attention deficit disorder (ADD), chronic asthma, diabetes, or even extreme obesity might be eligible under *Section 504* which defines handicapped in the following way.

A person is considered handicapped if he/she:

1. has a physical or mental impairment that substantially limits one or more major life activities,

2. has a record of such an impairment, or

3. is regarded as having such an impairment (LDA, 1995).

Additionally, *Section 504* provides for civil rights enforcement through the U.S. Department of Education, Office of Civil Rights (OCR). This means that parents and eligible students can file a complaint with the Office of Civil Rights that will be investigated by the agency. Generally, the alleged complaint is discrimination against an individual with a disability because minimum requirements set forth in law are not being implemented.

Types of discrimination that might occur in school situations are:

- denying credit to a student whose absenteeism is related to his/her disability,

- refusing to dispense medication to a student with a disability without a parental consent to waive liability,

- prohibiting a student from participating in extracurricular activities because of the person's disability,

- supporting student organizations that exclude students with disabilities, and

- locating students with disabilities in inferior facilities due to a lack of classroom space. (LDA, 1995).

Accommodation Plans

Section 504 requires districts to provide accommodations for students identified as being eligible for *Section 504*. Many of the suggested accommodations, such as modified homework or taped textbooks, are similar to modifications under *IDEA*. However, although there should be a written accommodation plan, the school district is not required to develop an IEP. *Section 504* does not provide for school districts to receive any additional funding to meet the needs of *Section 504* students. The lack of federal funding is one reason that some school districts are reluctant to identify students under *Section 504*. Students with autism qualify under *Section 504* and *IDEA's* more stringent regulations that provide federal funding.

This law also applies to students in postsecondary situations, meaning that students with autism or other disabilities, having college potential, may receive needed modifications or accommodations at colleges and universities. Such accommodations may include tape recording of lectures, assistance in note taking, or special accommodations for testing. Procedures vary at different colleges and universities. Parents and students should contact the specific postsecondary institution the individual plans to attend to learn the university's specific procedures required for identification and development of accommodation plans (NICHCY, 1991).

Public Law 101-336, The Americans with Disabilities Act of 1990 (ADA)

This law "guarantees equal opportunity for individuals with disabilities in employment, public accommodation, transportation, state and local government services, and telecommunications." (NICHCY, 1991). Essentially, it assures full civil rights for all persons with disabilities by prohibiting discrimination in programs or activities receiving federal funding. *ADA* assures individuals with disabilities the same rights and privileges that earlier legislation provided to women and minorities. It impacts public school programs by requiring schools to make programs accessible for students with disabilities. As students with autism begin community-based instruction or approach adolescence, *The Americans with Disabilities Act* becomes more relevant. As part of transition activities, students should learn about the rights and protections that are afforded them under *ADA* in the areas of employment, public services, public accommodations, transportation, and telecommunications.

Parents should also know that "employers with 15 or more employees may not refuse to hire or promote a person with a disability because of the individual's disability when that person is qualified to perform the job." (CEC, 1990). Additional employment provisions go into effect for employers with 25 or more employees.

ADA also prohibits employers from asking questions about disabilities on the application form. This includes questions about workers' compensation claims, previous treatment by a doctor, or other questions likely to elicit information about disabilities. Applicants do not have to answer these questions. If an application form includes these questions, it would be better to leave them blank than to answer the questions untruthfully. It is suggested that students with disabilities ask for an application form, fill it out at home, and then return it to the employer.

During the actual interview, employers cannot ask questions intended to elicit information about a disability. If the disability is obvious or if the individual chooses to tell the employer about the disability, the employer may ask questions about how the individual would do the tasks required for the job. Teachers and parents should prepare the student for the interview by talking to him or her about ways job tasks can be done. The employer may be impressed if the individual with autism is able to suggest possible accommodations or creative solutions to an anticipated problem (Parker, 1996).

The Vocational Education Act of 1984

Public Law 93-380, also often referred to as the *Carl D. Perkins Act* or the *Perkins Act*, provides federal funding to support vocational education programs. The law states that individuals with disabilities must be provided with equal access to recruitment, enrollment, and placement activities in vocational education. In 1990, this law was amended by passing *P. L. 101-392*, which changed the name to *The Carl D. Perkins Vocational and Applied Technology Education Act.* The amendments expanded the term, "special populations," to include individuals with disabilities, economically disadvantaged individuals, individuals with limited English proficiency (LEP), individuals in programs to eliminate sex bias, and individuals in correctional institutions. A key concept of this law is that individuals with disabilities have a guarantee of full vocational education opportunities.

Although this law guarantees full access to all vocational programs, I have personally had some negative experiences trying to get students with disabilities into vocational programs. In Texas, prior to the adoption of new rules in July of 1996, a vocational education supervisor or teacher had to be in attendance at the IEP meeting if vocational education was a placement option for students with disabilities. The first issue generally brought up was safety. Of course, with some students, certain classes were inappropriate because they involved welders, saws, and use of other potentially dangerous equipment. It was easy to understand why auto body shop, general construction of building houses, and some other vocational classes were not appropriate.

I had a problem with insistence by some homemaking teachers that students with disabilities could not be successful in homemaking classes because the educational activities in homemaking were often compatible with stated objectives in students' IEPs. Grades in their classes were based upon the results of very difficult written tests instead of students' performance in homemaking tasks. Even though the IEP committee recommended oral tests or evaluation based upon performance, some homemaking teachers were unwilling to have students with disabilities in their classrooms.

In two specific cases, students were placed in homemaking classes over the objections of the homemaking teachers. Unfortunately, students suffered while the special education staff learned a valuable lesson. If a classroom teacher does not want to accept a student in a classroom, the program may be sabotaged in subtle ways to ensure that students are not successful. In these two specific instances, both students failed the course and had to retake another elective for high school graduation.

In the above situations, the students' parents could have filed for due process hearings or registered complaints with the Office of Civil Rights because the students' IEPs were not being followed. However, the parents of these two children were neither knowledgeable about their rights or assertive enough to follow through with due process procedures.

Special educators now have a court case that can be cited regarding a teacher's specific refusal to modify or follow the IEP in regular education classes. In a Kentucky court case, a high school teacher was fined $5,000 in compensatory damages and $10,000 in punitive damages because he refused to allow the student to take oral tests. The power and authority of the IEP Committee and the written IEP document were demonstrated. (Walsh, 1993b). For additional information about this specific case, see modifications on pages 93 to 95.

The Attorneys' Fee Bill

Public Law 99-372, The Handicapped Children's Protection Act of 198,6 is significant to parents of students with autism because it provides for reimbursement of attorney's fees to parents who prevail in administrative hearings or court disputes with a school system concerning the child's right to free appropriate special education and related services. In most cases, the parents must prevail on only one issue to be eligible for reimbursement of attorney fees. I know of one case involving eighteen separate issues. Although the parent won on only one issue, the district was required to reimburse attorney fees.

The wording of the law refers to "reasonable attorney fees." In *Coleman v. Hudson School District* (1991, [Advocacy Inc., 1993]), the school district requested that reimbursement for the parent's attorney fees be reduced by 50 percent because the parents only received half of their request for reimbursement. However, the court disagreed and allowed parents to fully recover attorney fees because the parents had prevailed on the issue of appropriateness of the educational program.

Reasonable Attorney Fees

This has caused controversy because the perception of "reasonable" varies from individual to individual and school to school. "Reasonable" is not defined in this law. Consequently, the *IDEA Amendments* have provisions that limit the amount of attorney fees that may be reimbursed. Section 300. 513 addresses attorneys' fees. According to the *IDEA Amendments*, a court awards reasonable attorneys' fees under section 615 (I) (3) of the Act consistent with the following:

- **Fees must be awarded based upon rates prevailing in the community** in which the action or proceeding arose for the kind and quality of services furnished.

- **Attorneys' fees may not be awarded and related costs may not be reimbursed in the following situations:**

  * An offer is made within the time prescribed by *Rule 68 of the Federal Rules of Civil Procedure* or, in the case of an administrative proceeding, at any time more than 10 days before the proceeding begins;

  * The offer is not accepted within 10 days; and

  * The court or administrative hearing officer finds that the relief finally obtained by the parents is not more favorable to the parents than the offer of settlement.

- **Attorneys' fees may not be awarded relating to any meeting of the IEP team** unless the meeting is convened as a result of an administrative proceeding or judicial action, or at the discretion of the state, for a mediation that is conducted prior to the filing of a request for due process.

- **Attorneys' fees and related costs may be awarded to a parent** who is the prevailing party and who was substantially justified in rejecting the settlement offer.

Reduction of Attorneys' Fees

- **Attorneys' fees may be reduced if the court finds that**:
    * The parent, during the course of the action or proceeding, unreasonably protracted the final resolution of the controversy;
    * The amount of the attorneys' fees otherwise authorized to be awarded unreasonably exceeds the hourly rate prevailing in the community for similar services by attorneys of reasonably comparable skill, reputation, and experience;
    * The time spent and legal services furnished were excessive considering the nature of the action or proceeding; or
    * The attorney representing the parent did not provide to the school district the appropriate information in the due process complaint in accordance with this *IDEA* requirement.

- **Attorneys' fees will not be reduced if** the court finds that the state or local agency unreasonably protracted the final resolution of the action or proceeding or there was a violation of section 615 of the *IDEA Amendments.*

Chapter Four

The Guiding Star: Appropriate Assessment

Lost people frequently use the North Star to guide them in the appropriate direction. Appropriate assessment, like this guiding star, must direct the development of appropriate IEPs. **If the assessment is not comprehensive and appropriate for the student, the development of the Individualized Educational Program will be flawed.**

In the area of assessment, the *IDEA Amendments* have reaffirmed certain rights. Federal regulations continue to require nondiscriminatory evaluations. Selected assessment instruments should be designed for the intended purpose and not be culturally or racially discriminatory. The evaluation must be conducted in the native language of the student. Additionally, it is specified that "no single procedure shall be the sole criterion for determining an appropriate educational program for a child." (*IDEA, Federal Register*, 1992, 1999).

IDEA Amendment Changes to Assessment

Significant changes were made related to assessment of students with disabilities in the *IDEA Amendments*. Major changes include the following:

- **Parental consent** is required for the **initial evaluation and reevaluations** of a child with a disability. Previously, only notice was required for reevaluations—not notice and consent.

- **The team** that determines eligibility for special education shall **include the parent**.

- The team may use the **term developmental delay** for children aged 3 through 9 if the state and LEA adopt a policy to use the term. A specific eligibility category does not have to be identified.

- Parents will be given a **copy of the evaluation report.**

- The evaluation must include information related to enabling the child to be involved in and **progress in the general curriculum.** For preschool children, the child's ability to participate in appropriate activities must be addressed.

- Schools must use assessment instruments and strategies that directly assist persons in **determining the educational needs of the child.**

- **Reevaluations must begin with a review of existing evaluations.** Based upon that review and input from parents, the IEP team will identify what, if any, additional data is needed to determine:

  * eligibility for special education;

  * present levels of performance and educational needs;
    whether the student needs (or continues to need) special education and related services; and

  * whether any additions or modifications are needed to enable the student to meet measurable annual goals and to participate, as appropriate, in the general curriculum.

- If after reviewing existing evaluation data, the IEP team decides that additional data is not needed to determine whether the student continues to be eligible for special education, the **district must notify the parent of:**

  * The determination and the reasons for it; and the parents' right to still request an assessment.

  * The school will not be required to conduct a reevaluation unless the parents request it.

- The parent and the IEP team can agree that a **student does not need a comprehensive reevaluation every 3 years.**

- The district must **conduct an evaluation before dismissing a student** from special education except for students who are being dismissed by graduation.

- Students with disabilities will be required to **participate in state and or district-wide assessments or alternate assessments** by July 1, 2000 (*IDEA*, 1997, Section 300.138, *Federal Register*, 1999, p. 12429).

Purposes of Assessment

Parents' Search for a Cause

Most parents of children with autism begin looking for answers during the child's infancy or toddler years. They want to know why the child is not developing normally and what they can do to correct the problem. Their voyage to discovery generally follows a path that begins with medical personnel. Some parents see several medical practitioners before finally seeing someone knowledgeable about autism. Since many family doctors have minimal training about autism and little occasion to see individuals with pervasive developmental disorders, they lack the knowledge to make appropriate diagnoses.

Hearing an actual diagnosis of autism for your child is generally a very traumatic experience—a major crisis in any family. For many years, the diagnosis was associated with little hope of progress. However, with new technology, treatments, and success stories of adults with autism, some parents hope that their child will also be able to "rise above" autism in the same way that Grandin ([1995]; Grandin & Scariano [1986]); McKean (1994, 1996); and others have learned to cope in spite of their sensory dysfunctions associated with autism.

The search for a cause or diagnosis of abnormal development is linked to the concept of treatment. Parents hope identification of the cause will lead them to appropriate treatments or a "cure" for the child. Unfortunately, at this time, there are no "miracle cures" for autism. However, an accurate diagnosis does give parents a starting point. It gives direction to their search for the best methods, treatments, and strategies to improve their child's functioning. A good evaluation from a qualified medical professional will not only tell parents what is wrong, but also what can be done for the child (Siegel, 1996, p. 83).

The diagnosis may also open the door to additional services such as early childhood intervention or public school programs. Although parents generally mourn for the loss of their "dream child" who never was or will be, many also report a sense of relief. Their search for the cause of the child's abnormal development is over. They at least know the basis of the child's problems. For some parents, the uncertainty of not knowing what is wrong is more difficult to handle than knowing that the child has autism.

Unfortunately, there are still some medical personnel and psychologists who have little hope for individuals with autism. At the 1995 Autism Society of America conference in Greensboro, North Carolina, I met a parent whose child had been diagnosed three years earlier at the age of two. At that time, the medical professional told the parents to put the child in an institution, go home and have another baby. Rejecting the professional's advice, the parents went home and immediately began searching for appropriate treatments. Professionals such as this one show little regard for the effect that a diagnosis of autism has on the child and the family.

If you, as a parent, believe that your child might have autism, you should go to a physician who is an expert on autism. Your local pediatrician or family doctor should be able to suggest one. If the medical professional is unable to provide this kind of information, contact a local chapter or the national office of the ASA to obtain this type of information. Parents' search for knowledge and appropriate treatments may help them accept the child. Frequently, the journey for additional knowledge and information becomes an avenue for the eventual recognition and acceptance of the child's diagnosis. Acceptance does not imply that the search for effective treatment is over. It generally means that parents are ready to search for appropriate treatments and methodologies that continue to be developed and investigated. At this stage in the young child's life, a developmental evaluation will be done.

Developmental Evaluations

Developmental evaluations generally include:

- A developmental history including health/medical, genetic, and social information;

- Observations and descriptions of the child's behavior;

- Hearing evaluation by an audiologist to ensure that behaviors are not related to a hearing impairment;

- Vision evaluation by an ophthalmologist to determine if there is a visual impairment;

- Assessments of social relatedness and intelligence;

- Assessments of communication (by a speech-language pathologist) including evaluations of expressive and receptive language usually performed with formal and informal assessment techniques, including observations of methods the child uses for communication of wants and needs;

- Medical tests such as genetic testing for fragile x syndrome;

- Evaluation of the need for medical management of child;

- Administration of autism rating scales (usually a parent report form);

- Assessments of behavioral and adaptive functioning.;

- Educational assessments

- Assessments by occupational and physical therapists of motor functioning and sensory integration.

A developmental assessment performed by a team of persons knowledgeable about autism is very important in the initial diagnosis of autism. Most early intervention programs and early childhood public school programs will utilize the results of the developmental assessment. However, as the child grows older, the focus of school assessments will be on educational services and benefit.

School Evaluations for Students with Disabilities

A comprehensive individual assessment (CIA) must be performed when a child is initially referred for special education. McLoughlin & Lewis (1994, p. 4) define the process of a comprehensive individual assessment for students with disabilities as "the systematic process of gathering educationally relevant information to make legal and instructional decisions about the provision of special services." Educational assessments for students with disabilities are performed for one or more of the following purposes:

- to find a cause (of the disability);

- to identify individuals who may need further assessment;

- to determine eligibility (does the child qualify for special education?);

- to determine if there is a need for special education and related services;

- to obtain data to plan for the IEP (i.e., strengths and weaknesses and present levels of performance and educational needs of the student);

- to determine whether any additions or modifications to the special education and related services are needed to enable the child to meet the measurable annual goals set out in the IEP of the child and to participate, as appropriate, in the general curriculum.
- to monitor and measure student progress; and
- to evaluate program effectiveness.

School Screening

School screening is not required by the *IDEA Amendments*. However, Child Find programs are required. Some schools use district-wide school screening programs as part of their Child Find procedures. These screening programs typically use short and easy to administer assessment instruments which are given to all students to determine if there are indications of a disability. Because the same assessment is given to all students, parent permission for testing is not required. Low performance on school screening test measures generally indicate a need for further assessment of specific students, but the instruments are typically not used for diagnostic purposes. Children who exhibit a need for diagnostic testing are referred for comprehensive individual assessments through special education services.

Most school screening programs take place in the primary grades. Not all schools have school screening programs. With the trend toward inclusion, many school districts dropped screening programs. If a student's disability was not noticeable to the classroom teacher, the philosophy was that the student did not have a severe enough disability to justify removal from the general education classroom. If the teacher noticed a need for assessment, the classroom teacher could refer the child for special education assessment.

Entering Special Education Services in Public Schools

Although children may be diagnosed with autism or autistic disorder prior to the provision of school services, the school system or other public agency serving the child still has a mandate to determine eligibility for services when the child reaches school age. In some instances, schools may accept the report of the professional making the original diagnosis if it is a current evaluation. In other situations, school administrators may prefer to complete their own comprehensive individual assessment (CIA) using federal, state, and local guidelines for eligibility to determine whether the child meets criteria for autism and special education services.

Referral

If the child meets the age criteria for services in the state where he or she lives, the school must provide a CIA to determine whether the student is eligible for special education services. Section 300.121 of the *IDEA Amendments* requires states to ensure that all children with disabilities aged three through twenty-one have the right to a free appropriate public education. However, the obligation to make FAPE available to all children with disabilities does not apply to children aged three, four, five, eighteen, nineteen, twenty, and twenty-one, if that application would be inconsistent with state law or practice (Section 300.122, *Federal Register*, 1999, p. 12427).

This initial assessment should be completed by a team of qualified professionals. The first step in this process generally is a referral for an evaluation for special education services. Some states also require an observation of the child's behavior in the school setting, with written documentation recorded by someone other than the classroom teacher. A complete referral generally includes information from the classroom teacher or school records, a health history, information from the parents, and in many states, a vision and hearing screening. The referral can be made by medical professionals, by school personnel, other agency staff, or by parents.

Notice of Assessment

Prior to the assessment of a student suspected of having a disability, parents must receive notice of the school's intent to assess. The *IDEA Amendments* require parental consent for the initial evaluation and all reevaluations. Notice and consent requirements for assessments do not apply to evaluations that are completed at least annually to measure progress on IEP goals and objectives, if the purpose is to measure progress on goals and objectives.

An OCR ruling (School Admin. Unit No. 29 {NH], 20 IDELR 1011) in 1993 (LRP Publications, 1994c) reiterated that notice and consent are not required for standard post-placement tests which the district uses for all special education students. In this case, a student returned to the district from an out-of-district placement. The diagnostic reading and spelling tests that were administered to him without notifying his parent were not a violation of student and parental rights because the administration of these tests was standard district procedures for measuring the IEP progress; i.e., the school district used these tests for all special education students entering new placements to determine their current levels of performance at the beginning of the new placement.

The notice of assessment should be written in understandable language—not educational jargon. Notice must be provided in the native language of the parent unless it is clearly not feasible to do so. Generally, when schools have large populations of parents and students from minority and ethnic groups, special education forms are generally printed in English and several languages. For example, in the southwestern United States bordering Mexico, states have large Hispanic populations. There, most school forms are available in English and Spanish. In northern states bordering parts of Canada, schools may need to have forms available in French. Districts with large Asian populations would need forms in the specific language of the parents, which may be difficult to provide, because there are so many different dialects spoken by individuals from Asia.

In situations where school districts have only one or two children with special needs from a specific ethnic or minority group, districts may follow alternate procedures allowed in federal law. (*IDEA*, Section 300.505 [c]). Personally, I have been in situations involving parents who only spoke Choctaw Indian or Laotian. In each instance, we contracted with an interpreter from another town to orally translate the notices, assessment reports, and IEP meetings and documented that the parents understood the notice as translated.

Native language also applies to individuals with hearing impairments whose mode of communication is sign language. Notices and meetings may have to be translated into sign language for parents with hearing impairments. However, most individuals with hearing impairments can read the notice forms written in English. Interpreters are generally needed for the actual meetings because the meeting is oral, not written. Therefore, schools have a duty to inform parents in their native language, and parents may request information in their native language if the school has not prepared for such an occurrence.

Statewide Assessments

An emphasis in the *IDEA Amendments* is accountability for all students and involvement in the general education curriculum. Consequently, federal law now states that students with disabilities must participate in statewide and district-wide testing for all students. If a student is unable to participate, the student with a disability must participate in an alternate assessment. States are mandated to have alternate assessments completed by the year 2000. Schools generally do not have to notify parents about this type of testing because all students must participate. Notice requirements generally apply to assessment that is special and individualized—not to testing done with all students.

Determination of Needed Evaluation Data

When appropriate as part of an initial evaluation and for all reevaluations, there must be a review of existing evaluation data by the IEP team and other qualified professionals. (*IDEA* does not require a meeting for this review). This team will:

- Review existing evaluation data on the child, including:
    * Evaluations and information provided by the child's parents;
    * Current classroom-based assessments and observations; and
    * Observations by teachers and related service personnel.

- On the basis of that review of existing data and parental input, the team will identify what additional data, if any, are needed to determine:
    * Whether the child has a particular category of disability, or in the case of a reevaluation, whether the child continues to exhibit the disability;
    * The present levels of performance and educational needs of the child;
    * Whether the child needs special education and related services; and
    * Whether any additions or modifications to the special education and related services are needed to enable the child to meet the measurable annual goals set forth in the child's IEP and to participate, as appropriate, in the general education curriculum.

61

What if the agency determines that no additional assessment data are needed?

The public agency notifies the child's parents of that determination and the reasons for it; and of the parents' right to request an assessment to determine whether the child continues to be a child with a disability.

In the preceding question, what if the parent requests that the public agency perform the assessment?

Unless the parent requests an assessment, the public agency does not have to perform additional assessments. If the parent requests that an assessment be performed, the public agency will have to provide the assessment.

Determination of Eligibility

Once the tests and other evaluation materials have been administered, a group of qualified professionals and the child's parents must determine whether the child has a disability. The public agency must provide a copy of the evaluation report and the documentation of eligibility to the parent. A child may not be determined to be eligible under this part of the *IDEA Amendments* if the determinant factor for that eligibility determination is:

- lack of instruction in reading or math; or
- limited English proficiency; and
- the child does not otherwise meet the eligibility criteria.

Can the school dismiss my child from without performing an assessment special education services on the basis that he is no longer a child with a disability?

No. The school must perform an assessment if the team of qualified professionals determines that the student is no longer a child with a disability. That determination must be based upon current assessment data. The exception to this situation is graduation. Students who are being dismissed from special education services because they graduating from school with a regular high school diploma do not have be evaluated.

How often do reevaluations have to be performed?

If conditions warrant a reevaluation, they should be performed every three years. The team must at least review existing data to determine that a reevaluation is not needed. However, the child's parent or teacher may request that a reevaluation be performed before the three year period is over.

Evaluation Procedures

- Tests and other evaluation materials used to assess individuals

  * are not culturally or racially biased; and

  * are provided and administered in the child's native language or other mode of communication, unless it is clearly not feasible to do so.

- A variety of assessment tools and strategies are used to gather relevant functional and developmental information about the child.

- Assessment instruments are validated for the specific purpose for which they are being used.

- Assessment instruments are administered by trained and knowledgeable personnel, in accordance with any instructions provided by the producer of the test.

- No single procedure should be used as a sole criterion for determining whether a child is eligible as a child with a disability or for determining an appropriate educational program for the child.

- The child is evaluated in all areas related to the suspected disability including

  * health,

  * vision and hearing,

  * social and emotional status,

  * general intelligence,

  * academic performance,

  * communicative status, and

  * motor abilities.

- The evaluation should be sufficiently comprehensive to identify all of the child's special education and related services needs.

What if an assessment is not conducted under standard conditions?

The assessment report should describe the extent to which standard conditions were not used. For example, the report should provide or have attached the qualifications of the person administering the test and/or the method of test administration.

Formal Assessment

Formal assessment includes standardized assessments or norm referenced assessments. Norm referenced tests are developed using a large normative sample population. They compare the individual's performance to that of the normative population. Norm referenced tests such as intelligence tests and academic achievement tests are generally used for eligibility determination. Individuals with pervasive developmental disorders generally do not perform well on standardized tests that must be administered in a specific way with no modifications. If the specific instructions of the test manual are not followed, the resulting scores will not be valid. However, individuals with high-functioning autism or Asperger's Disorder may score very high on intelligence tests.

Many individuals with Autistic Disorder or low-functioning autism are unable to be assessed with standardized instruments because of levels of functioning in the area of language or difficulties responding to requests of the individual performing the assessment. In such instances, the test administrator may not be able to get a valid score. Therefore, checklists and observational scales are frequently used for eligibility determination.

CASE EXAMPLE

Larry, a nine-year old student, was seen by a neuropsychologist for his three-year comprehensive evaluation. The psychologist completed the eligibility portion of the assessment, while school personnel completed assessments of Larry's present levels of performance needed for IEP program planning. His mother related the events of the psychologist evaluation to me. First, the evaluation was conducted at the psychologist's office

Continued on next page...

CASE EXAMPLE continued

instead of on the school campus, which meant Larry had to adjust to a new environment. Larry did not appear to relate well to the psychologist. Larry's mother said she watched as he visibly shut down. Of course, he was identified as having autism and mental retardation. I personally don't believe that he has mental retardation. However, he has classic characteristics of autism with many sensory dysfunctions. His behaviors, which can generally be attributed to sensory dysfunctions characteristic of autism, get in the way of his performance on standardized assessments and in the classroom.

Continued on next page…

Intelligence tests are often not true measures of intellectual functioning in students with autism. They measure performance on one assessment instrument on one day in a particular setting. Many factors may influence students' performance on these instruments. Is the setting strange? Is there something in the setting that is bothersome?

Are there noises that others don't hear that are irritating? During administration of a hearing test, a student yelled, "Stop, stop." Alarmed, I asked, "What's wrong? He answered, "someone turned the copier on in the next room." Although I couldn't hear it, someone had turned the copier on. It was necessary to turn it off in order to complete the evaluation.

Does the evaluator wear a particular type of perfume that is bothersome? Does the student have difficulty with motor planning and initiation of motor movements? Is the student having a bad day? Did things happen earlier in the day that are affecting his or her current performance? Many students with autism are resistant to change and the test administration is a change of routine.

Therefore, we must acknowledge that lack of performance in test situations does not necessarily mean lack of ability. A test score in the intellectual range of mental retardation may not be a true indication of the student's actual intellectual abilities. Unfortunately, however, school districts and psychologists usually do not have the time to retest several times to determine best levels of performance. The reliability of scores would also be impacted because of the practice effect on test performance. I sometimes indicate on the written assessment report that "observations of the student in the classroom are not consistent with the results of his assessed intellectual functioning as he appears to be capable of performing at a higher level." Then, specific descriptions of higher level functioning can be included. We must begin to look at the capabilities of the student—not the disabilities. Focus on abilities and strengths.

As part of Larry's multidisciplinary team, the teacher and I were to assess his academic functioning levels in reading and math. To do this, we used the *Quick-Score Achievement Test (Q-SAT)* (Hammill, Ammer, Cronin, Mandlebaum, & Quinby, 1987). First, we administered *the Q-SAT* by exact manual directions and received little response from Larry. Had we stopped at this point, his assessment report would have indicated that he functioned at the preschool level in reading and math.

CASE EXAMPLE continued

Rejecting the test results as inaccurate, we retested Larry after modifying the assessment in the following ways. We placed the first ten math problems on index cards, one problem per card. The next problems were enlarged and put on a full sheet of paper with three problems to a page. These were then presented to him as part of his daily tasks in his one-to-one work sessions. The reading test was also modified by enlarging the words and only having ten words per page. This was also presented as a regular work task during one-to-one work time. The spelling task was modified so that he had to select the correct word from three words instead of writing or typing the word from memory.

The results were very interesting. As originally tested, Larry scored at the first percentile in everything. He could not do the spelling at all, he read three words, and did two math problems. With the described modifications at a later date, he could select several correct words. His behaviors in math surprised us and told us a lot about him. He did nothing on the index cards, which had the easiest problems. We realized later, Larry has never had problems presented in this format before. When he got to the paper problems presented the same as his typical daily work tasks, he answered enough correct items to establish a basal. Therefore, we gave him credit for all of the items below the basal. In spelling, he was able to identify a few spelling words.

I reported the results of both evaluations on the written report. I noted that standard procedures for testing were not used because of characteristics associated with autism. In one column, Larry's standard scores as he performed without any modifications were reported. In a second column, his test scores as he performed with modifications were reported. The narrative described the modifications and listed the words that he could read, the types of math that he could do, and his competencies in recognizing the correct spelling word. This report was much more beneficial for IEP planning than a report stating that he was unable to perform the assessment, even at the easiest level. For planning purposes for the IEP, areas of competency are needed, not the grade level or standard scores used in determining eligibility.

Determining Educational Performance Levels and Program Planning

The multidisciplinary team must assess current performance levels. As J. Keith (TCASE, 1998) states, "If you don't know where a child is now, how can you develop an annual goal?" The report of educational performance levels should indicate the student's present level of functioning. These levels should indicate if the student has problems in school; how far the student is behind other students the same age; and the reasons that the student is exhibiting problems in school. The results are then used by the IEP team to plan an appropriate program. Although there are several methods that can be used for assessment of performance levels, one recommended by Jose Martin (TCASE, 1998) is to **"use the specific short-term objectives mastered by the student in the last year to denote the present level of performance."** The following discussion describes other methods.

Informal assessments

Informal assessment methods or alternative assessments are typically more appropriate for students with autism. Although standardized assessments are preferred for determination of eligibility, informal assessments generally provide more information for planning IEP goals and objectives. We will discuss various forms of informal assessments that may be used.

Criterion-referenced assessments

Criterion-referenced tests are used frequently in school settings. The purpose is to determine mastery of a specific skill or measure the individual's achievement relative to a specific standard. Therefore, the tests are useful in assessing specific objectives on IEPs. A number of criterion-referenced tests are used with students with autism. These tests generally have an objective bank with objectives listed in a developmental sequence. Teachers then observe to determine whether the student can perform each of the items listed.

Curriculum-based assessments

These assessments are informal and may assess skills directly. Types of tests include informal inventories, teacher-made evaluations, and teacher observations.

Checklists and rating scales

Checklists and rating scales are structured instruments with specific questions. The person completing the checklist usually selects a response such as yes/no or 1-2-3 instead of writing comments to the questions. There are several checklists related to autism which are used diagnostically. Rimland's *E-2 Checklist* is the oldest of those commonly used with children with autism. Others include the *Childhood Autism Rating Scale (CARS)* by Schopler and his colleagues, the *Autism Behavior Checklist (ABC)*, and the *Gilliam Autism Rating Scale (GARS)*.

Portfolio assessments

Portfolio assessments consist of a representative collection of student work over a period of time—for instance, the year between IEP meetings. An example of a student work sample that might be included is this letter written on a computer by an eight-year old with Asperger's syndrome to Mr. Aaron. He is describing his experience with horseback riding.

 CASE EXAMPLE

Deer Mr Aaron

I rihd the Horse.

The horse is brown.

The horse is sneez.

Chuby is gos naaa.

The horse is in the traler.

The horse is feel happy.

I feel happy with horse.   Jed Hall

This work sample provides the evaluation team with information as to Jed's functioning in the language arts area. From this short example, we can make the following deductions:

1. Jed's thinking is very concrete.

2. He uses a very basic sentence structure - subject, verb, modifier.

3. He understands that sentences begin with a capital letter and end with a period.

4. He is not using commas, i.e., Deer Mr. Aaron does not have a comma after it.

5. He can spell many words.

6. He uses some phonetic rules to irregularly spell words that he doesn't know.

7. He has some difficulty with verbs - Chuby is gos naaa.

8. Either he is beginning to view perspectives of others or he is projecting his own perspective on the horse in, "The horse is feel happy."

9. He is expressing his feelings in "I feel happy with horse."

Some possible products that might be selected for inclusion in a portfolio are:

1. Work samples in various academic areas with the student's name and date written on it. Some teachers might want to include an analysis similar to the one above with the work sample.

2. For students who can't write, samples of marks on paper or drawings can be selected.

3. If students cannot make marks on paper, but do concrete tasks such as sorting, a photograph of the student doing the task could be selected. A written description of the task should be included.

4. In art, actual drawings or photographs of art projects could be included.

5. Some teachers also include an audio tape with a sample of students language/communication from various points in the year. Each time, prior to recording the student, indicate the date and situation in which the recording is to take place.

6. Videotapes are excellent methods of viewing student progress. However, some states require that parent permission be provided before students are videotaped.

7.   For behavior and social interaction, if audio or video tapes are not a possibility, record descriptions of behaviors once per six weeks. It would be very helpful to include baseline data at the beginning of the year and updated data at the end of each grading period.

In many cases, portfolio data provides a much more accurate evaluation of the student's abilities. Also, the portfolio is a great tool for the IEP team to use to determine present levels of functioning and progress made toward objectives.

Language Sample Analysis

In language sample analysis, the evaluator records a student's communication (either with a tape recorder or a video camera). The student's communication is then analyzed to determine the functions of communication, grammar use, length of sentences, etc. For nonverbal students, the language sample records the gestures or movements that the person uses to make their wants and needs known to others.

Functional assessments

Functional assessment is generally used to analyze the student's behavior by looking at the antecedents and consequences of the behavior. Functional assessments of behavior are now required by the *IDEA Amendments* when a student's behavior impedes his learning or the learning of others. The outcomes of functional assessments should include:

•   a functional description of the purpose of the behavior,

•   an operational description of the behavior and how it is measured, and

•   indications of when and under what circumstances the behaviors occur.

Functional assessments of behavior will be discussed in more detail in Chapter Eight, "New Behavioral Perspectives."

Play-based assessments

Play-based assessments involve observations of students with autism in structured and unstructured play situations with either a facilitating adult, the parent, another child, or children. It is typically used with children from birth to six-years-of age and provides opportunities for developmental observations of the individual's cognitive, social-emotional, communication and language, and sensorimotor domains. This model is usually implemented by a team that includes parents and representatives of several disciplines. The model can be used for determining student performance levels and as an assessment for various types of related services.

Ecological assessments

Ecological assessments involve looking at the student's environment and developing a task analysis of the specific skill to be performed. After the task analysis is complete, the observer asks the student to perform the task. The student's performance is then compared to the task analysis to determine the skills that must be worked on. This may also involve going to specific environments in the community and determining the necessary skills for the student with autism to function successfully in the environment. The student's present functioning levels are compared with skills needed to function in the environment. The discrepancies identify skills to be targeted.

Determining the Need for Special Education and Related Services

The team of qualified professionals along with the parent must determine whether the child has a need for related services. If specific needs are indicated, appropriate, related service personnel should perform an evaluation for the specific service. This team must also determine what special teaching methods might be used, and whether supplemental aids and supports are needed. This may involve identifying learning styles and strengths and weaknesses of the student with autism. Most of the current information strongly suggests the use of visual methods.

Measurement and Monitoring of Progress

In order to determine the effectiveness of the goals and objectives, criteria must be established for measuring and monitoring progress. The criteria may be stated in the form of percentages for mastery or in a discrete trial format such as eight out of ten times. An alternative to measurable objectives under the new regulations is the establishment of benchmarks that describe the amount of progress the child is expected to make within specific segments of the year. Benchmarks establish expected performance levels that allow for regular checks of progress that coincide with the reporting periods for informing parents of their child's progress toward achieving the annual goals. Measurement may occur informally with teacher observation, with the use of curriculum-referenced instruments, or with standardized instruments. The final regulations

71

of *IDEA* indicate that monitoring of progress should be reported to parents at the same frequency that parents of nondisabled children receive progress reports (report cards).

Assessment of Special Needs

Sensory Needs

Sensory needs may overwhelm individuals with autism. Consequently, it is very important that sensory needs are addressed in the assessment of needs because they may profoundly impact the behaviors of individuals with autism. The multidisciplinary team should evaluate the child to determine whether sensory dysfunctions in each of the sensory channels are present. Does the child exhibit tactile defensiveness? Does he object to light touch? Does he need deep pressure?

Proprioception provides information about the relative positions of parts of the body. Children with dysfunctions in this area may exhibit wrist flapping or wrapping their arms inside tee-shirts. Adult individuals with autism have described in detail dysfunctions in the auditory and visual channels. It is very common for individuals with autism to have hypersensitive hearing. Sounds that are too loud may actually be painful. Observe to see whether the child avoids certain areas of the school or exhibits more disruptive behaviors in areas such as the cafeteria and gymnasium, which are typically noisier areas of school.

Williams (1994, 1996) describes her dysfunctions in the area of visual input. She describes a history of fragmented vision. Other individuals with autism meet visual sensory needs by flicking their hands in front of their eyes, flipping pages of books, gazing at lights, or playing with shiny objects. Individuals with sensory needs in the gustatory area may mouth or lick objects to meet those needs. Individuals with olfactory dysfunctioning may constantly be smelling objects or people. Students with autism who need additional vestibular stimulation may exhibit this need by rocking their bodies or spinning and twirling in swings.

The assessment team should be identifying these needs and making recommendations for meeting these needs in more appropriate ways. Too often, the only IEP consideration is extinguishing these behaviors through behavior management. Unfortunately, extinguishing does not assist the individual in meeting sensory needs and more inappropriate behaviors may develop. The IEP team should look at alternative methods for meeting these needs.

Assistive Technology

An evaluation should contain recommendations related to the need for assistive technology devices and services. The assessment team should evaluate the student and make recommendations in a written report to the IEP Committee. If the team does not provide this type of evaluation, parents may request that it be done.

Extended School Year (ESY) Services or Extended Year Services (EYS)

States use varied terminology to refer to services that are generally provided during the summer and have different requirements as to how the need for services is determined. Ask your local school district or State Office of Special Education for guidelines for your specific situation.

What About the Parents' Role?

Parents should actively participate in the evaluation and function as a member of the assessment and IEP team under the *IDEA Amendments*. Parents know more about their child than anyone else. During the referral process, parents should provide medical, social, and developmental history information. Parents can also provide behavioral information for assessment of current behavior and other performance level information about skills in the home and community environments. Some parents may be asked to participate in play-based assessments because the child interacts more with the parent present. One purpose in specifying evaluation criteria is to enable parents to participate in monitoring of IEP goals and objectives. Home-school communication is important for facilitating active involvement of parents in the process of assessment and evaluation.

What if You Don't Agree With the Evaluation?

If you don't agree with the school evaluation, you should first confer with school staff. You may request that an Independent Educational Evaluation (IEE) be performed at public expense. You will generally be asked to state your areas of disagreement with the school evaluation. **The school district must either provide an IEE or request a due process hearing to deny the request for an IEE.**

If you think the assessment was incomplete, you may request additional testing. If the school does not agree, you still have the option to request an IEE.

If you obtain your own IEE and want the school district to pay for it, you must follow the procedures of the state and local district. This sometimes requires notifying the district of your intent to get an IEE. You should also obtain a copy of the local district's IEE procedures. School districts may have qualifications regarding geographical area and cost. Court decisions have limited the amount of reimbursement when they determined that the cost of the evaluation was unreasonable.

Chapter Five
What Happens at the IEP Meeting?

What happens once the assessment is complete? An IEP meeting should be scheduled to report results of the assessment and to determine whether the child is "a child with a disability." According to the *IDEA Amendments* (Section 300.534), a group of qualified professionals and parents of the child must determine whether the child is a "child with a disability." Additionally, a copy of the evaluation report and the documentation of determination of eligibility must be provided to the parent. If this team does determine that the student is in need of special education services, a meeting to develop an individualized education program (IEP) must be scheduled within 30 calendar days *(IDEA, Federal Register*, 1999, Section 300.343). Some states have separate meetings for determination of eligibility and developing the IEP. Other states perform both functions in one meeting.

Some assessment personnel choose to meet with the parent prior to the team meeting to go over the written evaluation report in privacy. If parents hear a diagnosis such as autism, mental retardation, (or both) for the first time during the review of assessment data in the initial eligibility determination meeting, they may become so emotionally upset that they are unable to continue the meeting.

CASE EXAMPLE

Eddie is a twelve-year-old child with autism. Although he exhibits many challenging behaviors, is nonverbal, and functions at a low level, his mother had not considered that Eddie might have mental retardation because she attributed his functioning levels to his autism. During the review of assessment data, the educational diagnostician stated that the psychological report indicated that Eddie had autism and mental retardation. Eddie's mother stated later that she heard nothing after she heard the words, mental retardation. The rest of the meeting was just a blur. She could not remember anything past that point. The meeting was recessed and convened at a later date.

Prior to the *IDEA Amendments*, I recommended that parents request, in writing, a copy of any assessment report to be reviewed in the IEP meeting. However, the *IDEA Amendments* require that parents receive a copy of the evaluation data. Although no timelines have been established for parents to receive a copy, it is advisable that the report be sent at least five school days before the scheduled meeting. This allows parents to study the report and be able to participate in discussions related to the evaluation results. Allowing time to study the evaluation results enables parents to prepare questions about the evaluation report.

Assessment reports usually do not contain test protocol forms. Some parents want to see these forms. However, most school personnel do not put these in student eligibility folders because of the possibility of violating copyrights. Many appraisal personnel keep the test protocol forms in their personal files as part of their personal notes.

Particularly, for initial evaluations, parents should be informed of the results prior to the formal meeting that is now required by the *IDEA Amendments* to determine eligibility. This provides parents with time to adjust to any surprises in the report prior to having to face a large group of people in an IEP meeting. Parents can request an informal meeting to go over assessment results at the same time that the parent signs consent for evaluation. It is best to make the request in writing for documentation purposes. It can be written on the consent form or in a separate note or letter. If a separate note or letter is sent to the special education department, mail it by certified mail with a return receipt requested for your own personal documentation that the request was received.

From my experience, many assessment specialists dislike discussing issues such as mental retardation or autism with parents. Therefore, they sometimes tend to skirt the issue. Eligibility is quickly glossed over during the meeting. When parents get home and begin to read the assessment report or IEP document, they realize how their child is labeled. Parents then want further explanations. However, if parents already know that their child has autism, they may not need as much preparation for the IEP meeting. Some parents may want a small informal meeting with the assessment team to be aware of current levels of functioning and assessment data for planning goals and objectives and delivery of related services prior to meeting in a formal IEP setting.

 CASE EXAMPLE

Several years ago, I was contacted by a parent who was very unhappy with the school program for her son. She asked that I meet with her prior to the start of the IEP meeting for her son. I agreed, and during our informal meeting, I reviewed an assessment report with this parent who had filed a complaint with the state education agency. According to this mother, it was the first time anyone had ever really explained assessment information in language that she could understand. She was much more agreeable with school suggestions once she understood her child's current levels of performance. However, she was angry that no one had bothered to sit down and explain her child's functioning levels outside of the official IEP meeting

It behooves school districts to privately discuss assessment reports with parents prior to the IEP meeting so that lengthy discussions can take place in an informal, non-threatening setting. It also enables parents to adjust to assessment results and prepare physically and emotionally for the IEP meeting. Allowing parents to work through emotional reactions in private prior to the initial meeting is beneficial for school staff and parents. Although it takes more time initially, it may eventually save time and effort by preventing future problems.

Reasonable Notice

IDEA requires that school districts provide reasonable notice to parents about the IEP meeting. "Reasonable notice" may be defined differently in different states. Section 300. 345 of the *IDEA Amendments* (*Federal Register*, 1999, p. 12441) requires that schools notify parents early enough to allow them the opportunity to attend. The meeting should also be scheduled at a mutually agreeable time and place.

Some parents may need more notice than what is specified by law because they have jobs that require that they give advance notice if they need time off.

CASE EXAMPLE

One parent that I worked with worked two jobs. She could not attend the IEP meeting unless the meeting was scheduled on her regular day off, which varied from week to week. If the meeting was not on her regular day off, she had to have at least two weeks notice to get her bosses to schedule that day as her regular day off. She simply could not afford to take the day off without pay. As long as the school would work with her schedule, she participated in the IEP meetings. However, if the meeting was scheduled on one of her regular work days, she did not participate.

According to Section 300.345 of the *IDEA Amendments*, notice to parents about IEP meetings must (*Federal Register*, 1999, p. 12441):

- Indicate the purpose, time, and location of the meeting.
- Indicate persons who will be in attendance at the meeting.
- Inform the parents of the provisions of the regulations relating to the participation of other individuals on the IEP team who have knowledge or special expertise about the child.
- For a student with a disability beginning at age 14, or younger, if appropriate, the notice must also:
  - * Indicate that a purpose of the meeting will be the development of a statement of the transition needs of the student, and
  - * Indicate that the agency will invite the student.
- For a student with a disability beginning at age 16, or younger, if appropriate, the notice must also:

*   Indicate that a purpose of the meeting is the consideration of needed transition services for the student,

*   Indicate that the agency will invite the student, and

*   Identify any other agency that will be invited to send a representative.

The purpose of the meeting may be to discuss initial evaluation results, to review the IEP, to discuss a change of placement, to discuss transition services, or to discuss behavior and/or discipline, etc. As stated above, transition must be included as an area of discussion on the notice if it is to be considered at the IEP meeting. In Texas, the notice should also indicate that parents may request a discussion of the provision of any educational or related service not identified for discussion in the notice from the district (Walsh, 1994a, p. 2). Although not required by federal law, agencies might use a letter (Figure 5.1) to convey to parents that the public agency personnel want the parents to feel comfortable as equal partners in the IEP process.

Figure 5.1 Sample letter to parents.

Dear Parents,

It is time to review your child's progress and develop a new Individualized Education Plan (IEP) for your child. As a parent, you are an important person with valuable information about your child. Any input you can provide will be a desirable contribution in the planning process for your child's educational program.

Your child's teacher will be evaluating your child's progress on the past year's goals and objectives. New objectives or benchmarks will be developed. We would like to identify skills and objectives that are important and attainable. Please indicate objectives that you consider necessary for your child to make progress next year. Please write them in the spaces below.

1.

2.

3.

4.

Return this information to your child's teacher prior to the IEP meeting or bring it with you to the meeting. If you have any questions or concerns, please feel free to call me. We look forward to having you participate as a partner in the development of your child's IEP.

Sincerely,

Special Education Director or Sp. Ed. IEP Team Member (Agency Representative)

Federal law does not require parents to notify school districts about most issues they plan to bring to the IEP meeting; however, Walsh (1994a) reported on a case in Richardson, Texas, involving a 15 year old student with PDD. The hearing officer ruled that parents **do** have to notify school districts about issues they plan to discuss at the IEP Committee meeting. Unlike many students with PDD, this student was not disruptive or aggressive. He was high-functioning with difficulties in social interaction and extreme anxiety or panic attacks. "The hearing officer observed that the student became extremely anxious if he did not understand assignments, or felt that he was falling behind." (Walsh, 1994a, p. 1). At the parents' request, the school met with the parents one day after their initial request. At this time, the student's parents requested residential placement.

The committee members refused to make a decision on the request without school district administrators present. They recommended that a central IEP meeting be held at a later date. Although federal law requires school districts to have a representative at the meeting who can commit the district to carry out the IEP, the hearing officer noted that the school representative may vary depending on the circumstances.

For a child with a disability who requires only a limited amount of special education, the agency representative could be a special education teacher. For a child who requires extensive special education and related services, the agency representative might need to be a key administrator in the agency (Walsh, 1994a, p. 1).

The hearing officer offered this interpretation of the parents' duty. To select an appropriate agency representative, the school district must gather information on the issues to be decided. As members of the IEP committee, parents have an obligation to provide pertinent information to the district so appropriate persons can be assembled for the meeting. Since this student's parents knew they would be asking for a private placement, they should have informed school personnel. Then, one meeting, with the appropriate administrators present, could have been arranged.

According to the *IDEA Amendments*, Section 300.403 (*Federal Register,* 1999, p. 12445), parents should notify the school district if they plan to remove the child from public school and place the student in a private school placement. In this situation, the cost of reimbursement may be reduced or denied if:

- At the most recent IEP meeting that the parents attended prior to removal of the child from the public school, the parents did not inform the IEP team that they were rejecting the placement proposed by the public agency to provide FAPE to their child, including stating concerns and their intent to enroll their child in a private school, at public expense.
- At least ten (10) business days (including any holidays that occur on a business day) prior

to the removal of the child from the public school, the parents did not give written notice to the public agency that they are rejecting the child's current placement.

- Prior to the parents' removal of the child from the public school, the public agency informed the parents, through the notice requirements of *IDEA*, of its intent to evaluate the child (including a statement of the purpose of the evaluation that was appropriate and reasonable), but the parents did not make the child available for evaluation.

- Upon a judicial finding of unreasonableness with respect to actions taken by the parents.

There are four circumstances in which there are exceptions to the above reasons for limitation of reimbursement. Reimbursement cannot be limited or reduced for parental failure to notify the school of their intent if :

- The parent is illiterate and cannot write in English,

- Notice to the public agency would result in physical or serious emotional harm to the child,

- The school prevented the parent from providing the notice, or

- The parents had not been informed of the requirement to provide notice to the school of their intent to remove the child from public school. (*IDEA*, Section 300.403 (3) (e) (4), *Federal Register*, p. 12455).

Annual Review

IDEA (*Federal Register,* 1999, p. 12440) states that the IEP must be reviewed periodically, but not less than annually. Many districts review IEPs in the spring of each year as school personnel plan for the next year. However, in a *Letter to Sheridan* (20 IDELR 1163, OSEP 1993), the Office of Special Education Programs (OSEP) stated that "the annual review can occur at any time during the year" (LRP, 1994a, p. XIV-158.). The district can elect to schedule the IEP meeting on the anniversary date of the initial IEP meeting or during the summer prior to the beginning of school. However, most school districts prefer not to hold summer IEP meetings because necessary personnel are not working during summer vacation. Some districts schedule the IEP meeting on the student's birthday.

The key factor is that annual reviews of the student's IEP must be conducted each year. The purpose of the annual reviews includes determining whether the annual goals for the child are being achieved and to make any necessary revisions in the IEP as appropriate to address any lack of expected progress toward the annual goals and in the general education curriculum. Thus, the *IDEA Amendments* reaffirm the commitment to access to the general education curriculum, quality education, and accountability for students with disabilities. IEP meetings or annual reviews should also review the results of any reevaluations that have been conducted since the last IEP meeting.

Is Everybody Here?

The IEP is a written document that describes the decisions of the IEP team. It is developed, reviewed, and revised in a meeting in accordance with the *IDEA* regulations. It specifies present levels of performance, annual goals and short-term objectives or benchmarks, and specific special education and related services to be provided. In this sense it is also a compliance and monitoring document because it can be used to determine whether the actual program is in compliance with the educational services that were written into the IEP. Student progress is also documented in the discussion of current performance levels and attainment or mastery of the previous year's goals. The committee meeting itself serves as a vehicle for communication between the parents and the school. The process is designed to provide an opportunity for resolving differences between the parent and the school. Two major purposes of the IEP are to establish learning goals for the student and to state the services that will be provided by the school district.

The first requirement when the IEP team meets is to have all required members present. According to the *IDEA Amendments* (*Federal Register*, 1999, p. 12440), the IEP team has changed and now includes at least one regular education teacher of the child. **For most students, the IEP team will consist of:**

- the parents of the child;
- at least one regular education teacher of the child;
- at least one special education teacher of the child or a special education service provider;
- a representative of the public agency who:
    * is qualified to provide or supervise the provision of specially designed instruction to meet the unique needs of children with disabilities;
    * is knowledgeable about the general curriculum; and
    * is knowledgeable about the availability of the resources of the public agency;
- an individual who can interpret the instructional implications of evaluation results, who may be a member of the team described in the preceding list; and
- at the discretion of the parent or the agency, other individuals who have knowledge or special expertise regarding the child, including related service personnel as appropriate; and
- if appropriate, the student with a disability.

Although the *IDEA Amendments* emphasize the involvement of parents in the child's educational program, IEP meetings can take place without the parents present. **Parents must receive notice of the meeting.** If the public agency cannot convince the parents that they should attend, the meeting can be held without the parents. However, the public agency must have a documented record of attempts to arrange a mutually agreed on time and place. **Acceptable documentation** includes:

- Detailed records of telephone calls made or attempted and the results of those calls;
- Copies of correspondence such as IEP notices sent to the parents and any responses received; and
- Detailed records of visits made to the parent's home or place of employment and the results of those visits.

Whether the parent is present or not, the local education agency must provide the parent with a copy of the IEP. It is recommended that parents receive a copy of the draft IEP prior to the IEP meeting.

The *IDEA Amendments* require that **a regular classroom teacher is present at the IEP meeting**. The regulations state that the teacher should be a teacher of the child. With the emphasis on involvement and progress in regular education, regular classroom teachers have an increasingly critical role in IEP meetings. If the child is, or may be, participating in regular education, the IEP team must include at least one regular teacher. There is a possibility that every child might participate in regular education, so the intention of the law is that every IEP meeting has a regular teacher present.

> **If a child with a disability attends several regular classes, must all of the child's regular education teachers be members of the child's IEP team?**

No. However, all teachers should have the opportunity to provide input to the IEP team. If participation of more than one teacher would be beneficial, it would be appropriate for each of the teachers to attend the meeting. The regular education teacher who is responsible for implementing a portion of the IEP should be the designated representative for the regular education teacher. If more than one teacher implements portions of the IEP, the local education agency may designate which teacher or teachers will serve as members of the IEP team. Additionally, the local education agency must ensure that each regular education teacher has access to the child's IEP and is informed of his or her specific responsibilities related to implementing the child's IEP. Regular education teachers must also be informed of the accommodations, modifications, and supports that must be provided to the child in accordance with the IEP. (*Federal Register*, Appendix A, 1999).

> **What is the regular education teacher's role in the development, review, and revision of the IEP for a child who is, or may be, participating in the regular education environment?**

The regular education teacher participates in the development, review, and revision of the child's IEP, including assisting in:

• the determination of appropriate positive behavioral interventions and strategies; and

• the determination of supplementary aids and services, program modifications, and supports for school personnel that will be provided for the child.

This means that the teacher may not (depending upon the child's needs and the purpose of the specific IEP meeting) be required to participate in all decisions made as part of the meeting or to be present throughout the entire meeting or attend every meeting. However, this interpretation does present certain logistical problems. For example, is the regular classroom teacher going to be "shuffling" in and out of the meeting? Will the committee have to call this person to come back to the meeting each time a decision is made that requires that a regular classroom teacher be present? Another logistical problem includes how to document when the teacher is present and when the individual is absent. It may be simpler for the regular education teacher to remain in the meeting.

Do you have to have a regular education teacher at the IEP meeting for students with disabilities aged 3 through 5 who are receiving preschool special education services?

If the public agency provides "regular education" preschool services to nondisabled children, then the same requirements apply that apply to older students with disabilities. If the public agency makes kindergarten available to nondisabled children, then a regular kindergarten teacher could appropriately be the regular education teacher who would be a member of the IEP team. If so, as appropriate, the teacher should participate in IEP meetings for a kindergarten-aged child who is, or may be, participating in the regular education environment.

If the public agency does not provide regular preschool education services to nondisabled children, the agency could designate an individual who, under state standards, is qualified to serve nondisabled children of the same age (*Federal Register*, 1999, p. 12472).

Section 300.344(a)(3) requires that **the child's special education teacher participate as a member of the IEP team.** This requirement may also be met by another special education service provider, such as a speech pathologist, physical therapist, or occupational therapist, etc., if the related service consists of specially designed instruction and is considered special education under applicable state standards. Regardless of who participates in the IEP meeting, special education teachers and related service personnel who will implement portions of the child's IEP must have **access to the child's IEP** as soon as possible after it is **finalized, and before the person begins working with the child.**

Who can serve as the representative of the public agency at an IEP meeting?

Each public agency may determine which specific staff member will serve as the agency representative in a particular IEP meeting, as long as the individual meets the requirements set forth in the *IDEA Amendments*. It is important that the person selected is able to commit the resources of the agency and assure that whatever services are specified in the IEP will actually be provided.

Who determines whether an individual has special expertise and knowledge?

This determination is made by the parent or the public agency who has invited the individual to be member of the IEP team. Certainly, related service personnel would fit into this category of having special expertise and knowledge of the child. Although *IDEA* does not require related service personnel to attend the IEP meeting, it is certainly appropriate for those persons to be included if a particular related service is to be discussed as part of the IEP meeting.

Can parents or public agencies bring an attorney to the IEP meeting?

The *IDEA Amendments* strongly discourage bringing attorneys to IEP meetings because of the potential for creating an adversarial atmosphere that would not necessarily be in the best interests of the child. Furthermore, attorney's fees may not be awarded relating to any meeting of the IEP team unless the meeting is convened as a result of an administrative proceeding or judicial action (or at the discretion of the state) for a mediation conducted prior to the request for a due process hearing. This new regulation regarding fees probably means that fewer attorneys will be at IEP meetings.

An impartial due process hearing officer determined that an IEP team's review of the IEP for a 13-year-old student was null and void because the IEP committee did not include all of the members required by federal law. In this instance, the hearing officer did not rule this as a violation of FAPE because the student still had an IEP in effect for a few more months. However, this case is important because it emphasizes the need for school districts to include all required members at the IEP meeting. Had this particular student not had an IEP in effect, the situation could have resulted in a denial of FAPE, which was the claim of the parents. Therefore, an IEP Committee can consist of additional members with special expertise and knowledge of the child (at the discretion of the school or parents), but it cannot consist of less members unless the missing member is a parent who chooses not to participate.

IEP Meetings that Discuss Transition

When transition is to be discussed at an IEP meeting, the student should be invited to attend. The public agency should also invite a representative of any other agency that is likely to be responsible for providing or paying for transition services. If a representative from the invited agency does not attend, the public agency must take other steps to obtain participation of the other agency in the planning of any transition services.

IEP Meetings that Address Behavior

When a child's behavior is impeding learning, experts recommend that the agency have a person at the IEP meeting who is knowledgeable about positive behavior strategies.

Getting Off to a Good Start

To get the meeting off to a good start, you should have an agenda and follow it. Agendas help keep the meeting on track and ensure that all components of the IEP are discussed in an appropriate order. Agendas provide all participants with information as to when certain issues should be discussed. Figure 5.2 is an example of a detailed agenda that could be modified and used.

After introductions and statement of the purpose of the meeting, there should be a review of assessment data in IEP meetings for initial placements. In subsequent IEP meetings, if other assessments were performed since the previous IEP meeting, a discussion of those evaluations should take place. An individual knowledgeable about the child's assessment should discuss the student's evaluation, including any related service evaluations. This is an appropriate time for parents to present results of private or independent assessments or to discuss concerns for enhancing their child's education. There should also be a determination as to the need for further assessments to provide an appropriate program for the student. If appropriate, the results of the child's performance on state- or district-wide assessment programs should be discussed. If the student does not participate in state- or district-wide assessment programs, the IEP team needs to discuss alternate methods of assessment and the performance of the child on those alternate assessment methods.

Determination of Eligibility for Services

Once assessment data has been presented and discussed, a determination of eligibility is made based upon the assessment data. If eligibility has already been established in previous IEP meetings, this may be a formality in annual review meetings, although the IEP team, along with the parents, must still confirm that the child is still a "child with a disability" and that an educational need still exists. Assessment data should be complete and accurate because it should be used in the development of goals, short-term objectives, and benchmarks. Benchmarks may be used in the place of short-term objectives or in addition to short-term objectives.

Figure 5.2. Sample IEP Meeting Agenda

I.   Introductions.

II.   Statement of purpose of the IEP Meeting.

III.   Review of assessment data including:

     A.   The strengths of the child.

     B.   Information from parents and school, including concerns of the parents for enhancing the education of their child.

     C.   Reports of initial or most recent evaluations.

     D.   As appropriate, the results of the child's performance on any general state- or district-wide assessment programs.

     E.   Comments/questions from members regarding assessment information presented.

IV.   Determination of student eligibility for special education services based upon:

     A.   Whether the child is a "child with a disability."

     B.   Whether there is an educational need for special education and related services.

V.   Needs/development/revision of the IEP including:

     A.   Review of previous year's objectives.

     B.   Present levels of performance or competencies of the child including:

          1.   Physical.

          2.   Behavioral.

          3.   Prevocational/Vocational (if age appropriate).

          4.   Academic/Developmental.

          5.   How the child's disability affects the child's involvement and progress in the general curriculum.

          6.   For preschool children, as age appropriate, how the disability affects the child's participation in appropriate activities.

     C. The IEP team, if appropriate, shall consider the following special factors:

          1.   Positive behavioral interventions, strategies, and supports to address behaviors that impede learning.

          2.   The language needs of children with limited English proficiency.

          3.   The use of Braille for a child who is blind or has a visual impairment.

          4.   Communication needs of the child, and for a child who is deaf or hard of hearing, consider:

               a.   The child's language and communication needs.

               b.   Opportunities for direct communications with peers and professional personnel in the child' language and communication mode, academic level.

               c.   Full range of needs, including opportunities for direct instruction in the child's language and communication mode.

          5.   Whether the child needs assistive technology devices and services, and if needed, include a statement in the IEP that there is a:

               a.   Need for assistive technology services and/or devices to receive a free appropriate public education (FAPE).

               b.   Need for assistive technology services and/or devices to provide least restrictive environment (LRE).

          6.   Address transition for preschool children when age-appropriate.

1. Early childhood intervention services to preschool regular or special education.
2. Preschool special education to kindergarten or other school programs.

D. Address transition services:
   1. For students age fourteen or younger, a statement of the transition service needs of the student that focuses on the student's courses of study (such as participation in vocational education programs).
   2. For each student beginning at age sixteen (or younger, if determined appropriate by the IEP team), and updated annually, a statement of needed transition services for the student, including if appropriate, a statement of interagency responsibilities or any needed linkages.

E. Beginning at least one year before a student reaches the age of majority under State law, the student's IEP must include a statement that the student has been informed of his or her rights under *Part B of IDEA*.

F. Need for extended year services (EYS).

G. Include a statement of measurable annual goals, including benchmarks or short-term objectives, related to:
   1. Meeting the child's needs that result from the child's disability to enable the child to be involved in and progress in the general curriculum, or for preschool children, to participate in appropriate activities.
   2. Meeting each of the child's other educational needs that result from the child's disability.

H. A statement of the special education and related services and supplementary aids and services to be provided to the child, or on behalf of the child, and a statement of the program modifications or supports for school personnel that will be provided for the child to:
   1. Advance appropriately toward attaining annual goals.
   2. Be involved in and progress in the general curriculum.
   3. Be educated and participate with other children in extracurricular and other nonacademic activities.
   4. Be educated and participate with other children with disabilities and nondisabled children in the activities described *in IDEA*.

I. Schedule of services and modifications described in the IEP.
   1. Projected date for the beginning of the services and modifications.
   2. Anticipated frequency, location, and duration of those services and modifications.

J. Statements of:
   1. How the child's progress toward annual goals will be measured.
   3. How the child's parents will be regularly informed of:
      a. Their child's progress toward the annual goals.
      b. The extent to which that progress is sufficient to enable the child to achieve the goals by the end of the year.

K. Indicate participation/nonparticipation in State and district-wide testing programs.

VII. Determination of placement.
VIII. Justifications.
IX. Assurances of nondiscrimination.

X.   Closing statements and signatures.
    A.   Review/restate major recommendations of the IEP committee.
    B.   If mutual agreement is not achieved, discuss options available.
        1.   Collecting additional data to make further decisions.
        2.   Requesting a third party mediator or arbitrator.
        3.   Agreeing to disagree, but continue to carry out the IEP.
        4.   Recess and reschedule the meeting if necessary.
        5.   Parents can request a due process hearing.
    C.   Obtain signatures of all persons in attendance.
    D.   Obtain parent permission for placement if it is an initial placement meeting.

Student Needs and Development and Revision of the IEP

Discuss your child's needs and review progress on the previous year's objectives next. There should be a discussion of tests and observations that were performed to measure progress on IEP goals and objectives. This should include information as to whether objectives were mastered or not. An easy method for developing and writing present levels of performance is to use the specific short-term objectives mastered by the student in the last year. Present levels of educational performance should be addressed in all areas of the student's functioning that may include information about your child's:

- academic achievement (or developmental levels, if appropriate);
- behaviors in the classroom;
- social interaction and adaptation;
- prevocational and vocational skills, if age appropriate;
- self-help skills; and
- speech, language, and communication skills.

Present levels of performance should indicate your child's strengths and weaknesses—not just his disabilities. For students with autism, the **present levels of performance should include determination of abilities at school and at home.** The *IDEA Amendments* require that the IEP statements of the child's present levels of educational performance include how the child's disability affects the child's involvement and progress in the general curriculum. For preschool children, the IEP team must state how the disability affects the child's participation in appropriate activities.

These statements should address student performance in specific and meaningful ways. For example, it is not sufficient to say Barry is functioning at the primer level, or Barry can do simple addition. Reporting of grade levels is not enough. A very specific statement regarding his math performance would be:

- *Barry can do simple addition facts from 0 to 5 when work is presented as a task at his work station in left to right manner with boxes under each problem to provide visual boundaries for his answer.*

Examples of a behavioral level of performance might be:

- *Barry walks beside the teacher without talking when he goes to the lunchroom, music, and P. E. 80% of the time when he uses earphones to reduce noises and wears a weighted vest for calming purposes.*

- *In the classroom, Barry sits at his work station and independently works on assigned tasks for up to twenty minutes 3 days out of 5.*

In the area of language, Barry is learning to say "I like cookies" instead of "Barry likes cookies." *He correctly uses the pronoun "I" 70% of the time.* Barry is also learning to take turns in his conversations when he is talking with his teacher or paraprofessional in the classroom. A performance level related to this might be: *Barry takes turns in conversational speech with adults 50% of the time.*

For younger children, performance levels in the prevocational area might include descriptions of how long the child can sit and attend to tasks, how the child follows one or two step directions, etc. With older children, performance levels in the vocational area might include information as to sorting and filing abilities. whether the student can tell time, or whether the person can make change.

Physical levels of performance might include abilities in walking, running, jumping, and skipping. Any physical problems such as seizure disorders or motor difficulties should be addressed here. For instance, with Barry, we might say, *Barry colors in the lines on pictures 90% of the time.* This is a skill that he did not have at the beginning of the year. His mother is delighted with this skill because he will sit for hours at home and color. However, she is also concerned that coloring may become a new obsession for him.

Consideration of Special Factors

When behaviors impede the learning of the student or of others, the IEP team must consider positive behavioral interventions, strategies, and supports to address these behaviors. For many students with autism, challenging behaviors are a frequent concern. Consideration of behavioral interventions will be addressed more fully in Chapter 8 of this book.

<u>Assistive Technology</u>

Each public agency must ensure that assistive technology devices or services are provided to students with disabilities if required as part of the child's special education, related services, or as supplementary aids and services (*IDEA, Federal Register*, 1999, p. 12438). An assistive technology device is defined as "any item, piece of equipment, or product system whether acquired commercially off the shelf, modified, or customized and is used to increase, maintain, or improve the functional capabilities of children with disabilities." (*IDEA*, *Federal Register*, 1999, p. 12438).

Assistive technology services refers to assisting any child with a disability in the selection, acquisition, or use of an assistive technology device. This includes:

- the evaluation of the needs of a child with a disability, including a functional evaluation of the child in the child's customary environment;

- purchasing, leasing, or otherwise providing for the acquisition of assistive technology devices by children with disabilities;

- selecting, designing, fitting, customizing, adapting, applying, retaining, repairing, or replacing assistive technology devices;

- coordinating and using other therapies, interventions, or services with assistive technology devices, such as those associated with existing education and rehabilitation plans and programs;

- training or technical assistance for a child with a disability or, if appropriate, that child's family; and

- training or technical assistance for professionals (including individuals providing education or rehabilitation services), employers, or other individuals who provide services to, employ or are otherwise substantially involved in the major life functions of children with disabilities (*IDEA*, Section 300.6, *Federal Register*, 1999, p. 12421).

How does this impact the education of students with autism? First, there must be a determination that assistive technology devices are necessary for the student to receive a free, appropriate, public education. This is generally done through an assistive technology evaluation. In our area, we generally use a multidisciplinary team to evaluate the student and produce a written report with recommendations that can be addressed at the IEP meeting. There must be a relationship between the student's educational needs and the device or service. If a particular device is determined to be necessary, the public school should provide that device at no cost to the parents. If the IEP team determines that a child with a disability needs to have access to an assistive technology device at home as a part of a free appropriate public education, the device must be provided by the school district. *The IDEA Amendments*, Section 300.308, specifically state "on a case-by-case basis, the use of school-purchased assistive technology devices in a child's home or in other settings is required if the child's IEP team determines that the child needs access to those devices in order to receive FAPE." (*Federal Register*, 1999, p. 12438).

One family that I work with requested an assistive technology evaluation for their son because the parents believed that he would benefit from the use of a computer. Although his verbal language is limited, he has better use of written language. He does have limited access to an older model computer at school. The first evaluation by the school district did not indicate a need for a computer in order to receive FAPE. The parents then requested an independent evaluation for determination of the need for assistive technology. The school district contracted with a facility that is nationally known for assessing students with communication disorders. The second evaluation did indicate a need for access to a Macintosh computer for this student. The parents are now waiting to see if this will be provided as the new school year begins.

Another device that may be considered as assistive technology is a calculator. Students may need a calculator to facilitate learning mathematical processes if they are not able to memorize necessary math facts. Nonverbal students with autism may use a variety of communication devices. Some are low technology pictures on paper. Others are sophisticated voice output devices. Regardless of the device requested or considered, there should be adequate evaluation to determine if the device is truly appropriate for the student before purchasing expensive equipment.

Transition

Transition occurs at the preschool level and as students begin to prepare to move from school to the world of work and community. At the preschool level, there is a transition from early childhood intervention programs to preschool regular or special education programs. There may also be transitions from preschool special education to kindergarten or other school arrangements. Other school transitions include moving from kindergarten to first grade or moving from a special education class to an inclusive setting. The IEP team should address how the team and the school can facilitate any transition the student is to make.

For older students, the *IDEA Amendments* have some very specific requirements. These requirements are addressed in terms of preparing for the world after graduation from high school. The IEP team must begin to look at the best methods for preparing the student to live and work successfully in the community. When a child is fourteen (or younger, if determined appropriate by the IEP team), and updated annually, the IEP team must make a statement of the transition service needs of the student that focuses on the student's courses of study in high school. This might indicate plans for the student to participate in vocational education programs or community-based instruction. When a child is sixteen (or younger, if determined appropriate by the IEP team), the IEP must make a statement of needed transition services for the student, including, if appropriate, a statement of interagency responsibilities or any needed linkages.

Many programs are beginning to use some form of "person directed planning" to assess and address transition needs of students. "Person directed planning" is also referred to as "person centered planning." It is a planning process directed by the person receiving services. It is a way of helping individuals make desired changes in their life and empowering them to plan their future and organize the supports and services they need. There are many "person directed planning processes including: Person Futures Planning, Individual Service Design, Essential Life-style Planning, Vocational Profile, the PATH, and Circles of Support.

In conjunction with this transition process, the *IDEA Amendments* also require that the public agency informs the student of the transfer of rights that takes place when the student reaches the age of majority under state law. Additionally, the IEP must include a statement that the student has been informed of his or her rights under Part B of *IDEA. (Federal Register,* 1999, p. 12442)

Do parental rights stop when rights are transferred to the student at the age of eighteen (or the age of majority according to state law)?

Some parents are concerned about their right to continue to access and participate in the development of their child's educational program when the rights are transferred to the student. This is a particular concern for parents of students who continue to need educational and community supports. Many parents apply for legal guardianship of children who are unable to live and work independently in the community. According to recent clarifications, parents who are entitled by the Internal Revenue Service (IRS) to claim their child as a dependent may continue to have educational access to records and other parental rights. Consequently, in most cases, when rights are transferred to the student, schools must provide notice to the student and the parent whenever notice is required.

Extended School Year Services

Next, the IEP team should discuss the need for extended school year services. States have different procedures for extended year services. Guidelines from each state must be followed. However, most children with autism have a need for a structured environment and would benefit from summer services. The fact that students with autism would receive educational benefit from extended school year services is not enough in many cases for the public agency to provide them.

The *IDEA Amendments*, Section 300.309, state "extended school year services must be provided only if a child's IEP team determines, on an individual basis, in accordance with *IDEA* regulations, that the services are necessary for the provision of FAPE to the child."

Many states use regression information to determine the need for services. In this situation, the student is assessed at the end of the year on IEP objectives and at the end of the first six weeks of school. If the student has not regressed on objectives, he or she would not be eligible for EYS the following summer. Parents should document information related to regression during school vacations so that they are prepared to present this type of information to the IEP Committee when discussing the need for extended year services.

The *IDEA Amendments* specifically state that public agencies may not limit extended school year services to particular categories of disability; or to unilaterally limit the type, amount, or duration of extended school year services. Like everything else, extended school year services must be determined on an individual basis according to the identified needs of the child. The regulations go on to define extended school year services as services provided to a child with a disability that extend beyond the normal school year of the public agency and are specified in the student's IEP. These services must be provided at no cost to the parents of the child and must meet the standards of the State Education Agency where the child lives.

Summarization of Student Needs

The IEP must include a statement of measurable annual goals, including benchmarks or short-term objectives, related to meeting the child's needs that result from the child's disability to enable the child to be involved in and progress in the general education curriculum. For preschool children, the IEP must include a statement relative to the child's ability to participate in appropriate activities. The IEP team must also determine the special education and related services and supplementary aids and services to be provided to the child, or on behalf of the child. This includes a statement of the program modifications or supports for school personnel that will be provided for the child.

Modifications of Instruction

The summarization of needs will assist the committee in determining priorities for objectives. The summarization of needs should include needs in special education, needs in related services, and needs for modifications in regular classes. These needs should link directly to assessment results and the goals and objectives that are to be developed. A particularly important discussion involves the determination of modifications. Although we should look carefully at what the student needs, we should also consider whether the modifications are reasonably calculated and feasible for regular classroom teachers to follow.

Input from the regular teacher is very important in determining appropriate modifications. If the regular teacher is not present at the meeting, there should be a provision for the teacher to provide input in a different way. The IEP committee should be aware that the classroom teacher is responsible for implementing whatever modifications are written into the IEP. In some cases, IEP committees have just checked everything listed—as many as twenty-five or thirty modifications. Very little thought went into the student's true need for modifications. A case out of West Virginia illustrates the importance of identifying only modifications that are really needed. It also emphasizes the fact that teachers are responsible for providing those modifications, whether the teacher agrees that the modifications are necessary or not.

"For the first time, a jury ordered a classroom teacher to pay damages to a student as a result of the teacher's refusal to implement the IEP. This case involved Michael Withers, a history teacher and member of the West Virginia legislature" (Walsh, 1993b). In this case, Mr. Withers refused to provide the modifications written into the IEP, particularly the provision that testing be done orally in the resource room by the special education teacher. Mr. Withers also refused to comply with a written directive from the high school special education coordinator.

According to Walsh (1993b), when the West Virginia legislature met, Mr. Withers took a leave of absence and a substitute took over his class. Not knowing Mr. Withers' attitude toward the student's recommended modifications, the substitute followed the IEP. During that period of time, the student did well in class. When Mr. Withers returned to the classroom, he continued to ignore the recommendations for modifications from the IEP. As a result, the student failed his class. The parents filed a grievance with the West Virginia State Education Agency.

The West Virginia State Education Agency heard the case and agreed with the parents that the school had failed to carry out the IEP. It ordered the school to administer an oral History test to the student and to provide tutoring and reteaching to enable him to prepare for the test. The school complied with these directives, but the parents went on to sue the teacher, the principal, the superintendent, and the board for compensatory and punitive damages under 42 U.S.C. 1983. The judge threw out the complaint against the principal, the superintendent, and the school board. "That left the teacher's fate in the hands of six good and lawful West Virginia jurors" (Walsh, 1993b, p. 1). The jury ordered Mr. Withers to pay to the student the sum of $5,000 in compensatory damages and $10,000 in punitive damages.

"The lesson is simple: no one can individually override the IEP. Any educator can screw in the light bulb—unless the light bulb has a disability. In that case you need an entire committee." (Walsh, 1993b, p. 1). *IDEA* **does** infringe on the traditional authority of the classroom teacher. Although Mr. Withers may or may not be right about the student's need for modifications, it is not his decision to make. He cannot simply refuse to carry out the modifications specified in the IEP by the IEP team.

So, what could Mr. Withers or any other educators have done when they do not agree with the decisions of the IEP committee? According to Walsh (1993a), the teacher had one of three basic options.

1. Report to the principal that he believes that the modifications specified in the IEP are not necessary.

2. Submit his own written recommendations based on the student's needs to be reviewed at the next IEP meeting. The recommendations must be based on the individual abilities and disabilities of the student, not the teacher's attitude toward special education.

3. Ask to attend the next meeting so that he can voice his concerns to the IEP team.

Appendix A of the *IDEA Amendments* provide the following recommendations for a child's teacher who feels that the child's IEP or placement is not appropriate for the student. The teacher should follow the agency procedures for calling or meeting with the parents and/or request that the agency hold another IEP meeting to review the child's IEP or placement.

As stated previously, modifications are important and should not be taken lightly. Once modifications are determined, goals and objectives or benchmarks can be developed and written. Specifics on how to write goals and objectives will be provided in the next chapter.

After development of goals and objectives, criteria and time lines for evaluation of the objectives must be determined. For example, how will mastery be determined? Will it be 80%, 4 out of 5 times, 9 out of 10 times, etc? Additionally, will mastery be determined by teacher observation, specific data based upon a discrete trial format (recording each time the student does or does not do the task), or standardized testing? Although, short-term objectives may be evaluated as frequently as the IEP committee determines is needed, the objectives must be evaluated at least annually as stated in federal law. However, the *IDEA Amendments* require that the IEP team make statements describing how progress will be measured, and how the child's parents will be regularly informed of that progress toward the child's annual goals. The agency must also inform parents of the extent to which the student's progress is sufficient to enable the child to achieve the goals by the end of the year. Benchmarks, as described in the *IDEA Amendments* specify the amount of progress that the child is expected to make within specified segments of the year. "Generally, benchmarks establish expected performance levels that allow for regular checks of progress that coincide with the reporting periods for informing parents of their child's progress toward achieving the annual goals" (*Federal Register,* 1999, p. 12471). An IEP team may use either short-term objectives or benchmarks or a combination of the two depending upon the nature of the annual goals and the individual needs of the child.

Then, the IEP committee must specify a schedule of special education and related services. According to the *IDEA Amendments*, not only must the IEP team specify when the services and modifications will begin, but it must also state the anticipated frequency, location, and duration of those services and modifications.

 CASE EXAMPLE

The IEP team has determined that Denny should receive speech therapy and occupational therapy. The team must then determine how much speech therapy and occupational therapy he will receive. Some agencies indicate that the service will occur for 30 minutes twice a week. Others indicate so many minutes of the service per month. One agency specifies that the child will receive so many 30 minute sessions per year. Additionally, the IEP team must name the location. Will Denny receive services in his regular classroom or go to the speech pathologist's office for speech therapy?

Following the schedule of services, placement can be determined and justifications, assurances, and closing statements can be made.

A school representative or the parent should briefly restate the major decisions of the committee before adjournment to ensure that all members interpreted the information similarly. If everyone agrees at that point, documents are signed, and the meeting can be adjourned. If the parent disagrees with the school recommendations, the school should state the options that are available and provide the parent with notice that the IEP will be carried out within a certain time frame if the parent does not respond. In other words, parents serve as "equal participants" when they are given the opportunity for meaningful input and have the right to challenge any decisions with which they disagree (Walsh, 1994c). However, a school district can implement an IEP over the parent's objection with certain conditions. First, the school must have permitted "meaningful input." Secondly, the school has provided notice to the parents of the right to challenge the school's decision (Walsh, 1994c). For initial placements, most states require that parents sign permission agreeing to the child's placement in a special education program.

The *IDEA Amendments* state that the IEP team should work toward consensus. However, "the public agency has the ultimate responsibility to ensure that the IEP includes the services that the child needs in order to receive FAPE. It is not appropriate to make IEP decisions based upon a majority 'vote.'" If consensus cannot be reached between the public agency and the parents, the agency must provide the parents with written notice of the agency's proposals and/or refusals regarding the child's educational program. The parents then have the right to seek resolution of any disagreements by initiating an impartial due process hearing (*Federal Register*, 1999, p. 12473-12474).   Although parents have the right to proceed to due process, it is strongly encouraged that both parties try to work out the disagreements through voluntary mediation or other informal means.

Are There any Other Questions?

When must the IEP be developed?

The IEP must be developed before the child begins to receive special education and related services.

Can parents request meetings more frequently than once a year?

Yes, public agencies must grant any reasonable request for an IEP meeting.

Can the IEP meeting be audio- or video-tape-recorded?

The *IDEA Amendments* don't address the use of recordings at the IEP meetings. The regulations go on to state that no federal statute authorizes or prohibits the recording of an IEP meeting by either the parents or public agency officials. Consequently, the State Education Agency or public agency has the option to require, prohibit, limit, or otherwise regulate the use of recording devices at the IEP meetings.

The regulations further state that public agencies adopting policies that prohibit or limit the use of recording at IEP meetings must provide for exceptions if they are necessary to ensure that the parent understands the IEP or the IEP process. Additionally, any policy or rule regulating the tape recording of IEP meetings should be uniformly applied. Any recording of an IEP meeting that is maintained by the public agency is an "education record" and as such, is within the meaning of the *Family Educational Rights and Privacy Act*. This means that parents can request a copy of the tape recording in the same manner that they request copies of other records.

Can the IEP be developed and completed prior to the IEP meeting?

No. However, public agencies may draft an IEP. It must be made clear to the parents that the proposed IEP is only presented for review and discussion with parents. Any member of the IEP team, with the consent of other team members, may make changes in the proposed IEP.

My child is two. What kind of services is he or she entitled to?

IDEA ensures that states provide a free appropriate public education for children with disabilities aged three through twenty-one. States are not mandated to provide services for children with disabilities from birth through two. However, states may elect to provide services for children with disabilities from birth through three. Federal funding is available for "birth to three" programs. You must check with your state education agency, the local public school district, or parent advocate groups to determine what kinds of services might be available for your child in the birth through two age range in each state.

When will my three-year-old child with a disability be able to receive special education services?

According to the *IDEA Amendments*, an IEP or an Individual Family Service Plan (IFSP) must be in effect by the child's third birthday. If the birthday occurs during the summer, the child's IEP team must determine when the services are to begin.

Will my three-year-old child have an IEP or an IFSP developed?

According to Section 300.342, schools may use an IFSP in the place of an IEP if using that plan is consistent with state policy and agreed to by the agency and the child's parents. Additionally, a detailed explanation of the differences between an IFSP and an IEP must be provided to the child's parents. If the parents choose an IFSP, the agency must obtain written, informed consent from the parents.

How do I know if the IEP is appropriate?

The U.S. Supreme Court defined a free appropriate public education (FAPE) in *Board of Education v. Rowley* (102 S.Ct. 3034 [1982]). First, the agency must comply with the procedural requirements of the *IDEA* and its regulations. The procedural requirements are specified in the *IDEA Amendments* and published in the final regulations in the *Federal Register*, March 12, 1999. Second, the IEP must be reasonably calculated to enable the student to receive an educational benefit. This landmark case established the concept that an educational program must be appropriate, not the best.

The case of *Cypress-Fairbanks ISD v. Michael F.*, a Fifth Circuit Court decision, sets forth four factors to consider in determining whether an IEP is appropriate for the identified student.

1. Is the IEP based on the student's assessment and performance?
2. Is the individualized program administered in the least restrictive environment?
3. Are the services provided in a coordinated and collaborative manner by the key stakeholders?
4. Does the student demonstrate positive benefits both academically and non-academically?

If your child's IEP meets these criteria, it is appropriate according to legal criteria. Conflicts between school and parents generally occur when parents and school staff perceive the answers to these questions differently.

Chapter Six
Targeting Student Needs

Present Levels of Performance

A good Individualized Educational Program (IEP) should be based upon the identified needs of the student, not on a predetermined curriculum adopted by the special education program or school district. "The only appropriate education is an effective education." (Patrick, 1996, p. 11). Identified student needs determined from the assessment should be the foundation for goals and objectives. Present competencies should accurately describe the effect of autism on the child's performance in all affected areas of the child's life.

Present levels of performance should be directly linked to the other components in the IEP. Needs identified through present competency levels should directly relate to other components of the IEP. For example, if the student has difficulty with transition between activities, a goal should be structured to facilitate transitioning of the student from one activity to another with less difficulty.

Goals and Objectives

Goals, objectives, and benchmarks in the IEP should be helpful to parents and school personnel by providing a general way of checking on the child's progress in the special education program. Although the IEP should provide the basis for daily and weekly planning, objectives should not be as specific as daily lesson plans. Specifics about the child's daily and weekly progress need to be obtained through parent/teacher conferences, report cards, progress notes, or other reporting procedures used by the school. Some teachers choose to use home/school notes to communicate specific information to the parents on a daily or weekly basis.

However, *Appendix A* of the *IDEA Amendments* states that the purpose of short-term objectives and/or benchmarks are "to enable a child's teacher(s), parents, and others involved in developing and implementing the child's IEP to gauge, at intermediate times during the year, how well the child is progressing toward achievement of the annual goal" (*Federal Register*, 1999, p. 12471). Although IEP teams can continue to develop short-term objectives that break the annual goal down into smaller steps, the final regulations also provide that IEP teams may use "benchmarks" as an alternative to short-term objectives. As defined in the final regulations of the *IDEA Amendments*, "benchmarks" describe the amount of progress the child is expected to make within specified time segments of the year. "Generally, benchmarks establish expected performance levels that allow for regular checks of progress that coincide with the reporting periods for informing parents of their child's progress toward achieving the annual goal." IEP teams may use short-term objectives, benchmarks, or a combination of both.

CASE EXAMPLE

Ray, a child with autism, lives in Houston, TX with his parents and a sister who does not have a disability. Houston ISD sends parents of regular education students report cards at the end of every six weeks. Houston ISD is using benchmarks in the IEP that state the progress that the student is expected to make toward the annual goal for each six week reporting period. Consequently, at the end of each six week reporting period, when Ray's sister gets a report card, Ray's parents will also receive a progress report that informs them how Ray is doing in reaching his annual goals and benchmarks.

A direct link should exist between activities that occur daily in the classroom and IEP goals and objectives. Sitting in "circle time," a morning routine followed by the teacher's reading and discussion of a story, could link to several goals in student IEPs. For one child, the activity might link to an objective of learning to sit for a certain period of time. For other students, it might link to objectives related to social interaction or communication and language development.

IEP goals are long-term, broad-based, general statements such as "Mary will increase verbal communication and comprehension by 20%." Objectives and benchmarks are specific and include: behavior, condition, and criteria for evaluation or mastery. Behavior refers to what the individual will be able to do at the end of the IEP time period (usually one year), or in the case of benchmarks, at the end of a reporting period. Condition describes where and under what circumstances the student will perform the goal or objective. Evaluation or mastery criteria provide information to determine whether the student has attained the goal.

Positive, Measurable Goals Addressing All Domains

Annual goals and short-term objectives should be stated in measurable, positive terms, identifying or listing what the student is expected to do, not what the student should not do. For example, Jimmie should walk (objective behavior) beside the teacher when going to the cafeteria or physical education (condition) with 80% accuracy or eight out of ten observations (measurable criteria for evaluation). An ineffective and inappropriate objective is "Jimmie will decrease running behavior." This is not stated positively and fails to state conditions or evaluation criteria. (Pratt & Porco, 1994, p. 7).

A "red flag word" that is frequently seen in IEP objectives is "appropriate." This should be a red flag because there is always a question of who determines what is appropriate. For example, Jimmie will walk down the hall appropriately. Do we know what is expected? Does "appropriate" mean no talking or talking softly? We must be very careful as we write objectives that each one is truly measurable and tells specifically what the student is expected to do. Another "caution phrase" is "attend to task." What is meant by attend? If the student sits and stares at the task, is he attending? Does "listen to the teacher" describe what is expected of the student? How do we know that the student is listening? How will it be measured if we don't know exactly what kind of behavior is expected?

IEP goals for many students with autism should address all aspects and domains of the student's life. In addition to academic areas at school, goals and objectives should also address extracurricular or after-school activities, transition, extended school year services, and community, work, and home activities. Goals for communication, social interaction, behavior, and related services should be embedded within the context of school, home, and community activities. (Pratt & Porco, 1994, p. 7). However, the *IDEA Amendments* have placed a new emphasis on access to the general education curriculum and accountability for all students. Section 300.347(a)(2) requires that each child's IEP include "A statement of measurable annual goals, including benchmarks or short-term objectives, related to meeting the child's needs that result from the child's disability to enable the child to be involved in and progress in the general curriculum." The IEP must also meet each of the child's other educational needs that result from the child's disability (*Federal Register*, 1999, p. 12472). What exactly does this mean? According to Appendix A, it means that the public agency is not required to include IEP annual goals that relate to areas of the general education curriculum in which the child's disability does not affect his or her ability to be involved in and progress in the general curriculum. If a child only needs modifications or accommodations in order to progress in an area of the general education curriculum, a goal does not have to be included in the IEP for that area. However, the IEP must specify the needed modifications or accommodations.

 CASE EXAMPLE

Allen spends all of his day in the general education classroom. He reads better than most of his classmates and has no difficulty with most of the academic demands of the classroom. However, he gets very anxious during tests. The noise of the other students bothers him, and it takes him longer to take put his information on paper. The IEP team determined that he should be allowed to take his tests in a study carrel away from other students and that he should have extra time to complete his tests. Because his disability does not affect his participation in the regular education curriculum, he does not need to have annual goals in the academic areas. However, the IEP must specify the test accommodations that the IEP team determined would be appropriate for Allen.

Do Goals Provide for Participation with Age-appropriate Peers without Disabilities?

The *IDEA Amendments* emphasize participation in regular education. Even the present levels of performance must address how the child's disability affects the child's involvement and progress in the general curriculum. Section 300.347(a)(4) requires that each individual's IEP include "An explanation of the extent, if any, to which the child will not participate with nondisabled children in the regular class and in extracurricular and other nonacademic activities" (*Federal Register*, 1999, p. 12471). This is consistent with the concept of "least restrictive environment" which has been a basic concept since the passage of *Public Law 94-142* in 1975. All students with a disability must be educated with nondisabled children to the maximum extent appropriate. Students with disabilities should be removed from the regular education environment

only when the nature or severity of the child's disability is such that education in regular classes with the use of supplementary aids and services cannot be achieved satisfactorily. Although *IDEA* does not mandate regular class placement for every child with a disability, it does assume that the first placement option considered for every student with a disability will be the school the child would attend if not disabled, with appropriate supplementary aids and services to facilitate such placement. At the same time, it reaffirms a commitment to a full continuum of services so that all students may be successful.

Student needs must be addressed under both goals and objectives with the provision of special education and related services. The number of IEP goals and objectives should be limited to represent the top priorities that a team can commit to teaching intensively.

Questions to Ask

Parents frequently want to know how to determine the appropriateness of goals and objectives for their child's IEP. One way parents can help ensure the appropriateness of the IEP is to look at the following list. This should help pinpoint some critical goals and objectives for the child. (ASA, 1995).

1. Make a list of what your child with autism can do.

2. How old is your child? Look at same-age peers. What do they do? Make a list of things that children the same age can do.

3. Compare the two lists. Choose items from the list that other children can do that you would like your child to be able to do. Remember to choose the most important items. Your child can not work on everything at once.

4. If you have difficulty selecting the most important items, ask the following questions of yourself.

    a. Is my child toilet trained? Is my child old enough to be toilet trained? If your child is old enough, but is not toilet trained, that should be a priority goal.

    b. Does my child use any form of communication? If not, this is another priority goal. If your child uses gestures for communication, an appropriate goal might be development of a picture symbol form of communication. If your child uses language, you might wish to have him work on pronoun usage or expressing wants, needs, and feelings. Essentially, **look at where your child is and build toward higher levels of communication.**

c.   Can my child eat independently? If not, is this an important goal for him or her?

d.   Can my child sit still? For how long? Does my child need this skill?

For individuals with autism who function at a lower level with many challenging behaviors, activities of daily living and social/behavioral interactions provide many sources of goal and objective development. Don't spend time teaching skills that the individual will not use.

What about higher functioning students? If your child can perform most daily living skills appropriate for his age and also uses verbal communication to express his thoughts, how will you develop your goals? The basic process is the same. Observe your own child's abilities and compare them with skills of other children the same age. The areas of difficulty will be the targets for IEP goals and objectives. In this instance, parents may be targeting social interaction, communication, and academic goals in specific subject areas.

Longitudinal Planning

Are the goals based upon long-term planning? Has the IEP team looked at what future plans the student and parent have made? Are the goals longitudinal; i.e., is it appropriate for the student as he or she gets older? For example, if the objective is "Johnny will play a card game with Sammy during leisure time one day each week," will he be able to carry over use of that skill in future situations? If the teacher is going to spend time teaching a card game, the student should be taught a game such as *Uno* instead of *Go Fish*. Many of the principles are the same, but *Go Fish* is only appropriate for young children. *Uno* is a game that is played from childhood into adulthood. It makes more sense to teach a skill that can be used for years, rather than a skill that age-appropriate peers may not be doing by the time the student masters the objective. I have seen tasks set up with visuals in a right-to-left presentation that require the student to match the face cards in a card deck. The tasks were developed using two decks of cards, a file folder, and library card pockets so that students could eventually combine the activities of the tasks and apply them in a real card game such as poker—a game most individuals never get too old to play.

Prevocational, Vocational Needs, and Transition

Do the goals address prevocational and vocational needs of students? *The IDEA Amendments* stress the importance of the preparation of students with disabilities for transition from the educational environment into the world of work and community. The focus is on employment and other post-school activities. Beginning at the age of fourteen, (or younger if determined appropriate), the IEP team must make a statement of transition service needs of the student that focuses on the student's course of study. This is different  from the previous transition requirement for age sixteen because it only addresses courses of study. The focus is on the educational program and the types of vocational training that public agencies might provide to facilitate future transitions into the world of work for students with disabilities.

The requirement for transition services at the age of sixteen (younger if determined appropriate by the IEP team) includes participants and services from other agencies. At that time, responsibilities of other agencies are considered and written into the IEP. Representatives of those other agencies are also invited to attend the IEP meeting.

Some states, such as Texas, mandate that prevocational and vocational needs be addressed for students with autism at the age of twelve. Because their needs for transition and vocational services may be much greater than other students' needs, it is appropriate to begin looking at prevocational and vocational needs at a younger age. These might include objectives designed to teach appropriate work habits or specific skills instruction for jobs in the community. Many other objectives such as telling time, making change, preparing foods, etc. can also be considered under vocational needs.

Repetitious Goals

What about objectives found in the IEP year after year? Does this indicate that the school is doing a poor job, or that the objective is unattainable for the child and should not have been included in the IEP? In a court case reported by Walsh (1994e, p. 1), the judge ruled that the repetition of objectives from one year to the next was permissible. The court noted that the parents had repeatedly agreed to the IEPs, and that student progress had been made.

According to the court, the student had autism and slow progress was to be expected: "This Court recognizes that in some cases a student may never master a goal. However, if the goal is appropriate, it would be harmful to eliminate the goal just because it is repetitious." (Walsh, 1994e p. 1). A key factor in this particular case was the parents' repeated ratification of the repetition of short-term objectives by signing and indicating agreement with the IEP. Consequently, the lesson that parents should learn is to speak up immediately when you disagree with the IEP. **Don't sign that you agree unless you really do**. If you do not agree with the IEP, indicate your disagreement.

Parents may indicate disagreement and still let the proposed educational program be implemented. If disagreement is indicated, the agency should provide written notice to the parents that the proposed IEP will be implemented upon a certain date (usually within ten days) if the parents do not file a complaint with the state agency or request a due process hearing. If the parents do nothing, the IEP will be implemented even though the parents disagree. If the parents request a due process hearing, the student will remain in his or her current placement (as determined by the last agreed upon IEP) until the due process hearing is completed.

However, the *IDEA Amendments* do place more emphasis on accountability and quality education for students with disabilities. Repetitious goals are usually an indication that in at least one area, the student is not achieving expected progress as identified by the short-term objectives or benchmarks. If the student is not progressing toward stating the goals and short-term objectives on the IEP, Section 300.343 indicates that the IEP team should meet to revise the IEP to address lack of expected progress toward the annual goals.

Are Computer Generated IEPs Okay?

Many school districts use computer-generated IEPs because of the ease in which they are produced as opposed to handwritten objectives. This creates several problems. I have been in situations where the teacher just discussed the goals she had planned without the written document. The parent is then asked to sign an IEP with no goals and objectives. When the teacher brings the computer generated IEP to the meeting, it appears that the objectives were developed by the teacher, not the parent and committee. In such instances, the parent may be expected to approve the IEP with no opportunity for parental input.

I have worked with teachers who have a tendency to computer-generate all objectives listed for the student's grade level. The IEP usually ends up with pages and pages of objectives that may not be looked at all year. Another problem with computer-generated goals and objectives for students with autism is that the list of objectives may not be appropriate for them. These objective banks are generally developed for students with learning disabilities and may be appropriate for higher functioning students with autism or Asperger's Disorder, but not for low-functioning students with autism. Additionally, the computer lists rarely contain objectives for social skills and social interaction that are generally needed for all students with pervasive developmental disorders.

However, computer-generated goals are appropriate when the needs of the student have been identified and are contained in the bank of objectives, or the IEP team has flexibility to add goals and objectives for specific students. This still does not resolve the problem of presenting a finished copy of the IEP to the parent unless the IEP is actually printed during the meeting. Computer goals and objectives should meet the same criteria that individually developed goals, objectives, and benchmarks meet by being individually developed for the specific student based upon assessment results and identified needs of the student.

Who Receives a Copy of the IEP?

One copy of the IEP is usually placed in the special education student eligibility folder. According to the *IDEA Amendments*, the parent should always receive a copy of the IEP. (*Federal Register,* 1999, p. 12473).The parent should not have to request the copy. It should be provided automatically. However, if parents want to receive a copy of the draft before the IEP meeting, they may have to request it. Therefore, my recommendation to parents is to request a draft copy when they receive notice of the IEP meeting. This allows the parents time to study the proposed goals, objectives, and/or benchmarks prior to the IEP meeting. It is difficult to try to listen and read at the same time.

The final regulations also indicate that all teachers who work with the child, and all related service personnel providing services, should have access to the child's IEP. Each person should be informed of his or her specific responsibilities related to implementing the IEP, and of the specific accommodations, modifications, and supports that must be provided to the child in accordance with the IEP. These regulations state that instructional and related service personnel should have access to the IEP before they begin providing the services described in the IEP. A common way of providing access is by providing a copy of the IEP to each of the IEP implementers.

In the past, some school districts have been reluctant to provide copies of the IEP to regular education teachers because it contains confidential information. Other school districts have routinely provided a copy to every teacher involved with the student to ensure that every teacher knows the modifications and accommodations required for the student. The final regulations appear to take the position that the teacher has a "legitimate educational interest in the student" as defined by *FERPA*.

Some districts require that teachers sign an access record anytime that they look at a file to comply with *FERPA's* requirement of keeping a record of folder access so that parents may know who has seen their child's records. Other districts have classroom teachers sign a receipt for a copy of the IEP because the agency has been "burned" in monitoring visits. Although the teacher had been given a copy of the IEP, when the monitors questioned the teacher about the IEP, the teacher indicated that he or she didn't know anything about it. The special education department uses the receipt signature to document that the teacher received a copy. However, putting a copy in the teacher's hand doesn't guarantee that it is read. Some teachers who had signed receipt forms still replied with, "I've never seen the IEP for this student."

Methodology—TEACCH and Lovaas

Methodology is a frequent issue in programs for students with autism. Parents frequently have a preference in methodology and would like their preference implemented. This issue affects special education instruction and related services. The most common instructional issue involves two nationally known programs, the Division TEACCH program developed in North Carolina, and the Lovaas method developed by Ivar Lovaas at UCLA.

Division TEACCH

The Division TEACCH program is easier to implement in school environments than the Lovaas program. TEACCH uses structured teaching as an intervention strategy. Components of this program include: physical structure, schedules, individual work systems, visual structure, and routines. "Structured teaching is the main approach at Division TEACCH for developing skills and minimizing behavioral difficulties." (Schopler & Mesibov, 1994, p. 196). The TEACCH program can be used in a classroom with several students, and it does not require after school interventions. However, after-school interventions may also be established if the child's individual needs indicate it as a necessary strategy for educational benefit. Parents are trained to use the visual cues, physical structure, schedules, and supports in the home and in the community.

The Lovaas Method

The Lovaas method is an intensive behavioral therapy that requires a minimum of forty hours per week in one-on-one therapy. Dr. Lovaas actually states that sixteen hours per day of intensive therapy is better than eight hours. According to Lovaas, "intensive one-on-one teaching for developmentally disabled children starting at the age of two should be an entitlement." (Johnson, 1994, p.21). However, our federal laws related to education of students with autism do not provide that kind of entitlement. Therefore, this is an expensive program for parents or school districts to provide. Parents can be charged $1400 for a two-day workshop to learn the methods. Two months later, they could be expected to attend a follow-up workshop, which costs $700. Some parents pay one person $15,000 per year to oversee the whole program on a twenty- hour a week basis. The training coordinator supervises the volunteers or students who are employed (Johnson, 1994, p. 21). Many schools have personnel trained in intensive behavioral therapy techniques and have implemented intensive behavioral therapy as instruction for students with autism. However, it may not span every hour of the school day.

What do the Courts Say?

In general, the courts have said that methodology is the prerogative of the district. Goals and objectives are established by the IEP team. The methods for teaching the goals and objectives are then determined by professionals implementing the goals and objectives. However, one court case did award reimbursement for costs of in-home therapy due to improper placement for a child with autism

In *Capistrano Unified School District* (23 IDELR 1209 [SEA CA 1995]), "the hearing officer examined the student's individual needs, and found that he required 1:1 instruction in a structured environment, extensive language therapy, and instruction in social skills. Given those needs, the district's special day class placement was completely inappropriate." (LRP, 1996b, XIV-174). In this situation, all students were given the same instruction that exceeded the level of the student with autism. Additionally, the school district had not offered any other placement options. There was documented evidence that the student was receiving educational benefit from the home program of intensive behavioral therapy. Therefore, the district was ordered to reimburse the parents for the costs of therapy and to provide 25 hours of one-on-one in-home therapy per week for the remainder of the school year.

A related issue, teacher training, has also been addressed by the courts. In *Koupal v. Sioux Falls School District*, (ASA, 1994; 22 IDELR 26 [S.D. 1994]) parents of a six-year-old with autism challenged the district's refusal to include teacher training in the student's IEP. The United States Supreme Court refused to review the decision. "As a result, the South Dakota Supreme Court's decision, which held that teacher training is not a related service under the *IDEA* and is not required to be included within an IEP, will stand."

What Can We Learn from This?

If the school's program is appropriate, the choice of methods and materials is left to the local education agency. In most cases the courts will not select one appropriate program over another. Parents must be able to show why the school's program is inappropriate and justify why the preferred program will produce educational benefit. Parents trying to get a specific methodology implemented will need to ensure that needs are stated in terms that can be linked to major components of the preferred program. For example, for a Lovaas type program, indicate the need for highly structured, individualized therapy; for a Division TEACCH type program, indicate the need for established routines, visual supports and schedules, and other structured teaching components.

If parents want a sensory integration program established as part of the provision of occupational therapy as a related service, needs should focus on sensory dysfunctions of the child and goals should relate to sensory integration activities.

What Kind of Goals?

Goals should be established for each developmental area or academic content area that is to be provided through special education instruction. Additionally, goals should be prioritized and identified for in-home training and parent training. Although related services and special education instruction can share the same goals, the IEP must include the goals and should indicate that the specific goal is to be implemented by the related service professional and the special education instructor. Goals should cross all environments and address all the needs of the individual with autism. Careful attention ensures that the IEP includes behavioral goals, including social skills development and interaction.

The key to development of all goals, objectives, and benchmarks is that they relate to assessed needs and are linked to provision of appropriate services and implemented in daily and weekly instruction. Criteria and schedules for evaluation should also be established.

What is Special Education Instruction?

Section 300.26 of the *IDEA Amendments* defines *special education*. In general, special education means **specially designed instruction** that is provided to meet the unique needs of a student with a disability at no cost to the parents. This includes:

- instruction conducted in the classroom, in the home, in hospitals and institutions, and in other settings; and
- instruction in physical education.

Special education also includes the following:

- speech-language pathology services, or any other related service, if the service is considered special education rather than a related service under state standards;

- travel training; and

- vocational education (*Federal Register*, 1999, p. 12425).

The final regulations of the *IDEA Amendments* defines *at no cost* to parents as meaning that all specially designed instruction is provided at no charge. However, the school may charge incidental fees that are normally charged to nondisabled students.

The specially designed instruction refers to adapting, as appropriate, to the needs of the child with a disability, the content, methodology, or delivery of instruction. The purpose of specially designed instruction is to address the unique needs of the child that result from the child's disability and to ensure access of the child to the general curriculum. The goal is that the child will be able to meet the educational standards within the jurisdiction of the public agency that apply to all children.

CASE EXAMPLE

Kelly is in the regular education class. He gets very frustrated when he does poorly on his spelling test. The classroom teacher is modifying the *content* of his spelling lesson. While the other students are expected to learn 20 spelling words each week, Kelly is only expected to study and learn 10. Kelly's teacher modifies her *methodology of instruction* on a daily basis because she provided written visual cues for all directions that Kelly is to follow.

Physical education refers to the development of physical and motor fitness and fundamental motor skills and patterns. Physical education includes developing skills in aquatics, dance, individual and group games, and sports. It also includes: special physical education, adapted physical education, movement education, and motor development.

The *IDEA Amendments* define travel training as providing instruction to children with significant cognitive disabilities, and any other children with disabilities who require this instruction, to enable them to develop an awareness of the environment in which they live and to learn the skills necessary to move effectively and safely from within that environment. Travel training can take place in the school, the home, at work, or in the community.

CASE EXAMPLE

Gary, a student with autism, is beginning a new job next month. He will be using public transportation to travel from school to his job and then from his job to home. It would be appropriate for Gary's IEP team to recommend that he receive travel training to help him learn how to access the public transportation to get him to work and home.

CASE EXAMPLE

Evan is going to a new school for sixth grade. It is larger than his current school, and he will be changing classes. Travel training can familiarize him with the new campus.

Vocational education refers to organized educational programs that are directly related to the preparation of persons for paid or unpaid employment, or for additional preparation for a career requiring other than a baccalaureate or advanced degree (*Federal Register*, 1999, p. 12425).

Special Eating Needs

Some students with autism have special eating needs. Some individuals have food allergies. Others may have special health problems that require soft foods because they are unable to chew foods.

CASE EXAMPLE

Elliott, a sixteen-year-old with autism and Down syndrome, has constant reflux problems. This caused eroding and infection of his teeth and gums. As a result, the dentist removed all of his teeth. False teeth are not feasible because he would not keep them in his mouth. Consequently, all of his food must be soft.

Some students with autism refuse to eat certain foods. This may be because the person doesn't like the taste, but it may also be related to the texture or smell of the food. Some individuals won't eat a food because of the sound it makes when it is chewed. For most students, this is not a problem. The food is simply left on the plate. However, for some students, it creates major problems.

 CASE EXAMPLE

Jerry won't eat bread. If bread is placed on top of his meat, he will not eat the meat because he can still smell the bread. If the cafeteria worker places the bread on his plate, he gets visibly upset and will not begin to eat his other food until the bread is removed. This should have been a simple matter of having the bread left off the plate. However, when the teacher asked the cafeteria manager to leave the bread off the plate, she refused. The teacher had to remove the bread at the table.

What Can be Done?

Because most schools participate in breakfast and hot lunch programs, the school lunch program must abide by instructions issued in October 1994 by the U. S. Department of Agriculture, which provides for substitutions of foods on school food plates. "If a school is not a participant in this federal program, they may still be obligated to make modifications and substitutions based on the *Individual with Disabilities Education Act (IDEA)*." (Clark, 1995, p. 45). Schools may be required to provide meals outside of the regular meal schedule or to provide services that are not usually required by the child Nutrition program. According to *IDEA*, food modifications can be included on:

• an individualized education program (IEP),

• a student health care plan attached to the IEP, and

• a goal-and-objectives IEP related strictly to feeding and nutrition.

If a child does not qualify for *IDEA* services, students may still qualify for special food services as long as the student meets the requirements for having a disability under *Section 504*.

Chapter Seven

Bridging the Gaps with Related Services

IDEA (*Federal Register*, 1999) defines related services as "transportation and such developmental, corrective, and other supportive services as are required to assist a child with a disability to benefit from special education, and includes:

- speech pathology and audiology services,

- psychological services,

- physical and occupational therapy,

- recreation, including therapeutic recreation,

- early identification and assessment of disabilities in children,

- counseling services, including rehabilitation counseling,

- orientation and mobility services,

- medical services for diagnostic or evaluation purposes,

- school health services,

- social work services in schools, and

- parent counseling and training."

The law goes on to explain that "the list of related services is not exhaustive and may include other developmental, corrective, or supportive services (such as nutritional services, service coordination, and art, music, and dance therapy), if they are required to assist a child with a disability to benefit from special education." (*Federal Register*, 1999, p. 12479). These services are important for individuals with autism because they frequently make the difference between an appropriate or inappropriate IEP. Regardless of the type of related service, it must be based on assessment data and stated in the IEP with specifications for duration and frequency for the child to receive the service. In a *Letter to Copenhaver* (LRP, 1995a), The Office of Special Education Programs replied that the amount of services is to be provided in a manner appropriate to the service. The *IDEA Amendments* reaffirm that position and require that the IEP team determine and specify the frequency, duration, and location of the service. The length of time should be specifically stated. Consequently, stating a range for services such as one-to-two hours per week or three-to-four hours per month is inconsistent with the philosophy of precise daily amounts. If the precise daily allocations of time cannot be specified because of the child's disability and unique educational needs, "public agencies should determine weekly or monthly allocations for the amount of services." (LRP, 1995a, p. XIV-147).

What about Educational Benefit?

A question that must be answered is, "Does the student need the service in order to benefit from special education?" If so, the goals and objectives should be supportive of the educational need for the related service by linking related service goals and objectives to special education instructional goals and objectives. Related service goals and objectives must fulfill an educational purpose and provide criteria for evaluating the instructional goals and objectives. All goals and objectives should focus on identified areas of difficulty and needs of the student with autism. "In a case involving a student with a pervasive developmental disorder, the Texas hearing officer determined that the IEP was inappropriate because it failed to include goals and objectives for counseling, in-home training, and parent training." (Graham, 1996, p. 3). These services were needed for the student to receive an educational benefit from special education instruction.

Direct versus Consultant Services

Parents sometimes interpret consultation services as meaning less service for their child. For a true understanding of these services, one must look at the differences between direct and consultant services. "In direct service, a related service provider works directly with a student on particular IEP objectives." (Durkel, 1994). This does not necessarily imply one-to-one services. The service provider may work with the child individually or in a small group of students working on the same objectives. Therapy may be provided in the classroom, in the therapy room, in the lunch room, on the playground, at home, or in the community. Location will depend upon the specific objectives identified. A variety of activities can be used to attain specified objective(s). Durkel (1994) states "that what direct service does best is establish a skill that the student may go on to use in a variety of different environments and activities." For example, many objectives taught in a Lovaas program would be delivered as direct therapy or instruction in one-to-one settings. However, generalization of those same skills would take place in a group setting.

According to Durkel (1994), "consulting is the means by which a related service provider can help other professionals meet a student's IEP goals and objectives. The recipient of consulting is not the student but another professional." This type of service ensures that students with autism have multiple opportunities in a day to use particular skills. For example, the classroom teacher and the speech pathologist would work on the same language goals. The speech pathologist would consult with the classroom teacher to ensure that the student received daily instruction on the objectives in the natural environment of the classroom. The objectives can be reinforced in all activities during the day, not just in a thirty minute period twice a week.

Consulting services should be used when it is "the best way to meet the student's IEP objectives. It is not to be used as a way to decrease a particular professional's case load size." If consulting is done correctly, it may take more of the service provider's time than direct therapy because of the need to observe and interact with the student in the classroom.

Some parents are concerned about how consultant services are monitored. Progress reports should be sent on the same schedule that progress reports from a direct therapy service are sent. Some students with autism receive related services through a combination of direct therapy and consultant services. For example, the student may receive thirty minutes of direct service and thirty minutes of consultant services each week.

CASE EXAMPLE

Kelley had difficulty pronouncing certain sounds and interacting with other students. His speech pathologist saw him once a week in direct therapy to work on his articulation (pronunciation of sounds) and consulted with his teacher once a week to ensure that situations were set up to encourage him to verbally interact with other children. By consulting with the teacher, the speech pathologist and the classroom teacher were able to help Kelley generalize the skills learned in direct therapy to other environments.

CASE EXAMPLE

Gary received physical therapy once a week for thirty minutes. Gary's physical therapist was totally frustrated because he refused to work with her. Gary was not making progress and the physical therapist was not able to provide appropriate services because of his refusal to participate by exhibiting many challenging behaviors. He would have tantrums and physically resist all efforts at physical therapy. However, he would participate in the same activities with his classroom teacher. Consequently, it was determined that he would actually receive more educational benefit by having the physical therapist consult with his teacher rather than having a battle of wills each time the therapist came. The IEP team met and changed Gary's direct therapy to consultant services. With this change in service delivery, Gary began to make progress in his physical therapy objectives.

As with all services designated in the IEP, recommendations should be based on the individual education needs of the child. Whether the student receives direct or consultant services should depend upon the identified goals and objectives and whether or not the goals and objectives can be best attained with direct therapy, consultant services, or a combination of both. The IEP should also establish the specific amount of services needed. How much service and how often the service should be provided are required elements of the IEP. As parents, you should never accept a recommendation for "services as needed." There is no way to monitor this because each member of the committee may perceive "services as needed" very differently. Additionally, the *IDEA Amendments* also state that the location of the service must be specified. Therefore, the IEP team must determine whether the service is to be provided within the classroom setting or a different location.

Professionals providing consultant services should keep records of when and with whom they consult. These records should include information about the recipient of the service, what was discussed, the next date of service, and what will be done during the next visit. Parents can examine these records and verify that the frequency of the visits is the same as specified in the

IEP. As stated before, professionals providing consultant services should also be sending progress reports for consultant services with the same frequency that occurs with direct therapy.

Specific Related Services

Parent Training

IDEA (*Federal Register*, 1999, p.12424) defines "parent training and counseling" as:

- assisting parents in understanding special needs of their child,
- providing parents with information about child development, and
- helping parents to acquire the necessary skills that will allow them to support the implementation of their child's IEP or IFSP.

Parent training is for parents and other primary family members or care givers. The purpose is to increase the family's knowledge about autism and to provide information on specific interventions and instructional techniques. It could be considered to be "survival skills for the parent." If identified as an educational need by the IEP committee, goals and objectives should be developed with frequency and duration of the service specified. The intent is to help parents work as active participants in their child's educational program, not as passive observers. A variety of methods specific to the child's needs and the environment may be used (Palomo, 1994).

In my personal opinion, parent training usually needs to be provided individually. Group instruction is frequently inappropriate because student and environmental needs differ from family to family. The first year I began providing parent training, the school district and I had the mistaken idea that we would get the parents together, see what night they wanted to meet, and provide behavior management sessions for them. As we sat discussing their needs, it was quickly obvious that our plans were not going to work. Instead, we developed individualized plans that met the needs of each family and student. In some situations where parents requested it, I met with a couple of parents together. In most cases, parent training sessions are individualized and specific to the child's family. Some public agencies, however, might be able to group parents with like needs together.

119

CASE EXAMPLE

Mike's parents needed the physical therapist to provide instruction on lifting him into the bath tub. A 9 year old with autism, epilepsy, and mild cerebral palsy, he could not get into the tub without assistance and he was getting too large for his mother to do this by herself. This training was most effective in the home situation where the physical therapist could actually see the bath tub and the room arrangement. It would not have been effective to provide this type of training anywhere except in the home environment. This was not a need for other parents so it would not have been appropriate to group this mother with other parents to learn this skill.

Service delivery may vary greatly in each situation. Some examples of different types of service delivery for parent training include:

- individual training with parents related to specific needs in the home and community;

- group sessions with parents on common issues such as behavior management and toilet training;

- classroom observations and/or participation in the child's classroom or in another classroom where certain techniques and strategies are being used;

- viewing videotapes of child/teaching situations;

- conferences and workshops provided at the local, regional, state, or national level;

- conferences with teachers and/or parent trainers either in person, by telephone, or through written communication; and

- any combination of the above.

Another question frequently of concern for both parents and school personnel is, "Who will provide the parent training?" Generally, the person providing the parent training must be knowledgeable about autism and the techniques and strategies to be taught. The parent trainer should be able to communicate in clear, understandable language, and must be sensitive to various family forms, family economic constraints, level of acculturation, and family educational levels. Although families frequently like to specify that a certain individual provide parent training, the selection of specific personnel, by law, is left to the discretion of the school program. However, school personnel are wise to consider the wishes of the parent. Parents should also cooperate with the services being provided and be realistic about the agency's resources and limitations.

Goals and objectives for parent training should be written into the IEP, and progress reports are required. Parent training is a related service, and all regulations that apply to related services apply to parent training. A goal might be worded as follows:

The parent trainer will provide support services and instruction in techniques to be used by parents and/or caregivers with the student in the home environment.

Objectives that might enable parents to reach this goal are:

- The parent will develop a picture schedule to be used with the child in the home and community.

- Parents will be able to increase their knowledge about autism by being informed about, and participating in, training opportunities related to autism and other topics relevant to the student's special needs in the local and regional area.

- Parents will increase their knowledge about autism through information provided by the parent trainer.

- Parents will model behavior management techniques demonstrated by the parent trainer as they interact with their child in the home and community environment.

In-home Training

In-home training is not specifically listed as one of the related services in the *IDEA Amendments*. However, the final regulations are very clear that the list of services is not exhaustive, and other related services may be provided if they are determined to be necessary for the child to benefit from special education. Additionally, hearing officers in several cases have required in-home training as part of the student's IEP. In-home training is different from parent training because it is provided to the student in the home, community, or natural environment. Ideally, a parent will work with the school trainer so that continued practice may occur in the home with parents guiding or supervising activities. The goal is to generalize skills learned at school to the home environment for maximum independence. If the IEP committee addresses in-home training as an educational need, it becomes an extension of the student's IEP. Specifics such as frequency and duration are documented in the written IEP (Palomo, 1994). Reports are sent home on the same time schedule that students without disabilities receive progress reports.

In-home training is typically provided by an individual skilled in behavior modification principles and language development. It may be appropriately provided by the student's special education teacher, instructional aide or paraprofessional, speech pathologist, or other related service personnel because these individuals know the activities and skills that the student has been able to perform in the classroom environment. An expert consultant is **not** required. Since the goal is generalization, it is absolutely imperative that the in-home trainer is familiar with the student's functioning in the school environment.

In-home trainers should also be knowledgeable about autism, respectful of individual family values, and good communicators. The responsibilities of the in-home trainer include working directly with the student and teaching transfer and generalization of goals and objectives from the school setting to the home and community environment. The goals and objectives along with frequency and duration for in-home training should be specified in the IEP. The goals and objectives may relate to:

- behavioral functioning,

- social skills enhancement,

- self- control and calming strategies,

- self-help skills,

- communication skills,

- choice making,

- sensory processing and motor skills enhancement,

- recreation/leisure activities, and

- vocational activities.

Although not absolutely required, parent participation during in-home training will facilitate transfer of skills from the school to home and community environments. In-home training may be provided independent of parent training or in combination with individualized parent training. It may also be provided within the community either individually or within a small group.

Speech-Language Pathology Services

Speech-language pathology services, commonly called "speech therapy" by many parents and professionals, is a common area of contention in the IEP. Numerous parents have told me that district evaluations indicated that their child with autism could not benefit from speech therapy because the student was nonverbal. Parents of verbal students with autism sometimes report that their children do not receive speech-language pathology services because the school specialist reports that the student can talk plainly and his oral functioning is commensurate with his intellectual functioning. To address this common problem, one must look at *IDEA's* definition of related services, speech-language pathology services, and the characteristics of autism.

Although provision of services must be determined individually based upon assessment data and decisions of the IEP Team, some myths associated with speech pathology and autism can be dispelled. According to *IDEA*, (*Federal Register*, 1999, p.12424), speech-language pathology services includes:

- identification of children with speech or language impairments;

- diagnosis and appraisal of specific speech or language impairments;

- referral for medical or other professional attention necessary for the habilitation of speech or language impairments;

- provision of speech and language services for the habilitation or prevention of communicative impairments; and

- counseling and guidance of parents, children, and teachers regarding speech and language impairments.

I personally question how a professional in speech-language pathology determines that a child with autism does not have a language impairment or a communication disorder when definitions of autism in federal law and the *DSM-IV* specify that individuals with autism have disorders in language and/or communication. Most speech-language pathologists in public schools spend a majority of their time working with students with speech disorders including articulation, voice, or fluency problems. The largest groups of students with speech disorders are those with articulation disorders. Speech-language pathologists usually have large case loads of kindergarten and first grade students receiving therapy in the pronunciations of the r, l, and s sounds.

You cannot teach a child to pronounce words correctly if he cannot say the words at all. But, nonverbal students have a great need to develop some form of communication. The speech–language pathologist can, and should, work with the student to develop more appropriate forms of communication, such as object swaps, picture symbols, written language, sign language, or oral communication. The speech pathologist should regularly consult with the teacher and parent to promote generalization in the use of a communication system at school, at home, and in the community.

Another common issue in the development of a speech-language pathology program is the delivery of speech-language pathology services. Should the student receive one-on-one therapy, group therapy, or consultation with the professionals working with the child? For many years, the preferred delivery system was pull-out type programs where the speech-language pathologist worked individually with the child or in small group instruction. Best practices in service delivery are now moving toward more integrated systems.

The delivery of services should be addressed after the goals and objectives of therapy are established. Services are currently provided in different ways in varying situations. Some goals need to be worked on in one-on-one or small group settings. However, since students with autism do not typically generalize information from one setting to the other, it can be beneficial for at least part of the student's therapy to occur within the classroom setting. This also allows for involvement with the classroom teacher, who can also work daily on the same targeted objectives in the classroom.

Many professionals now provide all speech pathology services within the student's classroom. Even one-on-one therapy can be provided in a small area of the classroom. This is preferable for many students with autism because the student practices skills within the context of the natural environment. If the goals include social interaction skills such as learning to communicate with others, they can generally be better met when other students are available to simulate normal play and conversation patterns. This type of delivery also avoids problems of generalization from the speech therapy room to the classroom.

Students with high-functioning autism who are highly verbal may not use language appropriately. For example, they may have difficulty with word retrieval or may not understand turn-taking in conversations. Topic maintenance and pronoun usage are also frequent problems. A good way to determine the student's level of functioning in this area is to conduct a language sample analysis. The evaluator observes the student in interactive situations and records at least 50 student utterances. It is also important to record the situations in which the language occurred, and ways the student interacted with others.

Many evaluators prefer to tape record or videotape the language sample so they may interpret the session later. This ensures that important events are not missed. Videotapes generally provide more information, but not all children will act normally when they know they are being videotaped. My very talkative four-year-old granddaughter totally shut down when I was trying to prepare a demonstration language sample for my university class. Finally, I had to audiotape her because it could be done without her knowledge. Therapy goals and objectives should target the areas of need identified in a complete assessment of the student's speech and language.

School personnel should perform comprehensive assessments of communication and language for any student with autism. Speech and language pathology services involve more than just articulation, voice, or fluency (stuttering) therapy. The assessment should focus on the communication and language of the student within the social (pragmatic) context of language. Parents who do not agree with the school's recommendations for therapy should obtain their own speech and language evaluation or request that the school provide an independent educational evaluation of the student in the area of speech and language. The results of the parent-obtained evaluation or the independent educational evaluation should then be presented to the IEP team along with the school's evaluation report. This way a fully informed decision can be made as to the need for speech-language pathology services.

Occupational Therapy

Occupational therapy is another related service that I consider to be crucial in educational programs of students with autism. Occupational therapists generally have more training in the area of sensory integration (SI) than any of the other related service personnel. Since sensory integrative dysfunctioning has been well documented in individuals with autism during the past few years, it is my opinion that any comprehensive evaluation of an individual with autism should include an evaluation by an occupational therapist trained in the area of sensory integration.

Lorna Jean King (Hutchison, 1995, p. 18-19) defines it in the following way. Sensory integration dysfunction is what happens when the brain is not able to put together the information from the various senses in order to get meaningful information. It is as if the brain is not connecting what we hear, what we see, and what we experience from the body. Experience, therefore, lacks meaning or is distorted.

According to *IDEA*, occupational therapy refers to services provided by a qualified occupational therapist and includes:

- improving, developing or restoring functions impaired or lost through illness, injury, or deprivation;

- improving ability to perform tasks for independent functioning when functions are impaired or lost; and

- preventing, through early intervention, initial or further impairment or loss of functioning (*Federal Register,* 1999, p. 12425).

Generally, occupational therapists focus on upper body movements and strength. They also work with the improvement of daily living skills, such as feeding, independent eating, leisure activities, and other fine motor skills. Occupational therapists receive training in sensory integration, an intervention approach that uses play to motivate the child to work on skills designed to build muscle tone, perception, attention, and coordination. Sensory integration therapy includes calming techniques and sensory defensiveness programs. According to King (Hutchison, 1995), occupational or physical therapists do not have "to be certified in sensory

126

integration therapy in order to treat a child. The certification in sensory integration refers to the ability to give and interpret the *Southern California Sensory Integration and Praxis Test*; it doesn't refer to treatment." Although younger children may make faster progress, anyone with autism can begin a program as soon as the individual is identified with a sensory integrative dysfunction.

School districts throughout the United States are receiving more and more requests for sensory integration therapy. As with other issues involved in the implementation of *IDEA* through public education, local districts and public agencies are responding in varied ways. Some provide the service, while others act as if they have never heard of sensory integration therapy. Most therapists agree that if progress is not made in the first three-to-six months of therapy, sensory integration is not likely to help that specific child (Partners Resource Network, Inc., 1996). Sensory integration therapy is primarily provided by occupational therapists or physical therapists. More special education teachers are working with therapists to use some of the methods in their classrooms. Many of the activities that form the "sensory diet" (Willbarger, P., & Willbarger, J. L., 1991) can be easily implemented in the school setting or home environment. A sensory diet consists of various activities that are regularly scheduled throughout the day to improve the student's ability to function successfully.

In defense of school districts who do not want to be involved with sensory integration and calming activities, I must note a recent 8th Circuit court case that involved the use of a blanket-wrapping technique to calm and relax a nine-year-old student. In this case, the student's parents filed a complaint against the district, its employees, board members, and the physical therapist who recommended the technique. The parents claimed that the technique was being used as a means of physical restraint. The circuit court found that the blanket-wrapping technique was not an unreasonable restraint that violated the student's constitutional rights. (LRP, 1996c). To avoid situations like this, I usually recommend that school district personnel fully explain techniques used in sensory integration to parents. It is a good practice to ask parents to sign a consent form agreeing to this form of intervention. This is a protection to the school district, but also provides the parent information about techniques with which they may be unfamiliar.

How do you know that your child needs this type of therapy? Children who have difficulty processing sensory information, trouble with motor planning, or exhibit sensory defensiveness (i.e., tactile defensiveness) may be candidates for an occupational therapy evaluation. Although historically, sensory integration therapy was developed for students with learning disabilities and emotional disturbance, it is now used to treat a number of disabilities including autism and other pervasive developmental disorders. Currently, I am aware of more students with autism or other pervasive developmental disorders receiving this form of intervention than students with other disabilities such as learning disabilities.

In some situations, parents make the mistake of asking for sensory integration therapy which is not identified as a related service under *IDEA*, (although *IDEA* regulations do specify that the list of related services is not inclusive). Parents may be more successful if they request evaluation for, or provision of, occupational therapy services, because sensory integration is just one intervention approach that occupational therapists may use. Parents have the right to request occupational therapy services, but the IEP committee and the occupational therapist determine whether sensory integration intervention or another method is appropriate. (Partners Resource Network, Inc., 1996). The determination will depend upon whether an "educational need" is identified. Parents and educators must remember, however, that "educational need" may apply to such areas as "social intervention, attention span, and self-help skills" if identified by the student's IEP committee. (Hanft, as cited in Partners Resource Network, Inc., 1996).

According to the case of *Fond du Lac School District*, SEA, Wisconsin 1993 (Lowe, 1994), the district had to pay for an occupational therapy independent educational evaluation because the district evaluation was inappropriate. "It did not even address gross motor functioning and failed to discuss sensory areas, and only minimally addressed activities of daily living." Additionally, the district was required to reimburse the parents for the independent occupational therapist's assistance in the development of an appropriate IEP based on her evaluation. All areas appropriate to teaching were addressed in the evaluation performed by the independent occupational therapist. These areas of an appropriate occupational therapy evaluation included:

- sensory input,

- visual motor activities,

- manipulative materials,

- fine and gross motor activities, and

- activities of daily living.

My interest in sensory integration training intensified a few years ago when a colleague and I went to Arizona to provide auditory integration training to eleven individuals. While there, I observed parents using joint compression to calm their children. I was fascinated with one young boy about nine years of age who tended to get so excited that he dug his fingernails into our skin. We were amazed to see him calm down within a couple of minutes when his mother used deep pressure to rub his arms or did joint compression. We quickly learned to provide deep pressure so that he would calmly sit and listen to the music. All of the students we worked with had also received private occupational and speech therapy in a joint therapy situation from professionals trained in sensory integration theory. We were very impressed with the benefits the children seemed to exhibit as a result of this sensory therapy.

As soon as we returned home, we contacted the occupational therapists we were working with to discuss the possibility of implementing sensory integration programs with our students with autism. Since that time, our regional education service center has provided several workshops related to sensory integration for the professionals and parents in this area. Many of the students are now involved in sensory defensiveness therapy programs, which include brushing and/or joint compression as developed by the Willbargers (Willbarger,P. & Willbarger, J. L., 1991) and other sensory integration activities. The first time I watched the occupational therapist brush a very low-functioning child whom I observed frequently during the past seven or eight years, I was astounded. He sat on my lap and listened to us talk for at least fifteen minutes. I had never seen him so calm. We have observed many other students exhibiting positive responses to sensory integration therapy.

CASE EXAMPLE

Arnold slips on a weighted vest each time he leaves his classroom because it helps him to remain calm and also inhibits his running responses. He also has a weighted quilt and bean bag in a "safe place" in the classroom. When Arnold begins to get overwhelmed by sensory overload, he is able to go to his "safe place," lie down on the bean bag, and cover himself with the weighted quilt until he is calm enough to resume his regular activities. Rubber tubing is also available for him to chew on when he feels the need for oral-motor sensory input. Generally, Arnold self-regulates the use of the rubber tubing. Additionally, an exercise bicycle and a mini-exercise trampoline have been added to the classroom so that biking and jumping on the trampoline can be integrated into his daily schedule as part of his sensory diet.

Another clear indication of some individuals' need for deep pressure was related to me on my first home visit to one family. As we were discussing the type of problems their twelve-year-old child was exhibiting, they talked about several problems that were disturbing to them, such as bumping into walls and jumping on the bed and living room furniture. The most disturbing and bizarre behavior dealt with the child's interactions with the family dog.

CASE EXAMPLE

Henry plays and aggravates the dog until the dog bites into Henry's skin leaving scars on his arms. As we discussed this problem, I asked if Henry had ever jumped on a trampoline because jumping on the trampoline provides individuals with natural joint compression. (Willbarger,P. & Willbarger, J. L., 1991). His parents said they had a trampoline, but the cover wore out and could not be used any more. Henry had jumped on it for hours daily until it wore out. As we verbally explored the situation, they realized that his current inappropriate behaviors did not begin until after the trampoline had worn out. It appeared that the trampoline met a sensory need for this young man, which he was now trying to meet other inappropriate behaviors such as having the dog bite his arm to provide the deep pressure that he needed.

Henry had not been receiving occupational therapy. I requested through the special education director that his IEP team consider his need for an occupational therapy evaluation. His mother and I also discussed the child's need for occupational therapy so that she could make an official request at the IEP meeting. Since that time, the IEP team did meet and Henry does receive occupational therapy once a week.

Physical Therapy

Physical therapy is defined in the *IDEA Amendments* (*Federal Register*, 1999, p. 12424) as "services provided by a qualified physical therapist." This broad definition allows for much flexibility in the delivery of physical therapy. Physical therapy is very closely related to occupational therapy. However, where occupational therapists mainly work with the upper body and fine motor skills, physical therapists typically work with the lower body and gross motor movements. For example, a child with difficulty in walking or an unusual gait would probably see a physical therapist. Many children with cerebral palsy need physical therapy stretching exercises to keep their muscles loose.

Another difference between occupational therapy and physical therapy is that occupational therapists typically provide therapy through activities such as games; while physical therapists go straight to the objective and begin stretching or other direct activities. A friend, also a special education director, had to go through extensive physical therapy after an automobile accident caused severe injuries to one foot and leg. She sarcastically said that she now knew what "PT stood for: pure torture."

Although sometimes uncomfortable, the alternatives for students needing physical therapy are even worse. One student with a low-functioning, epileptic form of autism, who also has mild cerebral palsy, receives both occupational therapy and physical therapy. If he does not receive the physical therapy, the tendons in his legs get so tight that he might need surgery to prevent the development of contractures.

It should be stressed that physical therapy must be delivered consistently. I worked with one student who received physical therapy while attending our school district. We were so excited about the extent of improvement in his ability to walk with a normal gait during the year that he attended our school district. When he moved to another close-by district for the next school year, he received no therapy. Upon reentry in our school, he was right back where we had originally begun with a very abnormal gait. It was very disappointing to see that a much needed service had not been provided for this student in his absence from our school district.

In some rural districts, where a difficulty exists in obtaining related service personnel, the provider of the service for motor disabilities is listed as either an occupational therapist or a physical therapist. This allows the district flexibility to contract with either type of therapist and provide whatever services are identified. Although I recognize the reasons for this type of decision, some students need and receive both therapies. This generally does not happen when either/or service provider is written into the IEP.

Medical versus Educational Services

The landmark case of *Irving Independent School District v. Tatro* (Advocacy, Inc., 1993) established criteria for determining whether a related service was considered to be medical or educational. Although the Tatro case did not involve a child with autism, it is important because it was heard by the Supreme Court and established case law guidelines for determining whether services are medical or educational. In the specific case of Amber Tatro, her parents requested that the school provide catheterization services because Amber was not able to attend school without catheterization during the day. The school refused on the basis that this was a medical service. The case took several years to go through the court system. The guidelines that came out of that case are appropriate to use in the consideration of sensory integration and sensory defensiveness therapy with students with autism.

The Tatro guidelines, which are sometimes referred to as the "bright line" test, are:

- Is the related service necessary to allow the student to benefit from special education?
- Can the related service be performed during school hours?
- Does the related service have to be performed by a physician, or may it be performed by a nurse or trained lay person? (Advocacy, Inc., 1993).

Generally, the service is considered a school health service if it can be performed by a nurse or trained lay person. However, the case of *Bevin H. V. Wright* moved away from this criteria when parents requested that a full-time nurse be provided for the student. The court concluded that full-time nursing care was an excluded medical service due to the additional criteria of time and resources (Graham, S. B., 1996).

- How much time and resources are necessary to perform the service?
- What is the cost to the school district?

In one situation, a parent requested that school personnel perform brushing therapy for her child's sensory defensiveness. The child's occupational therapist outside of the school situation had recommended it. Her parents were doing it at home and seeing positive responses in her ability to remain calm. However, the school administrator determined that "brushing therapy" was a medical service. Consequently, district personnel were told that they could not provide any form of "brushing service." According to the Tatro guidelines, brushing therapy can be a related service because it does not have to be performed by a physician, and it can be performed during school hours. The parents' experience at home indicated that providing brushing therapy at school would enable the child to better benefit from her special education instruction because it enables her to be calmer.

I suggested that the parent get a written assessment with recommendations for school implementation of the brushing program from the occupational therapist who originally recommended the brushing treatment. Then, this parent should request an IEP meeting to officially request that this service be implemented. She had made an informal, verbal request for the service previously; not a request made in the IEP meeting. Therefore, she needs to formally present the request to the IEP committee. She also needs to present the written report verifying the need for this type of program at the official IEP meeting.

At the IEP meeting, the district could respond in one of several ways. It could request time to perform its own occupational therapy evaluation. If the district already had an appropriate evaluation, the IEP team should consider reports from both professionals and make a decision. Should the district decide to provide the service, the parent must ensure that it is part

133

of the written decisions in the report so that the district is accountable for ensuring implementation of the program.

If the district refuses to provide the occupational therapy service, written notice should be provided to the parent at the IEP meeting. The parent should also receive information relating to parental rights to request a due process hearing. At that time, the parent must decide whether to proceed with a due process hearing. If the parent does nothing within a certain time limit, the district may continue with the provision of services specified in the IEP, which would not include the requested program. Another option is mediation between school officials and the parents.

A recently decided Supreme Court decision has far reaching implications for school districts in the area of medical versus educational. The U. S. Supreme Court heard arguments regarding how much nursing care schools must provide to disabled students in the case of *Cedar Rapids Community School District v. Garret F.* In this case, Garret F. needs one-on-one nursing services because of paralyzing injuries received in a motorcycle accident when he was four. In a five to two decision, the Supreme Court held that nursing services were a related service. The Supreme Court justices used the Tatro guidelines to reach their decision. It was determined that "the requested services were 'supportive services' because Garret cannot attend school unless they are provided; and second, the services were not excluded as 'medical services' under *Tatro's* bright line test" because the services could be provided by a nurse or qualified layperson and did not require a physician. This landmark decision was a reversal of the conclusions made in the *Bevin H. V. Wright* decision.

Music Therapy

Music has a built-in structure in time and space and is naturally motivating and reinforcing. "A common observation throughout the literature is that children with autism show unusual interest, and often talent, in music." (Deling & Nastaszczuk, 1996, p. 284). As discussed earlier, Jean-Paul Bovee and Matthew, a student I worked with, could sing songs before they could talk. Music and rhythm are thought to be processed by the right hemisphere in the brain, whereas language is generally processed in the left hemisphere of the brain. Songs that

134

incorporate rhythm and language are thought to engage both hemispheres of the brain, thus providing bilateral brain processing.

Nowak's (1996) study about music and children with autism explored the effects of playing baroque music, a right-brain teaching method, during the learning of spelling words. Although results were not significant because of a small sample size, three of the four children learned more spelling words while listening to baroque music than they did with a traditional approach to spelling. Although further research is needed, Nowak suggests consideration of the use of baroque background music in academic areas with older students with autism. She also suggests playing baroque music when teaching speech and language to younger children.

Music therapy (MT) can be important for students with autism because it enables the student to receive maximum benefit from an individualized program. It is defined as "the use of music as a therapeutic tool for the restoration, maintenance, and improvement of psychological, mental and physiological health and for the habilitation, rehabilitation, and maintenance of behavioral, developmental, physical, and social skills—all within the context of a client-therapist relationship" (Boxill as cited in Deling & Nastaszczuk, 1996). This therapy is generally provided by a Registered Music Therapist—Board Certified (RMT-BC), who is professionally trained to use music and structure music strategies to assist individuals in meeting prescribed therapeutic and educational goals. Music strategies are developed to address specific educational goals and objectives while focusing on the unique strengths and learning styles of the individual with autism.

Music therapists can intervene by providing direct therapy in individual or group therapy settings and by providing consultant services to special education and music teachers. School districts may contract with music therapists to provide in-service training to teachers of students with autism. This may be more appropriate in areas of the country where trained music therapists are not available. For example, the closest music therapist available to serve our region is located in a metropolitan area 130 miles away. It is unlikely that one certified person will be able to provide for the needs of students with autism in a 200 mile radius. Therefore, although it would be desirable for every student to have a music therapist, it might be more feasible for the special education teacher or music teacher on the campus to be trained to provide music therapy.

If your child responds to music and you believe music therapy as a related service might improve his educational benefit in other areas, you must make the request to the IEP team. The decision to provide music therapy or an evaluation for music therapy is made by the IEP team based upon the identified individual needs of the student. If the team members are in agreement, the IEP team requests that an assessment for music therapy be performed by a registered music therapist. This individual then performs an assessment and makes written recommendations to the IEP team. The IEP team then reconvenes, reviews the assessment report for music therapy, and makes a decision based on assessment recommendations and individual needs of the student The music therapist, either in person or through a written report, suggests goals and objectives to the IEP team. The IEP team accepts or revises the goals and objectives and determines frequency, duration, and delivery of music therapy.

As with other related services, it may be provided through direct or consultant services. Direct services are usually provided in small groups scheduled at specific times during the week. Consultant services may be provided to teachers to use music therapy for teaching basic concepts, facilitating transitions, or as an accompaniment for reinforcement of other activities. For instance, a transition song might be "Play time is over. Play time is over. What do we do next? We put up our things and line up for lunch. Let's all line up." The primary goals usually focus on communication, socialization, and active involvement.

Teachers using music therapy in the classroom should use student goals developed in the IEP meeting and choose activities that will target the selected goals. Music sessions should be kept simple while allowing for expression of creativity. It should be remembered that repetition is not necessarily boring; it is essential for learning. Teachers can use activities with singing, movement, rhythm and melodic instruments. Routine activities should be established and teachers should note students' music preferences and aversions.

It is recommended that activities have a clear beginning and end. Visual cues and supports are used in conjunction with the activities. For example, in "Old McDonald's Farm," the teacher may have plastic animals for the students to look at or hold while they are singing. Kids Songs produces a video of "Old McDonald's Farm" and other common favorites. In "I Know an Old Lady," a tag board drawing of the old lady may be used with a clear plastic protector sheet for the old lady's stomach. Each creature (spider, fly, frog, cat, dog, etc.) is dropped into the pouch as the students sing about the old lady swallowing each one. Visual cues may be provided by having the songs on communication boards using picture symbols and words.

Counseling Services

"Counseling services means services provided by qualified social workers, psychologists, guidance counselors, or other qualified personnel." (*Federal Register*, 1999, p. 12424). I do not work with many students with autism who receive counseling services. However, I work with more low-functioning students than high-functioning students. Lower functioning students generally have consultants work with classroom teachers on behavioral management strategies rather than counseling. I believe counseling is more appropriate for students with high-functioning autism or Asperger's Disorder. These students generally have the cognitive and communication/language abilities to interact with counselors in meaningful ways.

Some areas that counselors could work on are feelings of anxiety and panic. Activities could be used to assist these individuals in developing coping skills to facilitate their daily functioning abilities. I also like to use bibliotherapy with students. I feel that all students with autism should receive exposure to books and other information about autism so that they can learn to understand their differences and accept themselves as the individuals that they are. I now have *Joey and Sam, Russell is Extra Special, Andy and His Yellow Frisbee, Captain Tommy, Having a Brother Like David*, and *Talking to Angels*. I have noticed that some other children's books have been published recently. Some of the older higher functioning students could read books written for parents about autism, particularly books written by individuals with autism.

Medical Services

Medical services means services provided by a licensed physician to determine a child's medically related disability that results in the child's need for special education and related services (*Federal Register*, 1992). This type of service usually occurs at the assessment stage of the child-centered process as students are identified with autism or other pervasive developmental disorders. Parents may also request a neuropsychological evaluation when there is obvious regression, or the student with autism has developed new behavioral problems.

Audiological Services

Audiology includes:

- identification of children with hearing loss;

- determination of the range, nature, and degree of hearing loss, including referral for medical or other professional attention for the habilitation of hearing;

- provision of habilitative activities, such as language habilitation, auditory training, speech reading (lip-reading), hearing evaluation, and speech conservation;

- creation and administration of programs for prevention of hearing loss;

- counseling and guidance of pupils, parents, and teachers regarding hearing loss; and

- determination of the child's need for group and individual amplification, selecting and fitting an appropriate aid, and evaluating the effectiveness of amplification. (*Federal Register*, 1999, p. 12424).

Students with autism and a hearing impairment will probably need audiological services. In states where a hearing evaluation is necessary prior to initiation of assessment, students with autism may need to have an audiological assessment to determine whether a hearing loss exists. Because of their lack of response to the environment, they sometimes appear to have a hearing impairment.

I took one of the students and her parent for an audiological evaluation this spring. It was time for her reevaluation. Although we did not suspect that she had a hearing loss, we could not verify the absence of a hearing loss, because she would not cooperate with school screening procedures. Even the audiologist had to modify his standard procedures. I almost laughed when he asked, "Is she generally this oppositional?" He was able to determine that she did not have a hearing loss because of the sophisticated equipment and sound room that he had in his office. I was not surprised at his diagnosis of normal hearing because we really believe that she has hypersensitive hearing, not a hearing loss.

Vision Therapy

Although vision therapy is not a specific related service defined in *IDEA*, it can be a related service. Walsh (1994e) describes a case that clarifies some issues related to vision therapy, although the major issue in the case involved reimbursement for private school expenses. The case is interesting to parents of students with autism because many adults with autism describe distortions in their vision. Although the hearing officer denied the parents request for private school tuition reimbursement, he did order that the school district provide vision therapy as a related service.

In this case, the student did not meet the state's criteria for eligibility as a student with a visual impairment. However, the hearing officer stated that the student's eyes "do not work together as a team." Because there was nothing in the state rules indicating that vision therapy must be limited to students who qualify as "visually impaired," he ruled that the school must provide vision therapy as a related service. Like all other related services, the eligibility determination must be based on the individual needs of the student.

Psychological Services

As defined in *IDEA* (*Federal Register*, 1999), psychological services include:

- Administering psychological and educational tests, and other assessment procedures;
- interpreting assessment results;
- obtaining, integrating, and interpreting information about child behavior and conditions relating to learning;
- consulting with other staff members in planning school programs to meet the special needs of children as indicated by psychological tests; interviews, and behavioral evaluations;

- planning and managing a program of psychological services, including psychological counseling for children and parents; and

- assisting in developing positive behavioral intervention strategies.

Most students with autism will receive psychological services during the assessment stages of the IEP process. Students with autism will generally receive consulting services in planning school programs to meet their special needs. These services might also include a functional analysis of behavior and assistance in developing positive behavioral intervention strategies, which is required by the *IDEA Amendments* when behavior impedes the student's learning or the learning of others.

In a Richardson Independent School District hearing (LRP, 1994c), the hearing officer awarded reimbursement to the parents for psychotherapy services for their fifteen-year-old son who had a pervasive developmental disorder classified as autism. "The student's IEP was found to be inappropriate because it lacked goals and objectives which addressed the student's anxiety, parent training, or in-home training" (LRP, 1994c). Classroom accommodations specified in the IEP were not being provided. The school district was ordered to provide individual psychotherapy.

Recreation Therapy

Recreation therapy is defined in *IDEA* (*Federal Register*, 1992, 1999) as a related service which includes:

- assessment of leisure functioning,

- therapeutic recreation services,

- leisure education, and

- recreation programs in schools and community agencies.

For children with autism, play is work and they need direct instruction to learn how to play. For recreational therapy to be included in the IEP, a professional must assess the student's abilities in this area. This is typically done by observing and assessing the student's functioning in order to answer the following questions:

- How does the student play?

- Does the student interact with others?

- Does the individual use appropriate social skills?

- Is the student motivated to play?

- What kind of coping skills does the student exhibit?

- What kinds of family and community support and resources are available?

Ashton-Schaeffer (1996, p. 6) defines therapeutic recreation as "the use of recreation activities to improve the social, cognitive, and physical functioning of students." Leisure education is defined as "a process through which students can learn and practice recreation and life skills." In therapeutic recreation, individuals with autism may learn turn-taking, sequencing, or eye-hand coordination by playing card games. Leisure education may include: (a) initiating an activity, (b) assertiveness, (c) cooperation, (d) decision-making, (e) planning, (f) problem-solving, (g) accessing transportation, (h) using school and community recreation time, and (i) becoming more independent use of free time. The goal is to generalize skills learned in physical education and other classes so that the individual applies skills in community leisure times outside of school. Students should learn to use their own resources to independently participate in recreation/leisure activities of their choice throughout their life span. This type of education should begin in the early years and continue throughout the school career.

This service can be provided by a Certified Therapeutic Recreation Specialist (CTRS) or by classroom teachers with training in this area. Specific requirements may vary from state to state. The CTRS may provide a direct service or consult with classroom teachers or other related service personnel. In areas where individuals certified as a CTRS are not available, adaptive physical education (APE) specialists may provide the service. Certified Therapeutic Recreation Specialists may provide training to classroom staff in the design of instruction for leisure skills, conduct evaluations of specific students, or provide direct services in extracurricular activities.

As with other related services, goals and objectives should be included in the IEP for this service. A sample goal might be: *Jill will choose from a selection of four leisure activities for free time in the classroom with same-age peers and follow through with that choice.* An appropriate

141

goal for an older student might be: *Bob will choose one extra-curricular activity (such as student government, sports, sports management, or art) and participate in that activity.* (Ashton-Schaeffer, 1996).

Successful recreation and leisure experiences are important to students with autism, because they enhance chances for academic success and life satisfaction. My experience has been that these goals and objectives are included in the IEPs of students with autism. However, they have most frequently been included as part of the special education instructional IEP which covers the major life domains of functional academics, vocational, domestic, community, and recreation/leisure, instead of a related service. Instruction has been mainly provided by a special education teacher or a physical education teacher because Certified Recreation Therapists are not available in our area.

Adapted Physical Education

Although adapted physical education was previously a related service, the *IDEA Amendments* include any form of special education including adapted physical education as **special education instruction.** However, many of the same comments apply to adapted physical education, even when it is instruction instead of a related service. Like recreation therapy, adapted physical education services should begin with an assessment of the need for the service and development of appropriate goals and objectives. The service is generally provided by a special education teacher with training in physical education or a physical education teacher with training in special education. The focus of adapted physical education is to provide physical education services to students with disabilities. Many students with autism are able to attend regular physical education classes with special modifications and adaptations.

CASE EXAMPLE

Larry, a student with whom I worked with extensively, attends regular physical education classes with age-appropriate peers. However, he wears earphones to muffle sounds because the gym is such a noisy place. If the class goes outside, he usually takes the earphones off and leaves them with the teacher, because the noise on the playground is tolerable. He also wears a weighted vest which is calming to him. If he is on the

CASE EXAMPLE continued

playground where he can swing or run, he may take the vest off, as swinging is a particularly calming activity for him. His other modification relates to his need for close supervision. Either the classroom teacher or the paraprofessional in the classroom provide one-to-one supervision during physical education. He attends a regular physical education class which is too large for the physical education instructor to individualize instruction and provide close supervision.

Children who have autism and hearing or visual impairments may need other modifications. For instance, a child with a visual impairment may need to use a ball with sound or a child with a hearing impairment may need an interpreter to relate instructions. Another modification that might be helpful is to have a peer tutor work with the student during physical education. The major goal is to facilitate the provision of physical education.

Rehabilitation Counseling Services

Rehabilitation services are defined in *IDEA* (*Federal Register*, 1999) as "services provided by qualified personnel in individual or group sessions that focus specifically on career development, employment preparation, achieving independence, and integration in the workplace and community of a student with a disability." The term also includes vocational rehabilitation services provided to students with disabilities by vocational rehabilitation programs funded under the *Rehabilitation Act of 1973*, as amended.

These services are more appropriate for secondary students with autism. They are generally provided in conjunction with transition services, which are a mandated part of the IEP when the IEP team addresses transition with other agency providers for the student who is sixteen, and annually thereafter.

School Health Services

School health services are services provided by a qualified school nurse or other qualified person. Most of the students with autism with whom I work receive school health services for medication usage. Many schools have policies that the school nurse must administer any medications used. These policies may also require a copy of the prescription and medication in

143

the original prescription bottle. Since local policies differ, parents of students must find out what their own local education agency policies state related to the administration of medication.

Social Work Services

Social work services in schools includes (*IDEA, Federal Register*, 1999, p. 12424):

- preparing a social or developmental history on a child with a disability,
- group and individual counseling with the child and family,
- working in partnership with parents and others on those problems in a child's living situation (home, school, and community) that affect the child's adjustment in school,
- mobilizing school and community resources to enable the child to learn as effectively as possible in his or her educational program, and
- assisting in developing positive behavioral intervention strategies.

Any student with autism may be eligible for these services if the IEP Committee determines that he or his family needs this type of service. As stated previously, the IEP team must address positive behavioral intervention strategies any time that the student's behavior impedes learning.

Art Therapy

Art therapy, not specifically defined in *IDEA*, can use art as a medium for developing other skills. Many individuals with autism seem to be very artistic, and this is one skill that can be developed and used as a career skill or for recreation/leisure.

Orientation and Mobility

Orientation and mobility services, included for the first time in the *IDEA Amendments*, mean services provided to blind or visually impaired students by qualified personnel to enable those students to attain systematic orientation to and safe movement within their environments in school, home, and community. It includes teaching students the following, as appropriate:

- spatial and environmental concepts and use of information received by the senses (such as sound, temperature and vibrations) to establish, maintain, or regain orientation and line of travel (e.g., using sound at a traffic light to cross the street);

- to use the long cane to supplement visual travel skills or as a tool for safely negotiating the environment for students with no available travel vision;

- to understand and use remaining vision and distance low vision aids; and

- other concepts, techniques, and tools.

Students with autism for whom orientation and mobility services would be important are those who have a dual diagnosis of autism and a visual impairment.

Transportation Services

Transportation includes (*IDEA*, *Federal Register*, 1999, p. 12424):

- travel to and from school and between schools,

- travel in and around school buildings, and

- specialized equipment (such as special and adapted buses, lifts, and ramps), if required to provide special transportation for a child with a disability.

Transportation should be provided as a related service if necessary to enable the child to benefit from special education. Unlike other related services, the IEP Committee does not have to develop goals and objectives for transportation if transportation is being provided solely to enable the student to travel to and from school. However, justification for the provision of transportation must be provided; i.e., why does this child need special transportation to benefit from special education? The reasons should relate to an assessed need for special transportation. If there are reasons other than home-school transportation, such as enabling the student to increase independence or improve behavior or socialization, then goals and objectives must be provided. (Matthews, 1996 [Letter to Smith, 23 IDELR 344 {OSEP, 1995}]).

The most frequent issue that I encounter related to special transportation is the length of time that students must stay on the bus. One parent I worked with went to mediation with a school district over this issue. The family lives about fifteen minutes from the school. However, when her son rode the special education bus, the trip took almost two hours each way because he was the first student picked up and the last student taken home. To prevent him from spending so much time on the bus, she elected to transport him herself. The school district paid her mileage for the two, daily round trips However, the school administrator wanted to limit the mileage reimbursement for the school year to one round trip per day even though she would still be making two trips each day. As a result of mediation, the school is still paying for two round trips daily.

Another bus issue involves the length of the school day. When a student spends two hours in the morning and two hours in the afternoon on the school bus, he or she does not receive a full day of instruction. OCR found that a student was denied a free appropriate public education because he missed two and one-half hours of instruction daily. OCR ruled this was a violation of FAPE because the school district failed to consider the impact of long bus rides on the education of students with disabilities (LRP, 1995d, p. XIV-28). OCR also ruled that schools cannot shorten students' school day because of transportation needs. It has been a common practice for the special education bus to run later in the mornings and earlier in the afternoons to facilitate transportation schedules. School days can be shortened if the student has such an educational need. However, the school day can not be shortened to facilitate transportation schedules.

As a special education administrator, I sometimes had difficulties with bus drivers because they wanted to leave students at the corner rather than at their home. I had to continually monitor this to ensure that students were left at their home. Courts have now interpreted that "door-to-door" actually means "curb-to-curb." In a New York case and a Minnesota case, parents asked school districts to provide staff to carry the student into the home and up a flight of stairs. In both cases, the hearing officer ruled that special transportation was required, but the school districts' responsibilities stop at the curb. It is the responsibility of the parent to get them from the curb and into the home. (Walsh, 1994d).

Other transportation issues include provision of air conditioners and wheelchair lifts for buses. If students who use wheelchairs need to use special transportation, the bus should be equipped with a lift. Transportation must be accessible. Two Texas Hearing Officers also ordered districts to provide an air conditioned bus to and from school and job sites. The warm bus caused seizures in one student. This same student also had asthma and allergies which supported the need for an air conditioned bus. The other student had difficulty controlling body temperature and was entitled to transportation in a climate controlled vehicle. (Matthews, 1996).

Regulations defining special transportation include travel in and around school buildings and specialized equipment that might be needed. In this context, a wheelchair might meet the definition of special transportation if it is required to assist the student with a disability to benefit from special education. In fact, one student needed a wheelchair for transportation around the school, because it takes him so long to get from one place to another because of his resistance to walking to different places around the school. In this situation, the district is not required to provide a wheelchair for personal use outside of school. (Matthews, 1996).

Discipline is another major issue related to school transportation. If the student's IEP calls for special transportation as a related service, the district cannot suspend bus transportation as a disciplinary consequence. The method of transportation can be changed, but the provision of the service cannot. Modifications to transportation might include:

•   limiting the number of other students on the disruptive student's bus,

•   adding a paraprofessional or bus monitor,

•   restraining the student with a harness or seatbelt,

•   providing special training for the bus driver and monitors,

•   air conditioning the bus, and

•   equipping the bus with a two-way radio or cellular telephone.

For special education students who use regular school bus transportation, suspension is an option. However, bus suspension cannot last longer than ten consecutive days, or it constitutes a change of placement. Any day that a student is suspended from special education transportation counts as a full day when counting suspension days for discipline purposes. An IEP team must meet to determine whether the behavior is related to the student's disability. If the student's misconduct is not related to the disability, the student can be suspended from the bus like any other student without a disability (Matthews, 1996).

Insurance Reimbursements

The *IDEA Amendments* address the issue of **children with disabilities who are covered by public insurance** (*Federal Register*, p. 12430). According to the final regulations, a public agency may use Medicaid or other public insurance benefits programs in which a child participates to provide or pay for services required under *IDEA* with regard to services required to provide FAPE to an eligible child under *IDEA*. However, the public agency:

- may not require parents to sign up for or enroll in public insurance programs in order for their child to receive a free appropriate public education (FAPE) under *IDEA*;

- may not require parents to incur an out-of-pocket expense such as the payment of a deductible or co-pay amount incurred in filing a claim for services provided by *IDEA*, but may pay the cost that the parent otherwise would be required to pay; and

- may not use a child's benefits under a public insurance program if that use would:

  * decrease available lifetime coverage or any other insured benefit;

  * result in the family paying for services that would otherwise be covered by the public insurance program and that are required for the child outside of the time the child is in school;

  * increase premiums or lead to the discontinuation of insurance; or

  * risk loss of eligibility for home and community-based waivers, based on aggregate health-related expenditures.

Children with Disabilities Who are Covered by Private Insurance

With regard to services required to provide a free appropriate public education to an eligible child under this part, a public agency may access a parent's private insurance proceeds only if the parent provides informed consent consistent with the final regulations of *IDEA*. Each time the public agency proposes to access the parents' private insurance proceeds, it must:

- obtain parental consent in accordance with *IDEA* final regulations, and

- inform the parents that their refusal to permit the public agency to access their private insurance does not relieve the public agency of its responsibility to ensure that all required services are provided at no cost to the parents.

148

To summarize, one or more related services must be provided when the student needs them to receive educational benefit from special education services. Related services do not have to be provided to a student who does not receive special education services. They do not have to be provided to enhance the quality of the student's program. They must only be provided when they are necessary for the student to receive educational benefit from special education. Therefore, goals and objectives and determination of need must relate to educational benefit.

Chapter Eight

New Behavioral Perspectives

Behavior management and discipline was an area of great change in the *IDEA Amendments*. Congress had great concerns about what has happened in our nation during the last couple of years related to school violence and safety. Consequently, there was much discussion and concern related to this area of the IEP as *the IDEA Amendments* were drafted into law. The behavioral area continued to be an area of conflicting opinions as the final regulations for the law were developed. Some of the final regulations still leave issues unclear in this area. Therefore, many of the hearings based on the *IDEA Amendments* will probably relate to behavior intervention and discipline. There are still threats that Congress will make amendments to the current *IDEA Amendments* that might threaten the guarantees of FAPE that have been in place since 1975. The comments and interpretations in this chapter reflect the current status of the regulations as of this writing.

Under consideration of special factors, the IEP team must consider behavior that impedes learning. In the case of a child whose behavior impedes learning, the IEP must consider appropriate strategies, including positive behavioral interventions, strategies, and supports to address that behavior. The *IDEA Amendments* incorporated prior court decisions and the Office of Education Department policy that held that:

- Schools could remove a child for up to 10 days at a time for any violation of school rules as long as there was not a pattern of removals.

- A child with a disability could not be suspended long-term or expelled from school for behavior that was a manifestation of his or her disability.

- Services must continue for children with disabilities who are suspended or expelled from school.

The *IDEA Amendments* expanded the authority of school personnel to remove a child who brings a gun or any dangerous weapon to school, and to the knowing possession of illegal drugs. This includes the sale or solicitation of the sale of controlled substances. It also allows schools to request a hearing officer to remove a child for up to 45 days if keeping the child in his or her current placement is likely to result in injury to the child or to others. Along with this expansion of the school's authority in the area of discipline, the *IDEA Amendments* also added new responsibilities. Schools must now assess a child's troubling behavior and develop positive interventions to address that behavior. The IEP team must also describe how to determine whether the behavior was a manifestation of the child's disability.

Removals of Up to Ten School Days at a Time

The regulations clarify that school personnel may remove a child with a disability for up to 10 school days, and for additional removals of up to 10 school days for separate acts of misconduct, as long as the removals do not constitutes a pattern. What is not clear is who determines when a series of removals constitute a pattern? Criteria for this determination are not clear. This will probably become the basis of a hearing in the near future as schools and parents may very easily disagree on what constitutes a pattern of removals.

Specifically, Section 300.520 states that school personnel may order the removal of a child with a disability from the child's current placement for not more than 10 consecutive school days for any violation of school rules to the extent that the removal would be applied to children without disabilities.

CASE EXAMPLE

Consider James and Harry. James is a student without a disability. Harry has been identified as having autism. James and Harry get in a fight. The school's policy states that any student getting in a fight can be suspended for 10 days. The principal suspends both James and Harry for fighting. This is possible because the punishment is the same punishment that a student without a disability receives for the violation of school rules. If this is the first time during the year that Harry has been suspended, the school does not have to provide any type of special education services because suspensions of 10 days or less do not constitute a change in placement.

After a child with a disability has been removed for more than 10 school days in the same school year, the public agency must provide services to the student for subsequent removals during the year. Therefore, in the above example, if Harry had already been removed from school for 10 days during the school year, the school would have had to provide some type of special education services during his suspension for fighting.

What if a student with a disability brings a weapon or drugs to school?

If a child carries a weapon to school or to a school function under the jurisdiction of the State or a local educational agency, the student may be removed to an appropriate interim alternative educational setting for the same amount of time that a student without a disability would be subject to discipline, but for not more than 45 days.

What about the 10-day rule?

Either before or not later than 10 business days after first removing the student for more than 10 school days in a school year or commencing a removal that constitutes a change of placement as defined in the *IDEA Amendments*, the following actions should take place.

1. If the local education agency did not conduct a functional behavioral assessment and implement a behavioral intervention plan for the child before the behavior resulted in the student's removal, the agency shall convene an IEP meeting to develop an assessment plan.

2. If the child already has a behavioral intervention plan, the IEP team shall meet to review the plan and its implementation. If necessary, the IEP team should modify the plan to address the behavior.

3. As soon as possible after developing the assessment plan and completing the assessments required by the plan, the local education agency shall convene an IEP meeting to develop appropriate behavioral interventions to address the behavior. The behavioral interventions shall then be implemented. If no additional evaluation data is needed, the review of assessment data and the development of the behavior intervention plan may take place in the same meeting. In other situations, it may be necessary for the IEP team to meet twice.

What happens when a child with a disability who has a behavioral plan and who has been removed from the child's current educational placement for more than 10 school days in a school year is subjected to a removal that does not constitute a change of placement?

In this situation, the IEP team members must review the behavioral intervention plan to determine if modifications are needed. If one or more of the IEP team members believes that modifications are necessary, the IEP team shall meet to modify the plan and its implementation, to the extent that the IEP team deems necessary.

In what circumstances would a hearing officer order the removal of a student with a disability to an interim alternative educational placement (IAES)?

A hearing officer may order a change in the placement of a child with a disability to an appropriate interim alternative educational setting for not more than 45 days if the hearing officer, in an expedited due process hearing, determines that the public agency has demonstrated by substantial evidence that maintaining the student's current placement is likely to result in injury to the child or to others. In this situation, the hearing officer must:

- Consider the appropriateness of the child's current placement.
- Consider whether the public agency made reasonable efforts to minimize the risk of harm in the child's current placement, including the use of supplementary aids and services.
- Determine that the interim alternative educational setting that is proposed by school personnel who have consulted with the child's special education teacher meets the requirements of the *IDEA Amendments*.

How do school personnel determine that an interim alternative educational setting is an appropriate placement?

First, the interim alternative educational setting must be determined by the student's IEP team. Additionally, any interim alternative educational setting in which a student with a disability is placed must be selected so as to enable the child to continue to progress in the general curriculum, and the student must continue to receive those services and modifications, including those described in the student's current IEP, that will enable the student to meet the goals set forth in the IEP. The interim alternative educational setting must also include services and modifications necessary to address the behavior for which the child was placed in the setting and that are designed to prevent the behavior from re-occurring.

Manifestation Determination Review

When actions are contemplated related to carrying a weapon to school or possessing or using illegal drugs, the local education agency must adhere to the following procedures.

1.   The parents must be notified of the agency's decision and provided the procedural safeguards notice not later than the date on which the decision to take that action is made.

2.   Immediately, if possible, but not later than 10 school days after the date on which the decision to take the action was made, a review must be conducted to determine the relationship between the child's disability and the behavior subject to the disciplinary action.

These procedures also apply when the school proposes to remove a child with a disability who has engaged in other behavior that violates any agency rule or code of conduct that applies to all children if the removal constitutes a change of placement.

Conduct of the Manifestation Review

The manifestation review must be conducted by the IEP team and other qualified personnel in a meeting. The IEP team and other qualified personnel may determine that the behavior was not a manifestation of the child's disability only if the IEP team and other qualified personnel consider all relevant information including

1.   evaluation and diagnostic results, including the results of other relevant information supplied by the parents of the child;

2.   observations of the child; and

3.   the child's IEP and placement.

The IEP team must then determine that in relationship to the behavior subject to disciplinary action, the child's IEP and placement were appropriate, and the special education services, supplementary aids and services, and behavior intervention strategies were provided consistent with the child's IEP and placement. The IEP team must also verify that the child's disability did not impair the ability of the child to understand the impact and consequences of the behavior and that the child was able to control the behavior subject to disciplinary action. **If the IEP team and other qualified personnel determine that any of the above standards were not met, the behavior must be considered a manifestation of the child's disability.** If the public agency identifies deficiencies in the student's IEP or placement, or in their implementation, it must take immediate action to remedy those deficiencies.

What if the IEP team and other qualified personnel determine that the child's behavior was not a manifestation of the disability?

If it is determined that the behavior is not a manifestation of the student's disability, the relevant disciplinary procedures applicable to students without disabilities may be applied to the child in the same manner in which they would be applied to a student without a disability. If the public agency initiates disciplinary procedures applicable to all children, the agency shall ensure that the special education and disciplinary records of the child with a disability are transmitted for consideration by the person or persons making the final determination regarding the disciplinary action.

What if the parent disagrees with the manifestation determination?

If the child's parent disagrees that the child's behavior was not a manifestation of the child's disability or with any decision regarding placement, the parent may request a hearing. If the parent challenges the interim alternative educational setting or the manifestation determination, the child must remain in the interim alternative educational setting pending the decision of the hearing officer or until the expiration of the time period provided for by the disciplinary action, whichever occurs first. If the parent and the state or local educational agency agree, the student may be placed in a different setting until the hearing is concluded. If a child is placed in an interim alternative educational setting, and school personnel propose to change the child's placement after the expiration of the interim alternative placement, the child must remain in the current placement (the placement prior to the interim alternative educational setting) pending the results of the hearing. Schools may request an expedited hearing if school personnel maintain that it is dangerous for the child to be in the current placement.

Can school authorities refer students with disabilities to local law enforcement agencies?

Yes, school officials may report a crime committed by a child with a disability to appropriate authorities. If a crime is reported to authorities, school officials reporting the crime must ensure that copies of the special education and disciplinary records of the child are transmitted for consideration by the appropriate authorities to whom it reports the crime. However, Section 300.529 (b)(2) (*Federal Register*, 1999, p. 12455) states that special education and disciplinary records may be transmitted only to the extent that it is permitted by the *Family Educational Rights and Privacy Act*. In practice, this means that schools will have to get parental permission to provide student records to law enforcement agencies.

If a child's IEP includes behavioral strategies to address a particular behavior, can a child be suspended for engaging in that behavior?

If the child's behavior impedes his or her learning or that of others, the IEP team must consider, if appropriate, development of strategies including positive behavioral interventions and supports to address that behavior. In certain circumstances, the IEP team, which includes the child's parents, might determine that the child's behavioral intervention plan includes specific regular or alternative disciplinary measures to address the child's behavior. Short suspensions, that would result from particular violations of school rules, along with positive behavior intervention strategies and supports can be part of a comprehensive behavioral intervention plan. Care must be given, however, to ensure that short suspensions are not implemented in a manner that denies FAPE to the child. Whether disciplinary measures are appropriate for a specific behavior must be addressed in the child's IEP and determined on a case-by-case basis in light of the circumstances of the incident.

If a child's behavior in the regular classroom, even with appropriate interventions, significantly impairs the learning of others, can the IEP team making the placement decision determine that regular classroom placement is inappropriate for that child?

The IEP team making a placement determination for a child whose behavior is interfering with the education of others must carefully consider whether the child can appropriately function in the regular classroom if provided with appropriate behavioral supports, strategies, and interventions. If the child can function in the regular classroom with appropriate behavioral supports, it would be inappropriate to place the student in a more restrictive environment. However, if the child's behavior in the regular classroom, even with the provision of appropriate behavioral supports, strategies, or interventions would significantly impact the learning of others, that placement would not meet the child's needs and, consequently, would not be appropriate for the child.

Functional Assessment of Behaviors

As stated in previous discussions, the IEP team must include the results of functional assessment of behaviors when the IEP team addresses the need for behavioral interventions. Functional assessment of behavior, sometimes called functional analysis of behavior, is essentially a process of gathering information about behaviors. Information is gathered to analyze the purpose or function that a behavior serves and the environmental variables that maintain the behavior. Behaviors may appear to occur for one reason when the behavior actually serves a very different purpose. By collecting information about the behavior, the IEP team should be able to develop effective interventions. By using functional assessments of behavior, we are assuming that behaviors exhibited by students are purposeful, and the behaviors serve a function for the student. Some common functions of behavior include:

- gaining attention;

- gaining acceptance or approval;

- gaining access to materials, activities, food, and/or other tangible rewards;

- escaping or avoiding an unpleasant situation;

- meeting sensory needs by providing sensory stimulation;

- exhibiting power or control of self or others;

- seeking justice or revenge; and

- expression of wants, needs, and feelings.

In order to effectively perform a functional assessment of behavior, the behaviors to be evaluated or assessed must be precisely defined. What is the behavior of concern? People must then conduct interviews of individuals who live and work with the child with a disability. Next, direct observation of a behavior in the natural setting is essential to developing reliable, functional assessment data. A problem with functional assessment is that it may be hard to isolate specific variables related to the behavior. After the behavior(s) is defined, some questions to address when conducting functional assessments of behavior include:

- How long does the behavior last (duration)?
- How often does the behavior occur (frequency)?
- How intense is the behavior (intensity)?
- When does the behavior occur?
  * At a particular time of the day?
  * Before or after a specific activity or task?
- Where does the behavior typically occur?
- How does the behavior occur?
- With whom does the behavior occur?
  * With only one person?
  * With certain people (consider categories of persons, hair color, voice quality, interaction style, smells, clothing, etc.)?
- What happened just before the behavior occurred?
- What happened immediately after the behavior occurred?
- Do any of the following environmental factors affect the student's behavior including:
  * excessive noise levels,
  * new or unusual smells in the room,
  * use of certain types of materials (color, shape, smell, texture, etc.),
  * touching the person unexpectedly,
  * presence of extra adults in the room,
  * presence of extra classmates/peers in the room,

*   transitioning from one activity to another, and

*   certain weather conditions (extreme temperatures, precipitation, cloudiness, windiness, thunder, lightning, etc.)?

- Does the behavior appear to serve a purpose for the child? If so, what purpose?

- Can the behavior be addressed by teaching a more appropriate response?

The IEP team receives answers to the above questions through interview and direct observation. The IEP team should look at the development of positive intervention strategies to address the identified behaviors. The IEP team should consider contextual modifications, curricular accommodations, and replacement strategies. Contextual modifications refer to changes that can be made in the environment and teacher behaviors. Curricular accommodations refer to changes in instructional materials and techniques. Replacement strategies refer to new behaviors that will be taught to the student. This is particularly important when addressing behaviors that are meeting sensory needs for the child.

Individuals with autism exhibit many problems in the area of sensory processing, which are frequently addressed with behavioral goals. Many "self-stimming" behaviors, such as hand flicking and rocking back and forth, are based in sensory needs and may actually help calm the individual. IEP goals and objectives directed toward extinguishing "self-stimulation" are not recommended. Current information about sensory integration challenges traditional perspectives about self-stimulation. Acceptance or substitution of more appropriate behaviors is encouraged–not extinguishing behaviors that meet sensory needs. If the intervention focuses on extinguishing a behavior without teaching a more appropriate strategy for meeting the sensory need, most persons will develop another behavior that may be even more inappropriate than the original behavior.

Table 8.1 describes our sensory channels; how "normal" people meet their sensory needs; and inappropriate responses to sensory needs. Consider that an individual is socially acceptable chewing on the end of a pencil or pen, but abnormal if he or she picks up a stick or other unusual object to chew on. Adults may suck on hard candy, but try to extinguish the behavior of an individual who sucks on his or her fingers. Normal people gaze at their fingernails or window

160

Table 8.1   I'm Okay, You Have a Mannerism

Sensory Channels	Miss Manners Guide to Appropriate Self-Stimulation	Creative Variations Which May Plug You Into a Written Behavior Plan
Tactile: information received by touch (throughout body surface) includes sensitivity to light touch, pressure, pain, and temperature.	Twirling hair, drumming fingers, playing with condensation on a drinking glass, fingering fabrics, rubbing eyes, pulling on beard.	Pulling hair, lying in front of the air vent, slapping face/ear, playing with spit, rubbing head.
Proprioceptive: information about the relative positions of parts of the body. This information comes through sensations arising in the muscles, joints, ligaments, and receptors associated with the bones.	Snuggling in quilts, cracking knuckles, jiggling/crossing legs sitting on your leg.	Burrowing into furniture, wrapping arms inside tee-shirts, wrist flapping.
Visual: information received through the eyes/seeing.	Gazing at your fingernails, hands and rings, watching television without the sound, window shopping, flipping through magazines, eye pressing.	Flicking hand in front of eyes, flipping pages of books, light gazing, playing with transparent or shiny objects, eye-poking.
Auditory: information received through the ear/hearing.	Humming, whistling, tapping a pencil on a surface, playing background music.	Vocalizing or making sounds, banging on objects. tapping objects together next to ear.
Olfactory: information received through the nose/smelling.	Wearing perfume, sniffing magic markers, scratch and sniff stickers, burning incense.	Rubbing feces on the body and smelling, smelling other peoples hands or shoes.
Gustatory: information received through the tongue/lips, tasting. Closely tied to the sense of smell.	Chewing flavored toothpicks, sucking on mints/hard candy, smoking, chewing on hair, sucking on pens/jewelry.	Mouthing objects, chewing on hair, sucking on fingers, licking objects.
Vestibular: information received through receptors in the inner ear which enables us to detect motion, especially acceleration and deceleration. Closely tied to the visual system which provides information to the vestibule located in the inner ear.	Rocking in chairs or rocking body, amusement park rides, dancing, twisting on bar stools, skating, sliding.	Rocking body, spinning, twirling in swings, head rocking.

Our brain seeks out stimulation through the channels of our senses. Each of us seek out this stimulation in a variety of ways. Society accepts some of these behaviors without question, yet feels very differently about others. This acceptance seems to be arbitrary in some cases. This chart shows examples of how individuals typically fulfill this craving for stimulation and how some self-stimulation behaviors of children with deaf/blindness (and autism) parallel these behaviors.

Reproduced with permission from Kate Moss & Robbie Blaha, Texas School for the Blind & Visually Impaired Outreach Department.

Moss, K. & Blaha, R. (1993). Looking at self-stimulation in the pursuit of leisure or I'm okay, you have a mannerism. *P. S. News!!!* 5 (3), 10 - 14.

shop. A behavior intervention plan is developed for a child who flicks his hands in front of his eyes or enjoys flipping pages in a book for the visual stimulation it offers. We must recognize that all people meet sensory needs in very different ways. Some just use more socially acceptable methods.

In the past, many IEPs included discipline plans but did not include positive intervention strategies and supports. The discipline plan generally did not address instruction for appropriate behaviors. It just spelled out specific steps to use when the student violated school rules or got out of control. Consequences were provided that typically focused on punishment. With the *IDEA Amendments*, we must not only look at punishment, but also consider positive intervention strategies. As we include positive intervention strategies, we must also include goals and objectives for development of new behaviors in the area of social skills and interaction.

Social skills and interaction problems need to be addressed positively. Many inappropriate behaviors are exhibited because individuals do not know appropriate responses.

CASE EXAMPLE

When Tony walked down the hall, he spit at other students when they passed by. Instead of trying to extinguish this behavior, he was taught to appropriately greet other students by saying "Hello" or "Good morning" to get their attention. With many opportunities to practice this skill daily, he soon began to greet other students appropriately. Had a behavioral approach been implemented to extinguish the spitting, he still would not have learned how to greet other students appropriately.

Social skills assessments and curriculums may also be used to identify appropriate objectives. Typical social skills goal areas might include:

- following instructions,
- accepting criticism or a consequence,
- accepting no as an answer,
- getting the teacher's attention,
- making a request,

- waiting in line,

- dealing with anger in appropriate ways, and

- requesting wants and needs.

Goals areas for social interaction skills include:

- sharing materials and toys;

- parallel play, such as two young boys building towers side-by-side;

- play that requires turn-taking, such as throwing a ball back and forth;

- playing board games with another student; and

- accepting that you can't always win.

Social interaction goals that involve communication skills include:

- turn-taking and topic maintenance in social conversations,

- looking and listening to people when they are talking,

- greeting people,

- saying "thank you,"

- giving and accepting compliments,

- saying excuse me, and

- apologizing.

Social skills can be learned. Goals for appropriate social behaviors must generally be taught through direct instruction, which may include modeling of appropriate behaviors, role play, and demonstration. Carol Gray's (1994) *Social Stories*, another intervention strategy for helping students with autism learn appropriate responses for problem situations, describes social situations in terms of relevant social cues. Some also define appropriate responses or address aggression, fears, obsessions, and compulsions. These stories can be used with nonreaders by accompanying the story with an audiocassette tape. Figures 8.1 and 8.2 are social stories developed for a young girl who would not get off the bus each day when she got home. Figure 8.3 is a small book designed to add Polaroid pictures to go with each page addressing the same problem.

Figure 8. 1. Going Home on the Bus

Some children ride home on the bus.

The bus picks them up at their school in the afternoon and takes them home.

Some children like riding the bus. They think it is fun.

Some children like to go home. They want to put on play clothes and play.

On school days, the bus will come to my school at the end of the day. I will walk quietly from my classroom to the bus.

Figure 8.2   Getting On and Off the Bus

After I walk from my classroom to the bus,
I quietly get on the bus.

I tell the bus driver and bus aide hello.

I walk to my seat.

I sit down quietly and watch where the bus is going.

When the bus gets to my house, I get up and
walk to the front of the bus by the bus driver.

Then, I walk down the steps.

After I get down, the bus aide gives me something
special for riding the bus so nicely.

Then, I go into my house and play.
Everyone is happy because I am home.

Figure 8. 3   A Book About "The Bus Trip Home"

The Bus Trip Home	This is _____ in her classroom.	This is ____ getting on the bus.
This is _____ sitting quietly in her seat on the bus.	This is the bus at her house.	This is ____ getting up and walking to the front of the bus.
This is _____ getting off the bus.	See her come down the steps.	This is ____ getting a reward for getting off the bus. Sometimes she gets chips. Sometimes she gets other things she likes.
This is ____ walking into her house. See her wave bye.		

What is a Behavioral Intervention Plan?

Behavioral IEPs include goals and objectives for improving students' behaviors. In some states, goals are also included for decreasing inappropriate behaviors. The *IDEA Amendments* require that behavioral intervention plans be developed any time that behavior impedes learning. Although consequences for student behavior and criteria for evaluation should be included, the final regulations are very clear that the behavioral intervention plan also includes positive interventions, strategies, and supports. Consequences should be developed for inappropriate and appropriate behaviors. When a student exhibits extremely difficult or challenging behaviors, the IEP team should establish goals and objectives and identify appropriate positive interventions relevant to the specific behavioral problems.

See an example of a behavioral intervention plan (Figure 8.4). All of the components necessary for adequate behavioral management are addressed. Appropriate goals and objectives are illustrated for increasing desired behaviors and decreasing inappropriate behaviors. This plan also includes a description of consequences of behavior. The behavioral descriptions provide information as to present levels of functioning in the IEP, as well as criteria for determining mastery. Specific interventions and a hierarchy of consequences are included to ensure that all personnel working with this student use consistent behavior management techniques.

Even though there are several problem areas of behavior, the behavioral intervention plan only addresses three major goals for increasing desirable behaviors and three objectives for decreasing negative behaviors. The IEP team felt that these behaviors should be priority goals with the other problem areas targeted at a later date. The bus management plan and social stories (Figures 8.1 and 8.2) were developed to meet special needs of the student.

Although not included in this plan, there have been instances when physical restraint was necessary. In these instances, individuals should be careful in the use of physical restraint. It should only be used in response to physical acting out behaviors. If the student is exhibiting verbal acting out behaviors, verbal interventions should be used. Even when the student is physically acting out, physical intervention should not be used unless verbal interventions are not working and the student is endangering himself or others.

If instructional personnel are in positions where physical restraint must be used, they should have adequate training in the use of physical restraints. This training should be documented, and there should be annual training to refresh their skills in this area. The use of physical restraints should be included in the behavioral intervention plan when it is apparent that such a strategy is needed with an individual child. Hopefully, one would never have to use physical restraints, but it is better to be prepared to use physical restraints and not need them, than to need physical restraints and be unprepared.

Figure 8.4   IEP SUPPLEMENT

BEHAVIORAL INTERVENTION PLAN

Name: _____   Date:

School: <u>Any School, USA</u>

REVIEW OF EXISTING DATA:

___, a Junior High School student, has continued to make progress in behavioral control this year. However, she still exhibits extreme impulsivity and distractibility. These characteristics underlie most of her problem behaviors in the classroom and at home. She is on medication for hyperactivity/attention deficit disorders. She is able to control her behavior much better when she is on medication.

She exhibited problems during the extended school year program; she frequently fought to stay on the bus. She did not want to get off the bus and go into her home. Several incidences occurred this summer. However, she did not have medication for a few weeks at the beginning of the session in June. After her medicine was received in late June, the school staff only gave her the morning medication because the students went home at noon.

Based on current data, the IEP team considering this student's educational programming and placement has made the following determinations regarding behavioral interventions:

1.   The student has the capacity to understand the school rules as outlined in the district's code on conduct.

2.   The student **does not have** the capacity to follow school rules as outlined in the district's code on conduct.

3.   Due to the student's disability, special behavioral intervention techniques are necessary.

FUNCTIONAL BEHAVIORAL ASSESSMENT:

Behaviors reported by parents:

1.   Noncompliance with directives/ refusal to do things.

2.   Inappropriate hygiene habits.

3.   Inappropriate verbal language.

Behaviors exhibited in the school environment reported by teachers:

1.   Noncompliance with directives.

2.   Talking out inappropriately in class (i.e., using inappropriate language).

3.   Physical aggression such as throwing, knocking things off the table, pushing others, etc.

4.   Not completing tasks/assignments.

5.   Running ahead of the teacher/paraprofessional while walking around the school campus.

6.   Out of seat behaviors.

7.   Inappropriate hygiene habits.

Behavioral observations of qualified personnel:

This student frequently refused to comply with instructions. She appeared to be talking inappropriately in class to gain attention. Incidents of physical aggression appeared to be related to anger or a need to demonstrate that she was in control. Some behaviors appeared to be related to her extreme impulsivity and inability to delay gratification. She has very little control over her behavior most of the time. See Report of Observation for more specific information.

Situations that generally happen before inappropriate behaviors are exhibited include:

1.   She was directed to complete a task.

2.   The teacher was directing her attention toward other students, and this student was not receiving any attention.

3.   Another student did something that irritated her.

Responses that generally occur after inappropriate behaviors are exhibited:

1.   She is warned about her behaviors.

2.   She loses access to a desired activity.

3. She is isolated and attention is removed if she continues to exhibit inappropriate behaviors.

Reinforcers that have been tried during the past year:

1. Verbal praise

2. Tangible reinforcements (food, candy, money, tokens, etc.)

3. Activity reinforcers

4. Premack Principle

None of the reinforcers consistently worked. Some would work briefly.

Consequences that were applied during the past year:

1. Positive reinforcement

2. Negative reinforcement

3. Student/teacher conference

4. Premack Principle

5. Loss of privileges

6. Isolation in area by herself away from other students

7. Removal from the bus

8. Sent home for calming down time

9. Teacher/parent conference

10. Conference with teacher, principal, and student

11. Reverse psychology (Whenever she is refusing to do something, tell her that's OK, someone else will do it. She will then sometimes comply.)

None of these reinforcers worked consistently. Nothing worked when she was extremely upset.

Time out is not used because she refuses to go and has to be physically moved to the area. Isolation or withdrawal of attention has been more effective. The IEP team agrees that corporal punishment would not be appropriate for this student.

Figure 8.4 *Continued*

GOALS AND OBJECTIVES

Goals/objectives for increasing positive behaviors:	**Mastery criteria**

1.   She will comply to instructions/directions no more than three verbal prompts   60%
requested to complete a task.

    a.   When given a task to do, she will stay in her assigned area   70%
for ten minutes.

    b.   When given a task to do in her work area, she will sit down   60%
at the table and work on the task for five minutes with no more
than three verbal prompts.

    c.   When given a task to do in her work area, she will sit down   55%
at the table and work on the task quietly for ten minutes
with no more than three verbal prompts.

2.   She will verbally respond with yes or no when asked a question,   50%
with no more than three verbal prompts.

    a.   When spoken to by adults, she will look at the person and listen   60%
without talking until the other person has finished asking the question.

    b.   When the adult has finished talking, she will respond with   65%
yes or no with verbal prompting.

    c.   She will verbally respond when asked a question with   70%
no more than three verbal prompts.

3.   At snack time, she will participate in a conversation with her peers.   50%

    a.   She will sit down at the snack table and say hello to one person.   60%

    b.   She will ask one friend, "Do you like your snack?"   60%

    c.   She will say something nice to someone at the table.   50%

Objectives for decreasing negative behaviors:

1.   She will refrain from using curse words when she is angry.   50%

2. She will decrease the amount of off-task behaviors.   50%

   (No more than 15 minutes in every 30 minutes).

3. She will decrease physical aggression when she is angry (throwing   40%

   objects, knocking things off the table, and pushing others).

POSITIVE INTERVENTIONS

Reinforcers that will be used by special education and regular education personnel include:

Tangible reinforcers, activity reinforcers, and extra privileges.

Recommended positive interventions, strategies and supports:

1. Establish consistent routines with visual schedules.

2. Set well-defined limits and rules and reinforce or consequent them immediately.

3. Set well-defined tasks expectations, for example, "_____, I need you to

   _____, or you will need to take a time out."

4. Ignore minor inappropriate behaviors, whenever possible.

5. Provide frequent verbal and nonverbal reinforcement for appropriate

   behaviors (give her additional staff time, edibles, go outside, etc.)

6. Provide many opportunities for success.

7. Use the Premack Principle. You must do "x," before you do "y."

8. Encourage her to communicate her feelings/needs/wants, etc. in an

   appropriate manner at appropriate times without talking out.

9. Redirect her into appropriate activities as needed (shape appropriate

   behaviors with reinforcements and ignore or redirect inappropriate ones.)

10. Use visual cues and supports to cue her into more appropriate behaviors.

11. Implement a social skills training program that will provide opportunities

    for her to practice appropriate behaviors in a nonthreatening situation.

12. Use social stories with her when she has difficulty with certain problems.

13. Implement the hierarchy of consequences whenever inappropriate behaviors

    are exhibited.

Hierarchy of consequences:

1. Redirect to assigned task.

2. Reminder of rules/restatement of instruction.

3. Redirection to appropriate activities and behaviors.

4. Warning (state verbal limits and options).

5. State Premack Principle. You must do "x," before you do "y."

6. Teacher-student conference.

7. Loss of privileges.

8. Use over-correction as a consequence.

9. Time-out from teacher/adult attention (five minutes) in room.

10. Redirect to a task.

11. Because she cannot be physically removed from the classroom, if misbehavior continues, remove the other students from the room.

12. Teacher/parent conference.

13. Call assistant principal/principal for assistance.

14. If she remains out of control, she may be removed from the class and sent home for a "calming down" period. This will usually be for the remainder of the day, but should not exceed two days.

15. When she comes back to school, she must conference with the teacher.

PROGRESS REPORTS

The goals and objectives will be evaluated at least once per six-week period. A report card detailing progress will be sent to the parents.

ASSURANCES

The IEP team assures that the requirements of statutory and constitutional due processes and due process under the *Individuals with Disabilities Education Act (IDEA) Amendments* have been met.

Figure 8.5   IEP SUPPLEMENT

BUS MANAGEMENT PLAN

Name: _____   Date:

School: Any School, USA

Behaviors reported:

The major problem exhibited on the bus is the refusal to get off the bus when she gets home. Sometimes, she also refuses to walk to the bus. This has been a sporadic problem for the past two years. However, there have been considerable problems occurring during the ESY program during the summer.

Relationship to disability:

She does have the capacity to understand school rules, but she does **not** have the capacity to follow the school rules as outlined in the district's code of conduct. Due to her disability, special behavioral intervention techniques are necessary.

Recommended interventions:

1.   Implement visual cues and schedules for going home on the bus.

2.   Use a social story about "Going Home on the Bus" during the school day.
       A picture book of her trip home may also be developed.

3.   Have the bus pick her up and take her home first so that she is alone on the
       bus with the bus driver and the bus aide.

4.   Use visual cues on the bus so that she can follow each step and
       predict what to do during each step. The steps are:

       a.   Walk from the classroom to the special education bus.

       b.   Get on the bus.

       c.   Sit down in the assigned seat on the bus.

d.   When the bus gets to her home, she gets up and walks to the front of the bus.

e.   She gets off of the bus.

f.   The paraprofessional will reward her for getting off the bus without physical prompting or restraint.

g.   She walks into her home.

5.   If the previous steps do not work, contact the Community School personnel, if necessary, to assist in physically removing her from the bus.

6.   Minor family members will not be asked to get on the bus to assist with her removal.

7.   Contact her mother if she has a problem on the bus.

8.   Document the incident using a bus report form.

9.   Take her home in a car.

| Teacher Signature | Parent Signature | Administrative Signature |

Chapter Nine
Placements for Success

Placement decisions must be driven by the Individualized Educational Program. The annual goals, short-term objectives, and benchmarks developed in the IEP are the foundation of educational programming. The placement decision should not be based upon the student's disability. We should not place a student with autism in a class for students with autism just because there is an established class.

The IEP team must examine developed goals, objectives, and benchmarks and determine the least restrictive environment (LRE) in which the goals and objectives can be met. The importance of IEP goals, objectives, and benchmarks is highlighted as they become the driving force for placement decisions. However, a core concept of the *IDEA Amendments* is that students with disabilities will have access to the general education curriculum. The intent of the law is that educational programs for students with disabilities will be as accountable as those programs for nondisabled students. The *IDEA Amendments* place great emphasis on involvement and progress of students with disabilities in the general education program.

Beginning with statements of the child's present levels of educational performance, the IEP team must address *how the child's disability affects the child's involvement and progress in the general curriculum.* Section 300.347(a)(2) requires that the IEP team make a "statement of measurable annual goals, including benchmarks or short-term objectives, related to meeting the child's needs that result from the child's disability *to enable the child to be involved in and progress in the general curriculum.*" Section 300.347(a)(3) addresses supplementary aids and services. The IEP team must include a statement of the special education related services and supplementary aids and services to be provided to the child, or on behalf of the child. The IEP team must include a statement of the program modifications and supports for school personnel that will be provided for the child to advance appropriately toward attaining the annual goals and *to be involved and progress in the general curriculum.*

Clearly, the intent is that most students with disabilities will be educated in the general education classroom with appropriate aids and supports. In fact, the IEP team must explain why students are removed from general education classes. Section 300.347(a)(4) specifically states that the child's IEP must include "an explanation of the extent, if any, to *which the child will not participate with nondisabled children in the regular class* and in extracurricular and other nonacademic activities. This emphasis is clearly consistent with previous regulations related to least restrictive environment (LRE) that required that each child with a disability be educated with nondisabled children to the maximum extent appropriate. However, *IDEA* does recognize that the regular classroom is not an appropriate environment for every student. It goes on to state that each child with a disability be removed from the regular educational environment *only when the nature or severity of the child's disability is such that education in regular classes with the use of supplementary aids and services cannot be achieved satisfactorily.* The LRE principle of *IDEA* is intended to ensure that a student with a disability is served in a setting where the child can be educated successfully.

The least restrictive environment may be the regular classroom for many students with autism. However, the least restrictive environment may be the self-contained special education class, or even a residential placement, for other students with autism. Some students with autism may benefit from a combination of time spent in the regular classroom and the special education classroom.

The decision must be individualized. What is right for one student with autism may not be right for another student, because of different functioning levels; different levels of support needed; and the goals, objectives, and benchmarks that need to be addressed. Disagreements between parents and school personnel sometimes occur when parents and the school differ on the best placement for a student with a disability.

One frequent controversy is that of inclusion versus self-contained classroom placement. However, schools that have tended to veer away from inclusion of students with autism will need to look very closely at their programs and individual students to determine what kinds of supports and aids can be provided to enable these students to function more successfully in the general education program. This may involve providing all general education teachers with more training in appropriate methods and strategies for working with students with autism and other disabilities.

Another placement-related issue is residential placement. Requests for residential placement generally result in conflict between the parent and public school district. When parents request residential placement, the school may object because of the financial cost of the residential placement compared to serving the student in a local setting at the school. If the school district requests residential placement, there are generally extenuating services. In making the request, the school is saying, "This school district cannot meet the overwhelming needs of this student." Most schools will try many options before recommending or requesting residential placement. One school tried a program with three adults (one teacher and two paraprofessionals) working with one student. When this did not work, the school requested residential placement for the student through a due process hearing. Another school district looked at the possibility of providing a respite worker in the home from three to eleven p.m. before requesting a residential placement.

Age-appropriateness may also become an issue in placement decisions. Many parents feel the need to have their children in protected settings; they may want the student to stay on an elementary campus instead of moving to a junior high or high school campus. Other parents want their child to be with age-appropriate peers. As previously stated, there is no one best placement for students with autism, even when considering groups of students with different levels of autism. I have been a member of IEP teams that have recommended residential placement, self-contained classes, resource classes, and inclusion. The specifics of each situation must be considered after carefully looking at the needs of the individual student and the continuum of placements. This continuum can be visualized like a ladder where each rung moves toward less restrictive placements, or a very tall house, where each floor is a different type of placement.

Instructional Arrangements

Section 300.551 (*Federal Register*, 1999, p. 12457) states that "each public agency shall ensure that a continuum of alternative placements is available to meet the needs of children with disabilities for special education and related services." This continuum of alternative placements listed in the definition of special education includes instruction in regular classes, special classes, special schools, home instruction, and instruction in hospitals and institutions. The final regulations indicate that the public agency must provide for supplementary services, such as resource room or itinerant instruction that would be provided in conjunction with regular class placement.

Beginning at the top with least restrictive alternatives and working down to most restrictive alternatives, possible school placements are as follows:

• Regular Classroom Placement. Students receive no special education services. They are general education students. If they had been in special education, this represents a dismissal from the special education program. This placement is generally more appropriate for students with Asperger's syndrome and high-functioning autism.

• <u>Regular Classroom Placement with Special Education Supports and Services.</u> This placement and regular classroom placement are considered to be "full inclusion" placements because the delivery of all special education supports and services occurs in the regular classroom. Most students with low-functioning autism placed in the regular classroom will need special education supports, such as assistance from a paraprofessional for portions of the day or speech therapy and other related services delivered in the natural classroom environment. Supports and services may also include modifications and accommodations of instruction for optimal student success in the classroom.

• <u>Regular Classroom Placement with Section 504 Services, Title/Chapter 1 Services, or State Compensatory Services.</u> All of these services are considered regular education services because of the origin of the funding. Section 504 has no funding attached and services are provided through regular education funding—either local or state. If federal funding is used, it is usually to provide Title or Chapter 1 services. The name keeps changing, but either name implies a federal funding source. These special classes operate in several ways, but are generally considered to be part of the regular education program. State compensatory classes generally operate in the same manner as Title 1 classes by providing tutorial and remedial instruction to students in the regular classroom. The difference is that the program is funded with state funds instead of federal. Some school districts also have co-teaching arrangements, which provide for a regular classroom teacher and a special education classroom teacher to team teach in a regular classroom that includes students with disabilities. The two teachers work together to provide content area instruction, such as science or social studies, with modifications and supports for students with disabilities.

• <u>Special Education Content Mastery, Resource Classes, and Related Services.</u> Most students using these forms of special education spend most of their day in the regular education classroom. Students placed in content mastery spend time in the regular class until there is a specific need for assistance on an assignment. At that time, they go to the content mastery class to receive tutorial assistance on their regular classroom assignment. Students in resource classes spend most of their day in regular education, but may go to special education resource classes for one to three periods per day. Students in resource placements generally spend less than 50 percent of their day in special education. Related services are typically delivered once or twice a week. The student spends the rest of the day in either regular education or special education classes. Related services may be delivered as direct therapy or consultant therapy and may take place in the regular classroom, the special education classroom, or a special room designated for the delivery of the related service.

• Partially Self-contained Classrooms. Students in these classes generally spend more than 50 percent of the day in the special education class, but may be mainstreamed for non-academic areas such as lunch, music, art, and physical education.

• Self-contained Classrooms. Students with disabilities in these classes spend all of their time in the special education class. The student receives all services in special education classes with instruction and related services delivered by special education personnel.

• Special Day Class. Students attend this class instead of attending school on their own campus. Theses classes are generally not located on the school campus and may be private schools or sheltered workshops contracted for by the schools.

• Homebound Instruction. This type of instruction is provided in the home. It is generally intended for students who have some type of illness. Students receive limited support at home. In Texas, homebound instructors provide four hours of instruction per week. However, there have been court cases throughout the nation in which schools have been ordered to provide much more than the minimum amount of homebound services for students with autism. Some parents have been successful through due process in receiving behavioral instruction in the home for extended lengths of time.

• Hospital Instruction. This form of instruction is typically provided to students who spend significant time in the hospital. The majority of students have been in regular classes and have temporary disabilities due to automobile or bicycle accidents, or sports injuries. A significant number of homebound students have mononucleosis, hepatitis, or other communicable diseases. Students with autism who have temporary illnesses would be eligible for this type of instruction. Also, students with autism may be served in this type of class if they are temporarily placed in a hospital setting for medical purposes. However, most states require that students are expected to be out for a minimum period of time before requiring districts to provide hospital instruction.

• Residential Placement. This form of instruction is very expensive. It provides a 24-hour-day, structured placement for students with autism. Differences regarding the need for residential

181

placement for specific students are often the reason that parents or school districts resort to due process hearings that involve students with autism.

Placement Decisions

Placement decisions are sometimes difficult because the decision frequently depends upon the personal philosophies of school personnel and parents. If the philosophies are similar, there is generally no problem. If the philosophies are different, conflict may occur. Regardless of personal philosophies, the *IDEA Amendments* still support a full continuum of placements for students with disabilities even though state and federal leaders encourage implementation of inclusive environments.

In determining placement, each public agency must ensure that placement decisions are made by a group of persons, including the parents, and other persons knowledgeable about the child; the meaning of the evaluation data; and the placement options. In conforming to the LRE provisions of the *IDEA Amendments*, the child's placement must:

- be determined at least annually,
- be based on the child's IEP, and
- be as close as possible to the child's home.

As stated previously, unless the child's IEP requires some other arrangement, the child should be educated in the school that he or she would attend if nondisabled. Section 300.552 (*Federal Register*, 1999, p. 12458) goes on to state that a public agency may not remove a child from education in age-appropriate regular classrooms solely because of needed modifications in the general curriculum.

Recommendations Geared to Currently Available Programs

As Reed Martin once stated, if the school district has made a district decision that all schools and programs will be inclusive, they are in danger of "tripping over the 'i' in IEP." Placement decisions must be made on the basis of what is best for the *individual* student to enable student mastery of the goals and objectives in the IEP. However, some schools tend to encourage parents to place students in "available" programs. If the campus program is inclusive, most of the recommendations are geared toward inclusion. If the campus program is set up with resource (pull-out) classrooms or self-contained classrooms for students with disabilities, the recommendations will probably be geared toward resource or self-contained special education instruction.

For example, a few years ago, friends with a daughter in kindergarten wanted their child in the regular kindergarten classroom with her same-age friends. Knowing that this might be a difficult meeting, the parents taperecorded the meeting and also brought two advocates from The Arc, an attorney and an inclusion specialist. The meeting progressed without too many problems until it was time to determine placement. All members of the IEP committee agreed that this child had specific needs for certain types of instruction and supports.

When the parents requested that this instruction occur in the regular classroom, the principal made the mistake of agreeing that the child would benefit from that type of program and supports, but stated, "We don't have that kind of program at this school." Of course, persons knowledgeable about federal law for students with disabilities know that is not an adequate excuse for not providing a needed educational program. If a student resides in the district and needs a specific type of instructional program, it is the duty of the school district to develop an appropriate program, whether the school currently operates that type of program or not. This meeting was recessed so that additional information could be collected prior to making the final decision.

Stay-put Provisions

The parents also refused to allow a trial period in resource placement because of the "stay-put" provisions in federal law. If this issue went to a court hearing, their child would remain in whatever placement was last agreed upon. Therefore, they insisted that their child remain in the general education classroom, the placement they wanted to continue.

If a hearing was necessary, the child would remain in the general education classroom until the hearing officer ruled on the issue. During the recess period, the district evaluated its position and determined that it was unlikely it could win a hearing with the comments made on the audiotape available for presentation. When the IEP meeting resumed, the school district agreed to provide the requested support services and leave the child in the regular classroom for instruction. Several years later, this child still receives support services in the general education classroom placement.

Age-appropriateness of Placements

Two situations related to age-appropriateness occurred this year. One parent was upset because the school district had placed her child on the middle school campus, an age-appropriate placement. She felt that he should have remained in his previous placement at the elementary campus for another year. She did not feel that her child was ready for the middle school campus.

At the same time, another family had a child in fourth grade. The IEP team recommended that he remain in his current placement, a self-contained classroom at the primary campus with classes for kindergarten though second grade. The family believed he was too old for the campus. Since he generally models behavior of the students around him, the family wanted him modeling behavior of fourth-grade students, not early childhood, first, or second-grade students.

Although special education professionals in the school district agreed with her, they had been told for years that there was no space at the intermediate campus for another classroom. Since this was the second year the parents had requested intermediate school placement at the IEP meeting, they became very persistent. The child was removed from school by his parents for two to three weeks until the school district worked out a way to move the classroom to the age-appropriate campus. Although it was a difficult decision to make, the student's parents felt it important enough to persist in their requests. Other students would benefit by having this class established on that campus for many years. Her persistence was actually appreciated because parents can sometimes cause things to happen in school districts that school staff members are unable to do.

How Do We Decide?

How should IEP committees go about making placement decisions? There are several questions that should be addressed and discussed prior to the final decision. First, the school's recommendations and parental preferences for placement should be discussed with both parties providing justification for their preferences.

Examine Goals and Objectives

Then, goals, objectives, and benchmarks should be examined to determine where they can best be met. If goals require social interaction with age-appropriate peers, it is generally necessary to provide some time in the general education classroom for this to occur. However, for some students who are extremely disruptive in the general education classroom, schools have provided a setting for social interaction in the special classroom by identifying a "circle of friends" from the general education classroom who come into the special classroom for social interaction periods. This is sometimes referred to as "reverse mainstreaming."

Consider Special Problems

Next, the committee should consider special problems of the student. For example, one young man cannot tolerate the general education classroom for long periods of time. He is much more comfortable having his "friends" come to his room for a period of time each day and really anticipates it. He can sometimes go into the general education classroom to watch a movie with the class, as long as he has the option to self-regulate when he needs to return to his room. At the end of the year, when he was moving to a different town, he went into the general classroom to say good-bye to his friends. He even allowed one of the girls to hug him.

This was very unusual; the previous year when a new student to the classroom came up without warning and kissed him, he reacted very differently. With scissors in hand, he immediately ran out of the classroom, down the hall, and out of the school building. The teacher found him standing on top of the air conditioner unit. After getting him down, she quickly took advantage of this "teachable moment" by providing on the spot, social skills instruction. She told him, "You don't have to run out of the room to avoid getting kissed. You can tell Bridget that you don't want to be kissed." When the teacher and Billy got back to the room, they wrote, "No more kissing" on the blackboard. The rest of the day, he repeatedly went to the board and pointed to the words. Then, he would turn to Bridget and say, "no more kissing." Billy has begun to realize that he does have some control over situations that are disturbing or irritating to him. When he went to say good-bye to his friends in the general education class, other students began crowding around him. He quickly indicated that it was time to go and left the situation that was becoming too stimulating for him.

In another situation, school district officials limited social interaction with other students because the young man with autism had physically attacked several students. He had torn a necklace off one girl's neck, causing the necklace to break. Other students did not like to eat with him because he grabbed food off their plates.

By requesting residential placement, the school district admitted that their program could not appropriately meet the needs of this student. The hearing officer ruled in favor of the school district request for residential placement because it appeared there was no way for the school and parent to collaborate and cooperate to provide a structured, consistent program for school and home. It was evident that the current program was not working when part of the school documentation presented in the hearing indicated some days when this student exhibited over 300 aggressive incidents.

Daniel R. R.

The case of *Daniel R.R.* provides some guidance (Martin, 1994) to parents and districts considering various placement options. This case involved a student whose parents wanted him placed in a regular classroom and the school district felt that he needed a more restrictive setting. The implications of this case have been adopted by the Eleventh and Third Circuit Courts of Appeals as well as the Eastern District of California. The following questions were developed in this case (Martin, 1994):

• Has the public agency tried placing the student in the regular education classroom with sufficient supplementary aids and services? According to the Circuit Court, modifications cannot be *mere token gestures.*

• Will the student receive educational benefit (including non-academic benefit) from placement in the regular education program?

• Will the child's overall educational experience in regular education be beneficial, considering the benefits of regular and special education?

• Will placement in the regular education setting, result in any foreseeable detriment to this the child?

• Will the placement of this child, and all that his program entails, have a negative impact on other students in that setting?

If the IEP team decides not to have the child in all regular settings and to have the student restricted for some portion of the school day, then the IEP team must examine the rest of the day to assure there are maximum opportunities for interaction with students without disabilities. The IEP team must also provide explanations as to why the student is not able to stay all day in the general education classroom.

Again, the school must consider what the student actually needs, not the available programs in the district. In looking at benefit, we must look to social areas, as well as cognitive and academic areas. If a potential harmful effect is identified, can it be addressed and ameliorated with supplementary aids and services or modifications? If the student exhibits disruptive behavior, can the student's behavior be improved by developing and implementing a behavior intervention plan? If the student requires major curricular modifications, will the child

186

take too much of the teacher's in-class time and be a detriment to other students? If the degree of necessary modifications makes the curriculum unrecognizable, then the student probably needs a placement other than regular class placement. Are the modifications unduly expensive? Is the need so great that other students would suffer because of the time required for the teacher and teacher's aide to attend to the student's needs? If so, could this be addressed through additional teacher training or by providing additional paraprofessional support? The Fifth Circuit stated that special education and regular education are not an "all or nothing" proposition. A combination of services can be used.

In the *Daniel R. R.* case, the public school district was allowed to place Daniel in a special class. They were able to do this because they had tried the regular class placement and had a tremendous amount of documentation showing why it was inappropriate for this student.

Baldwin County Board of Education

In the case of *Baldwin County Board of Education* (LRP, 1994b), the state hearing officer ruled in favor of the district. The parents had requested residential placement on the basis that the school district had improperly classified the student. He had been classified as having autism in a previous district. The current district classified him as having an emotional disturbance. However, the hearing officer ruled in favor of the district because the district had treated the student as a student with autism and his goals and objectives on the IEP were appropriate. It did not matter that the student was placed in a class for students with severe emotional behavior disorders because the IEP was appropriate.

Appropriate vs. Quality

Another issue in placement decisions is appropriate versus quality. Federal law requires a free appropriate public education. Schools do not have to provide a quality education. In *Christopher S. v. Round Rock ISD* (Walsh, 1994b), this typical argument took an unusual twist. The school district wanted to provide a residential placement, and the parents wanted to continue the homebound placement that was being provided. In court, the district tried to show that the residential placement was a "better" placement than homebound and would maximize the student's potential. Again, the hearing officer used the *Rowley* (Walsh, 1994b) argument that quality is not required, only appropriateness. In this case, the officer denied the district request for residential placement on the basis that the current homebound program was appropriate.

Change of Placement After Initial Permission

In another case reported by Walsh (1994c), the issue of change in placement after signing permission for initial placement was discussed. Although federal law requires permission for initial placement, once that happens, the school district can implement the proposed IEP, and can change the child's placement even over the parental objections. If the parents do not request a due process hearing, the district may leave the student in the changed placement. If the parents file a due process hearing, the last agreed upon placement is used, as the "stay put" provision is invoked.

Placement, like all other issues involving education of students with disabilities, must be decided on an individual basis. Although there are guidelines for determining special class placements versus regular class placements, there are rarely situations where the decision has a clear-cut answer. If there were, we would have fewer due process hearings. Each placement decision must consider the needs of the individual student and consider all factors involved in order for the IEP team to make informed, rational decisions that provide educational benefit to students with autism.

Dismissal from Special Education

We are usually very excited when a student has made enough progress to be dismissed from special education. However, students are sometimes dismissed prematurely; i.e., they are not ready to function successfully without the supports and services that have been provided. Consequently, the *IDEA Amendments* require that the public agency must evaluate a child before determining that the child is *no longer a child with a disability*. This ensures that decisions are made on valid data. This should make for better decision-making regarding students about to be dismissed from special education.

Graduation

According to federal law, graduation is a change of placement. Parents need to understand that graduation from high school *with a regular high school diploma* **releases a public agency from providing any further services,** even though the student may remain age-eligible for services. Consequently, graduation from high school requires that the public agency provide parents with written notice of the intent to graduate the student from high school.

Not all students who graduate from high school receive a regular high school diploma. In some states, students may graduate with a certificate of completion. The above provision related to termination of services for students graduating with a regular high school diploma does not apply if the student graduated without that diploma. However, in some states this issue is unclear because all students graduate with a high school diploma. Check with applicable state guidelines for your state's interpretation of this requirement. It appears that some states will interpret "receiving a high school diploma" as meeting all of the requirements of regular graduation. Additionally, graduation does not require an evaluation of the student, even though graduation is a form of dismissal from special education.

Private School Placement

There are several issues related to private schools. First, local education agencies have the same responsibilities for Child Find for students in private schools that they have for students in the public school. Each local education agency shall locate, identify, and evaluate all private school children with disabilities, including religious-school children residing in the jurisdiction of the local education agency (*Federal Register*, 1999, p. 12445.) According to *IDEA*, provision must be made for the participation of private school children with disabilities to be provided with special education and related services. Pursuant to this rule, a services plan should be developed and implemented for each private school child with a disability who has been designated to receive special education and related services under *IDEA* regulations.

However, Section 300.454 (*Federal Register*, 1999, p. 12445) states that "no private school child with a disability has an individual right to receive some or all of the special education and related services that the child would receive if enrolled in a public school." This means that private school students are entitled to some special education services. However, a private school student is not entitled to the same services that he or she would be entitled to if attending a public school. To receive a free appropriate public education (FAPE), the student must be enrolled in the public school.

According to Section 300.455, services provided to students in private school must be provided by personnel with the same standards as personnel providing services in the public schools. However, as stated above, "private school children with disabilities may receive a different amount of services than children with disabilities in public schools."

If a child with a disability enrolled in a private school is to receive services, there must be a services plan developed. Services may be provided on-site at a child's private school or at the public school. However, if necessary for the child to benefit from, or participate in, the services provided, a private school child with a disability must be provided transportation (Federal Register, p. 12446):

• from the child's school or the child's home to a site other than the private school, and

• from the service site to the private school, or to the child's home.

The local education agency does not have to provide transportation from the child's home to the private school. The cost of the transportation may be included in calculating whether the local education agency has met the fiscal requirements related to serving students in private schools. (Basically, the local education agency must spend the amount earned per child in the annual child count for federal funds. [See *Federal Register*, Section 300.453, p. 12445 for specific information related to expenditures for students in private schools.])

CASE EXAMPLE

Gregg, a bright young student in third-grade at a private school, has a speech impairment. He needs speech therapy to improve his speech. According to the public school, the funds that *IDEA* requires the agency to spend will only provide for speech therapy services at the private school once per month. However, if Gregg's parents enroll him in public school, Gregg would be eligible for speech therapy as frequently as the IEP team determines is necessary. If the public agency employs master-degree speech-language pathologists certified in clinical competence through the American Speech and Hearing Association to provide speech therapy in the public schools, an individual with the same qualifications has to provide therapy at the private school.

Public Charter Schools

Under Section 300.312 of the *IDEA Amendments*, children with disabilities who attend public charter schools and their parents retain all rights afforded students in public school districts under the final regulations of the *IDEA Amendments*. In states where public charter schools are considered to be a local education agency, public charter schools are responsible for ensuring that the requirements of *IDEA* are met, unless state law assigns that responsibility to some other entity. In that case, the other entity is responsible for ensuring that student and parental rights are provided.

Chapter Ten
Serving the Spectrum of Autism

Low-Functioning or Regressive/Epileptic Subtype

In differentiating subtypes of autism, Grandin and Hart (1993) identified high functioning autism as the Kanner/Asperger Type. The low-functioning subtype of autism was identified by Grandin as a regressive/epileptic subtype. Van Krevelen (cited in Wing, 1991) noted that the low-functioning child with autism "lives in a world of his own" (Williams K., 1995, p. 9). Characteristics of the regressive/epileptic subtype include the following:

1. Individuals sometimes have obvious **body movement problems** or difficulty with stopping and starting hand movements.

2. This subtype **appears to have no receptive speech**. Because incoming speech may fade in and out, incoming speech may be a jumble of sound. These individuals are more likely to be nonverbal.

3. **Sensory information from different senses may jumble and mix together** into noise or patterns that the individual is unable to distinguish.

4. These individuals **often have epileptic seizures**, abnormal EEG readings, an undersized brain stem, and immature central system development.

5. Although it is difficult to tell, individuals **may have more normal thinking and emotions**.

6. Many respond poorly to intrusive methods due to sensory overload. **Intrusive methods may cause confusion and pain.**

7. Individuals **may be able to attend to only one sensory channel at a time**. For example, they may not be able to listen and look at the same time. Information should be presented to only one sensory modality. They may actively avoid certain sounds and stimuli that may be attractive to individuals with less severe disabilities.

8. These individuals may exhibit **severe anxiety problems**.

9. They tend to respond best to beta blockers, epilepsy drugs, buspirone, clonidine, Vitamin B-6, and magnesium and DMG supplements. (Grandin & Hart, 1993, p. 209).

It is difficult to divide students with autism into groups by high- and low-functioning because they fit on a continuum, and there are students at all places on that continuum. However, those that may be grouped very generally as "low-functioning" may function better in a life skills curriculum than in an academic curriculum. As was discussed earlier in the chapter on developing goals and objectives, one of the best ways to identify appropriate goals is to do a comparative analysis. Compare the things that your child can and cannot do with the things that a child without disabilities of a similar age can and cannot do. No two students will have the exact same needs. However, some similar needs that I see regularly will be included in the following list.

1. In the area of **activities of daily living**, goals should focus around the child's ability to independently attend to toileting, self-feeding, and acquiring self-dressing skills. If the child has acquired these skills, activities such as picking up toys and following simple directions should be addressed.

2. In the area of recreation/leisure, the child should be able to **independently participate in recreation/leisure activities** for fifteen to thirty minutes. This area is difficult for parents because many children take almost constant supervision. Activities that are possible for these students might include the computer, coloring (if the student does not have severe fine motor difficulties), working puzzles, listening to music on the radio or tape player, or playing with special toys. Many students who function at this level enjoy interacting with the computer in cause and effect programs. The living storybooks are great because they allow for interaction at the cause and effect level, but also provide exposure to words and reading, which is even more important because the *IDEA Amendments* place a great emphasis on students having access to the general education curriculum.

3. In the area of communication, the most important goal is to **establish a form of communication.** Getting students who use gestures and objects to communicate basic needs consistently is a significant accomplishment for some students with autism. Having multiple communicative interactions is much more important than the form of communication that the child uses. Initiating communication to indicate wants and basic needs to others is very important.

4. In the **social/behavioral area**, there are several important areas for goal development. Students should learn to deal with frustration without becoming unduly upset. Following simple directions is extremely important and can be a safety issue if students don't comply when they are told to "stop." Interacting with others in social situations such as

playing on the playground is another important goal for many students with autism. For some children with extremely challenging behaviors, just being able to sit and work on a task or listen to a story without screaming is an important objective.

CASE EXAMPLE

Eddie exhibits many challenging behaviors. He drops to the ground and screams when he does not want to do something. The longest he will sit and listen to a story is three minutes. His behavioral issues are being addressed by having situations set up for him to play with age-appropriate friends on a daily basis. Eddie will bounce the ball with them and ride on the merry-go-round on the playground. He also has a goal of just being able to sit for five minutes and attend to a task or listen to a story without screaming. The occupational therapist and physical therapist are working with the classroom teacher to identify sensory methods that will calm him.

---

5.   **Academically,** simple put-in tasks, sorting activities, matching, and packaging activities predominate in most self-contained special education classrooms. Younger children should also be participating in story time and circle times with the rest of their class. All activities should emphasize the use of functional communication. With the new focus on access to the regular curriculum, we will have to look at the regular curriculum to determine when students can participate and when alternate activities or modifications are needed.

Basic methods that seem to be successful with these students include a structured environment with visual cues and supports and daily schedules that enable the student to predict what is happening next. Significant others in the student's environment need to consistently use the same methods and techniques.

Students with High-Functioning Autism

The potential of many students with high-functioning autism is unrecognized, particularly during the younger years. They tend to have major social, behavioral, cognitive, and sensory difficulties that limit their success in school. Direct instruction in specific skills may be necessary for successful functioning in the classroom and related school environments. It may also be necessary to teach these students how to cope with their sensory integrative dysfunctions. As these students get older, they should be able to self-monitor their needs for certain types of sensory activities and learn more appropriate ways to satisfy their sensory needs.

A **functional assessment of the student's behaviors** in various school and community environments should lead to identification of areas that need direct instruction, adaptations, and modifications. Diesback & Jester (1994) recommend that these high-functioning students receive direct instruction in various study skills. They may also need assistance in understanding assignments, class procedures, test formats, and grading systems. These students also need direct instruction in how to make and maintain friendships.

The obsessions and interests of high-functioning students should be focused and encouraged to foster talent development. For example, Dr. Temple Grandin (1996) has taken her obsession with cattle chutes and developed a career in the area of corral and plant design. She also took her talents and interests in this area to develop the "hug machine," which appropriately satisfies her need for deep pressure. The following recommendations apply to students with high-functioning autism and to many students with Asperger's Syndrome.

1. **Academic tasks** might focus on functional academics for some students whereas other students may be able to participate in regular academics with specific modifications identified by the IEP committee. The IEP team must first look at the regular curriculum and modify it only when it is apparent that the student needs modifications and supports that are not available through the regular curriculum.

2. **Activities of daily living** may involve instructional tasks, such as learning to look up information in a telephone directory; ordering from a menu, determining the cost and whether the student has enough money to pay for the ordered items, and preparing simple snacks and meals. Other students might be given tasks related to their obsession such as using a telephone directory to find a specific store that sells a certain brand of equipment. Students included in general education classes should have access to the curriculum for the general education class.

3. **Activities related to social interaction** must also be a major focus for these students. They need to learn how to interact with other students. In many situations, they need to learn perspective-taking. Many individuals with high-functioning autism say that they must learn appropriate social interactions by imitating others. They do not pick up on the subtle cues of people in their environments. Therefore, they need direct instruction on appropriate behaviors for social interaction and must have many opportunities to practice the appropriate behaviors in natural environments.

4. **Instruction in communication** should focus on communicative behavior in social or pragmatic situations. Does the student know how to maintain a social conversation? Has he or she learned the art of turn-taking in social conversations? Does the student need instruction in pronoun usage? Does the student interpret everything literally? Is instruction needed in the figurative use and meaning of language? Can the student deal with words with multiple meanings?

CASE EXAMPLE

Jason is in the regular classroom. Academically, he performs as well or better than the other students. However, he has great difficulty when words are used in ways different than he perceives them. For example, if someone says, let's take a "break," Jason gets very upset. He says, "Break means you break something in half. How can you take a break because you aren't breaking anything?" He also gets upset when school tasks are referred to as "work," because work is something that his Dad does at his factory job. Because his reactions to use of multiple meanings for certain words interferes with his ability to successfully perform in the general education classroom, an important objective for Jason is to learn that words have multiple meanings, and it is okay to use the words in different contexts.

As with all students, the specific objectives needed in IEPs will depend upon the student's level of functioning in each area as measured by comprehensive assessments and student progress measures. Objectives are not required for general education subject areas in which the student participates. When instruction takes place in the general education classroom, it is assumed that the student will participate in the general education curriculum. If modifications and accommodations are needed, they should be specified in the IEP.

Students with Asperger's Syndrome (AS)

I found much of the information on Asperger's Syndrome in the literature about learning disabilities, as many individuals with this disorder also have some form of learning disabilities. This disorder tends to be at the higher end of the autistic continuum, with individuals exhibiting average to above average intelligence. They also appear to have superior rote memories. Their lack of understanding of human relationships and the rules of social convention may result in inept social skills and eccentric behaviors, which cause them to be victims of teasing and scapegoating by peers. They tend to be naive, lacking in common sense, clumsy, and inflexible. These students may exhibit obsessive interests in obscure subjects (Williams, K., 1995). According to Grandin (1996), there may be several forms of high-functioning autism. Asperger's syndrome is one form. Volkmar and Klin (1994) have suggested that the neuropsychological profiles of individuals with Asperger's syndrome appear to closely follow the profile described by Byron Rourke as Nonverbal Learning Disabilities (NLD) syndrome. Twatchman (1996), indicates that people with Asperger's syndrome have intellectual skills that virtually eclipse the social-emotional and other deficiencies that are a basis for much of the aberrant behavior seen in the syndrome.

Each child with Asperger's syndrome has a very unique personality. They may be easily stressed and display emotional vulnerability. Like other pervasive developmental disorders, there is no exact recipe for classroom approaches that can be provided for every student with AS.

1. Students with Asperger's syndrome may be overwhelmed by minimal environmental change because of their highly sensitive reactions to environmental stressors. They sometimes engage in rituals and are anxious, tending to worry obsessively when they do not know what to expect. Stress, fatigue, and sensory overload easily throw them off balance. **Providing a safe environment** with a daily routine with minimal transitions and surprises will be beneficial for these students (Williams, K., 1995). Allay fears of the unknown by preparing the child for new activities, teachers, and classes.

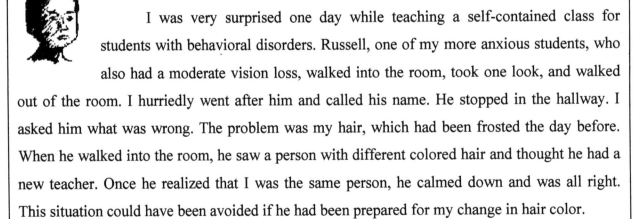

CASE EXAMPLE

I was very surprised one day while teaching a self-contained class for students with behavioral disorders. Russell, one of my more anxious students, who also had a moderate vision loss, walked into the room, took one look, and walked out of the room. I hurriedly went after him and called his name. He stopped in the hallway. I asked him what was wrong. The problem was my hair, which had been frosted the day before. When he walked into the room, he saw a person with different colored hair and thought he had a new teacher. Once he realized that I was the same person, he calmed down and was all right. This situation could have been avoided if he had been prepared for my change in hair color.

2. Many individuals with Asperger's Syndrome **have difficulty understanding complex rules of social interaction.** They are naive, extremely egocentric, and may not like

physical contact. Many do not understand jokes, irony, or metaphors. They may use an unnatural tone of voice and misinterpret social cues. Although they may have well-developed speech, they may exhibit difficulty in initiating and sustaining conversations. They may be easily taken advantage of because of their desire to be part of the social world.

These students need to be protected from bullying and teasing. When social ineptness is severe, peers need to be educated about students with Asperger's syndrome. Provide opportunities that allow students with Asperger's syndrome to show their strengths in proficient academic areas by using cooperative learning tasks.

3. **Teach students with Asperger's Syndrome how to react to social cues** and provide repertoires of responses to use in various social situations through modeling of two-way interactions and role-playing. These students must learn social skills intellectually because they lack social instinct and intuition. Use older students for buddies and foster involvement with others. Encourage active socialization and limit the time spent in isolated pursuits of interests by students with Asperger's syndrome.

4. Individuals with Asperger's Syndrome may appear to be eccentric with preoccupations or odd, intense fixations. They frequently ask repetitive questions about interests and sometimes refuse to learn anything outside their area of interest. **Limit their questioning behavior** by providing a specific time during the day when the child can talk about this. One teacher I work with implemented a "pretend time" at the end of each day as a reward for good behavior. **Set firm expectations** for completion of class work. Make it clear that the student must follow specific rules. Allow students time to pursue their own interests. If possible, give students with Asperger's syndrome assignments that link their interest to the subject being studied. Use the child's fixation as a way to broaden his or her repertoire of interests (Williams, K, 1995).

5. These students are often off-task and appear to be very disorganized and have difficulty sustaining attention in classroom activities. They have difficulty determining what is relevant; they tend to withdraw into complex inner worlds in a manner much more intense than is typical of daydreaming. This description is so typical of one of my former students. He was an expert on dinosaurs. That became his world into which he withdrew. I learned more about dinosaurs that year than I ever hoped to know. These students

should be **provided with external structure, frequent teacher feedback, and redirection, as needed.**

Many techniques appropriate for students with attention deficit disorder may help them to develop organizational skills. Some students may need to have modified assignments due to poor concentration, slow clerical speed, and severe disorganization. Board games provide structure and opportunities to practice social skills.

6. Although they have average to above average intelligence, individuals with AS frequently **lack higher level thinking and comprehension skills.** Set firm expectations for producing quality work. Develop a highly structured, individual program that capitalizes on the students' excellent memory. This facilitates success.

7. Although AS students have the intelligence to participate in regular education, they may not be able to cope with the demands of the classroom. They are often self-critical and unable to tolerate making mistakes. This causes stress. These students may **need direct instruction or counseling to learn coping mechanisms for stress.**

There are many good children's books available on dealing with stress. My favorites for use with young children are *Don't Pop Your Cork on Mondays* and *Don't Feed the Monster on Tuesdays.* These books provide students with fun ways to learn coping strategies, such as deep breathing or counting to ten. There are also games such as the *Social Skills Game* and the *Anger Control Game,* which would be good for teaching appropriate social behaviors.

Be calm and predictable in interactions with students with Asperger's syndrome while clearly indicating compassion and patience. Be alert to changes in behavior. If you observe symptoms of depression, a referral to a school counselor or mental health therapist may be appropriate. Adolescence is a key developmental period when depression is likely to occur when the normal stresses of adolescence are intensified. Students with AS may need emotional support in the school environment, which is difficult for some teachers who may see their role as strictly academic.

Like students with high-functioning autism, students with Asperger's Syndrome must have **access to the general education curriculum** according to the *IDEA Amendments*. The development of the IEP will depend upon the assessed strengths and weaknesses of each individual student.

CAUTION
SHE'S NOT
IN A GOOD
MOOD

Chapter Eleven

Heed the Warning Signs:

School District Errors

WARNING

A core concept of the *IDEA Amendments* is the involvement of parents and students with regular and special education personnel in making individual decisions to support each student's educational success. In the past, school districts have commonly made the mistake of not treating the parent as an equal partner in the child-centered process. Sometimes, just the nature of the IEP meeting inhibits true collaboration. We must recognize the barriers to equal partnerships between parents and professionals (See Figure 11.1). Our recognition of the barriers may be the first step in making improvements in IEP meetings.

Figure 11.1 Barriers to Equal Partnerships
Between Parents and Professionals.

1. Inadequacy of the IEP Meeting as a vehicle for communication.

    A.   Labeling the child is a legal necessity that may invoke unpleasant reactions.

    B.   Labeling of each other may reinforce negative feelings.

2. Late notices and inflexible scheduling.

3. Limited time for IEP conferences.

    A.   Time spent with families is essential; time spent now may save time later.

    B.   Schedule school/parent conferences on a regular basis outside of the IEP team.

4. Emphasis on documents rather than IEP participation.

    A.   Listening, but not hearing, what is being said.

    B.   Learn to ask the right questions.

5. Use of "educationalese" or professional jargon.

    A.   Use language parents can understand.

    B.   Speak clearly.

    C.   Use restatement and reflection of major concepts and decisions to clarify understandings.

First, take a look at the meeting itself. The parents come into a meeting where professionals outnumber them several times. After the basic introductions and identifications are concluded, presentation of assessment information begins. Generally, each professional tells parents the results of his or her assessment. Parents are rarely asked if they have additional assessment information to share. Once the information is discussed, the chair (agency representative) or assessment person asks if everyone agrees with the results. Naturally, it is expected that everyone will quickly agree and move on to the next agenda item.

IEP meetings do not have to be like this description. Many things can be done to make the parents feel that they are true partners in the educational process of educating their child. School personnel and parents must make the effort to establish true two-way partnerships.

A Two-way Relationship

Recognize the two-way nature of the relationship. Respectful, egalitarian relationships should be established with mutual problem-solving as the goal. Recognize that parents are experts on their child. They know the child's strengths and weaknesses and typical patterns of behavior. They have had several years to find out what does and does not work with the student. Take advantage of the parents' knowledge in the assessment and IEP process. Remember that partnerships take time; they don't happen overnight. The door is not always open—you may have to push it. Keep on trying to establish positive relationships.

If parents begin to question assessment results, many professionals become very defensive. Professionals must remember that questioning may be an indication that the parents really do not understand and just want clarification. It does not mean that their professional credentials are being questioned. I have seen instances where related service personnel are offended and believe their qualifications are being challenged if the parents question or disagree with their recommendations for frequency of service delivery.

Don't Take it Personally

It's okay to have differences of opinion, so do not take things personally. Professionals must learn that disagreement is not necessarily a personal reflection on them. Frequently, it is a reflection of differences between "educational" and "medical" service delivery models. In my experience, parents generally request more frequent services than school districts recommend. Parents often disagree with school recommendations for consultative services because they believe their child needs direct therapy.

Evaluate your own communication style. Be aware of your own paraverbal and nonverbal communication. What are you conveying? Do you appear to be rational and logical? Have you raised your tone of voice and quickened your speed of talking? This conveys anger. Slow down and speak quietly and calmly. Does your body language convey active listening? Are you making eye contact with the parent? What kind of facial expressions are you making?

Do you respect the parents' cultural values? Do not address African-American parents by their first names unless given permission (Lynch & Hanson, 1992). Even though you may intend it as a friendly gesture, it may imply disrespect.

I work with parents from a variety of cultural backgrounds. Most call me by my first name, and I use their first names. This is my signal to them that I consider them as equal partners in the process of developing appropriate programs for their children. However, I have worked with one African-American parent for several years. She calls me Miss Beth and I call her Mrs. Smith. For both of us, this is a sign of respect.

How do you interact with Hispanic parents? Do you speak to the wife or the husband first? If both are present, you should speak to the husband first. Even if the husband is not present, you should ask if the father is in agreement with the recommendations and plans. Begin with an informal, relaxed exchange of social communication before you begin the meeting. Don't show impatience or behave in a hurried manner (Lynch & Hanson, 1992). Regardless of the culture, learn about it and show respect by observing its important do's and don'ts.

Respect parenting styles. Recognize the stresses that families of children with autism face. Understand that their daily schedule may be:

Get up.
Eat.
Survive.
Go to bed and hope your child doesn't wake up until morning.

Consider in-home and parent training for students with autism to enhance the student's functioning in the home and school environments.

Recognize that educator parents of children with disabilities have their own special needs. It is particularly difficult to teach in a school system when you must advocate for your child's special needs. When I present workshop sessions for parents, the parent educators generally stay asking questions because it is so difficult to be an employee and your child's advocate in the same system. In fact, I advised my university students who had children with disabilities to work in a different system from the one their child attended in order to avoid this type of conflict.

<h3 style="text-align:center">Organizing the IEP Meeting</h3>

Parents report that IEP meetings are very intimidating experiences. School personnel should strive to make it a less intimidating experience. When conflicts do occur, the school staff can facilitate consensus and promote understanding and tolerance through utilization of the following recommended rules for the IEP meeting (Walsh, 1988; Walsh, 1992). These rules will enhance the communicative effectiveness of school personnel involved in the meeting.

1. **Plan the environment.** The room should be easily accessible for all parties, comfortable in temperature, and free from excessive clutter. Tables and adult-sized chairs should be utilized whenever possible. Since these meetings are sometimes very long, it is important that participants do not have to sit in chairs designed for elementary school children. The meeting should also be scheduled so that there are no interruptions.

2. **Provide enough time.** Although parents should not expect meetings to last for several hours, adequate time should be scheduled to present and discuss their concerns. Avoid making parents feel that they are restricted to the agenda or time line established. Schedule additional time when it is known that the parent has lengthy concerns to be aired.

3. **Designate a rapport builder.** This is generally an individual who has established a good relationship with the parent. It could be the regular or special education classroom teacher, a special education support staff member, or a school counselor. The task of this individual is to make parents feel as comfortable as possible and be free to participate as equal partners in the IEP process. If personality conflicts exist between school personnel and parents, utilize personnel who have established positive relationships with the parents.

4. **Invite the parents to assist in the development of the IEP.** Although federal law requires districts to provide notice of IEP meetings, many parents do not feel that the

school district really wants their participation in this meeting. One way to encourage participation and to make parents feel involved in the process is to send a letter (Figure 5.1, p.78) inviting parents to suggest objectives for IEP Committee consideration. This allows parents an opportunity to provide input for the IEP meeting. The *IDEA Amendments* have placed even greater emphasis on parental involvement in the educational process. Schools must make every effort to ensure that parents are involved in decisionmaking for their child.

5.   **Designate a documentarian.** This person's task is to record the minutes of the meeting. This should not be the person designated as chairperson or the individual responsible for completing all IEP forms.

6.   **Have the agency representative present.** State and federal laws mandate the presence of an agency administrator during an IEP meeting. This should be someone who has the ability to commit resources of the school district. It is equally important that the designated representative stay for the complete meeting and not be running in and out of the room taking care of other school business. The agency representative's absence from the room at critical times could invalidate the meeting proceedings. This is particularly important if parents file a complaint or the involved parties go to a due process hearing or federal court.

7.   **Have an agenda for the IEP meeting.** All persons present should have a copy of the IEP meeting agenda (Figure 5.2, p.86-88). Agendas keep the meeting focused and flowing smoothly. It informs parents of the topics to be covered while enabling them to know the appropriate time to present their concerns. It is important to set meeting guidelines (including reasonable time frames).

8.   **Put a blank or draft IEP in front of the parents.** Parents should receive a draft copy of the *proposed IEP* prior to the meeting or at the beginning of the meeting. This enables them to follow along as specific items are discussed.

9.   **Complete the IEP prior to the placement.** Federal law mandates that placement decisions be based upon the IEP. Therefore, goals and objectives must be completed prior to placement even when parents wants to discuss placement first.

10.   **The teacher should be knowledgeable about the content of the IEP.** Be prepared to discuss present competency levels including the child's strengths, weaknesses, and current progress. The teacher must be knowledgeable about the IEP objectives and their

appropriateness for implementation with the child. Reasonable evaluation criteria for each objective should be defined. The teacher should be able to address parental concerns related to IEP development.

11. **Speak in plain language;** don't use educational jargon.

12. **Present initial assessment information to parent's prior to the IEP meeting.**

13. **Use restatement to summarize decisions** made by the IEP team for clarification purposes.

Generally, the smaller the meeting the better. Parents are more likely to actively participate when there are fewer people. An extremely large number of IEP team members tends to overwhelm most parents and lessens the probability of active participation.

Become knowledgeable about autism and the legal mandates that apply to students with autism at the state and federal levels. Ensure that instructional personnel receive specialized staff development and training in methods designed to facilitate effective teacher-student interaction and instruction (Bossey, 1995). Be sure that the instructional staff knows the IEP. Teachers cannot implement an unfamiliar IEP. The final regulations of the *IDEA Amendments* require that all special education personnel and regular classroom teachers who provide services to a child should have access to the student's IEP prior to providing any services to the student. School personnel should not be expected to provide services until they are informed about the type of services to be provided.

Reed Martin (ADDA, 1996), a leading special education attorney representing parents, identified the top fifteen mistakes that school districts make in the IEP process. Proper notice is one area where frequent mistakes are made. Schools also fail to provide notice to parents of the IEP meeting. Schools may not have appropriate personnel at the IEP meeting. Sometimes schools fail to use assessment data as the foundation of the IEP. This may be a result of failure to meet state standards in administering the tests, refusal to consider a request for an independent educational evaluation, failure to evaluate the student in related services areas or refusing to evaluate because the issue is a medical issue, and failure to reevaluate within the three-year time frame specified in *IDEA*.

Section 504 is another area in which errors frequently occur. Schools may fail to recognize that *Section 504* and *IDEA* apply to all *IDEA* eligible students. *Section 504* requires an evaluation prior to changing a child's placement, particularly through expulsion. Students who don't qualify for *IDEA* eligibility should be automatically referred for *Section 504* eligibility.

Other Errors

Other commonly made errors include omitting basic components of the IEP or failing to provide related services based upon the needs of the child. A common mistake is discussing and deciding on placement prior to the development of the IEP. In this situation, the objectives are determined and developed based upon the program selected, rather than developed and used to make a determination of appropriate placement. Some districts fail to develop the IEP in a timely manner or fail to provide extended school year services when appropriate. Other common errors include failure to reasonably calculate the IEP to confer educational benefit or failure to ensure implementation of the IEP.

Transitions

Schools may also fail to have the IEP follow the student (ADDA, 1996). Since transitions are frequently difficult for students with autism, the district might send a detailed letter with the IEP to facilitate transition into a new setting. (This requires parental approval). The letter in Figure 11.1 was developed at the request of the parent and the receiving school district. It goes into much more detail than the forwarded assessments reports and IEP . The new instructional staff should have a better start with this student because the staff will already know the pitfalls experienced by the sending district.

Figure 11.2   Letter to Receiving School District

May 11, 1999

Special Education Director
Any town, USA

Re: Frank B.

Dear Special Education Staff:

I want to help make Frank's transition to your school district easier. We have brainstormed the things that we feel you need to know about Frank. I have really enjoyed

Figure 11.2 *Continued*   **Letter to Receiving School District**

working with Frank the past three to four years. Although he can be very challenging, he is also unique and special. I will really miss him, but I am happy for him because he is really excited about moving back to your town and going to your school district.

Some of his **characteristics** are very typical of children with autism. They include:

1.   Changes are generally upsetting to him. Try to prepare him for changes and transitions that you know will be occurring. Any type of change at home or at school will require time for adjustment.

2.   A need for consistent routines, schedules, and visual cues and supports.

3.   Hypersensitivity to sound, smell, and touch (tactile defensiveness).

4.   Fondness of bright lights.

5.   Pretending that he is an animal (he wears a sock in the back of his pants for a tail.)

Things that Frank is afraid of:

1.   Thunderstorms and the sound of thunder. We have done the social story on lightening and storms, but he is still afraid of them. If the room has no windows, he will get very upset when the lights go off and will run and scream. We generally take him to a hallway with a doorway where he can have some light and see out.

2.   Yellow liquid soap. If your school uses yellow soap, this may be a problem because Frank does not like it. However, he loves pink liquid soap. He is also afraid of water in the toilet that is colored blue with toilet cleaners.

3.   Bones in meat. Any meat must be deboned before it is given to him. He will fall on the floor and have a tantrum if he is given any meat with bones.

4.   Stapler. He is afraid of the stapler, but also obsessed with it. We keep the stapler out of sight. At first he was terrified of it, but has become better after he and his teacher have repeatedly discussed it. However, if your stapler looks different from the one that he has gotten used to, he may become very agitated and run out of the room when you take it out.

Things that Frank does not like:

1.   The color yellow. He says that yellow markers and yellow tempera paint smell. However, he will use them. Just be prepared for his comments.

2.   Bread. He used to think that the crust on bread was a bone. He has learned it is not and will eat toast without crust. He will not eat soft bread, or hot dog or hamburger buns. The

Figure 11.2 *Continued*   **Letter to Receiving School District**

lunchroom must not put the bread on his tray. If the menu is hot dogs, he should just be given the weiner on his tray. If they place the bread on his meat or other food, he will not eat the other food because he can smell the bread on it. He will sometimes eat a roll. If rolls are on the menu, ask him if he wants one. If he doesn't, don't put it on the tray.

3. If there is something on his tray that he wants removed, you can usually cover it with a napkin and that will satisfy him.

4. Loud noises (whistles) and strong odors.

5. Soft touches are irritating to him. He does much better with firm touches that provide deep pressure.

Things that Frank uses for calming:

Frank is really doing well with the calming techniques that we have been using. He has learned to self-monitor when he does, and does not, need the calming supports.

1. Earphones or ear muffs to reduce the sound in situations like the bathroom, the cafeteria, and the playground or gymnasium. He rarely needs them in the room. However, there are times in the room that Frank will go over and put them on. He will at times remove them in other places if he determines that it is not as noisy as he anticipated.

2. Chewing Tubes. Frank has learned to go and get one of the rubber chews when he is becoming agitated. If they are out, he will just get one. If they does not see his chewing tube, he will ask his teacher for the chewing tube.

3. There is a stationary exercise bicycle in his room that he generally rides early in the morning. This is also scheduled into his schedule for breaks and rewards.

4. There is a mini-exercise trampoline in the room. This is also included in his daily schedule. When Frank gets really hyperactive, he jumps on it for a few minutes.

5. Frank also generally wears a weighted vest (4 3/4 pound weights) when he leaves the room to go to the cafeteria, gymnasium, assemblies, etc.

6. Frank has a safe place to go to in the classroom that has a bean bag, chair, a large pillow, and a weighted quilt with two weights in it. It is calming for him to go lie on the bean bag and cover with the weighted quilt.

7. Bazooka Bubble Gum is also calming. It is the best brand of bubble gum we have found because it is tough to chew. He has been taught to chew it and not eat it. He has to show

Figure 11.2 *Continued*   **Letter to Receiving School District**

it to the teacher before he spits it out and gets another piece.

8.   Swinging. This is generally what he chooses to do on the playground. It is a good activity for Frank because it stimulates his vestibular system and is calming to him.

Don'ts

1.   Don't leave any kind of hand lotion or glue in the classroom. He may try to eat it.

2.   Don't leave any kind of videotape in the classroom where he is aware of it. He will obsess on it until it is removed from the room.

3.   **Never use earphones with a tape recorder, record player, or computer. Frank has had auditory integration training two times and the use of earphones with music can cause the treatment to reverse and cause him to become more sound sensitive.**

4.   Do not give him stuffed animals. He will lie on top of them and rub his stomach in inappropriate ways. His mother asked the occupational therapist not to use this kind of therapy with him because he will exhibit the same inappropriate behaviors in public places .

5.   He is obsessed with Disney movies and has memorized every word. **Do not have them available in the room.** He can not handle it. It has been much better since we took these away at school. We tried to use them as a reward, but it didn't work because he obsessed too much about them. You can use educational movies related to thematic topics.

6.   Don't leave Dr. Pepper or other soft drinks out. Regardless of who the drink belongs to, he will drink it.

DO'S

1.   Frank loves to use the computer. He particularly likes the living story books and any Disney stories. He must be supervised at the computer or he will begin stimming on the computer buttons. His teacher has been unsuccessfully trying to get him to use two hands on the keyboard.

2.   He loves to do simple, wooden puzzles and excels at this. We don't know how he would respond to a jigsaw puzzle, but it might work well with him.

3.   He likes science stories and real life pictures. He has been interested in topics like weather, animals, and animal habitats. Two stories that were used for his reading this year are *Who Wants a Ride* and *A Book About Your Skeleton*. These stories are typically

Figure 11.2 *Continued*   **Letter to Receiving School District**

read to him first and then he goes back through and retells the story. He has an excellent auditory memory and can repeat verbatim practically any Disney movie dialogue.

4.   Frank loves to use a single hole punch. We have allowed him to do this as it is good exercise for his hands.

5.   He likes books that play music and often brings them on the bus. We make him leave them on the bus for the ride home because he obsesses on them when he brings them into the classroom.

Bathroom Procedures

1.   When he goes to the bathroom, Frank usually wears headphones to mask the sounds.

2.   He is sent to the bathroom on schedule. The visual symbol must be on his schedule. He also uses a mini-visual schedule for the actual bathroom tasks.

   a.   Morning after breakfast. He uses the bathroom (urinates) and then washes his hands.

   b.   Before lunch. He uses the bathroom (urinates) and then washes his hands.

   c.   After lunch. He usually has a bowel movement. However, he must be told to go "poop." Say, "Frank, go poop in the pot." Note: *At the beginning of the year, he was having accidents on a daily basis. He has since taken some medicine which has helped his problem with diarrhea. He has also learned the routine of the bathroom. Now, Frank rarely has an accident. He has also learned to clean himself up which has been a big help.*

3.   He can now go and take care of himself, but he must have someone to watch him.

   a.   Make sure that he doesn't go into the hall without clothing.

   b.   Mirrors are distracting for him.

   c.   He always tucks the front of his shirt in under the button of his jeans.

   d.   If the jeans are tight, he may need help buttoning the jeans.

4.   His procedure.

   a.   Flush only one time. He used to obsess on flushing the toilet over and over, but now has learned to only flush one time.

   b.   He can only use one squirt of the liquid soap—but it should not be yellow.

   c.   He has been allowed to use two paper towels.

209

Figure 11.2 *Continued*   **Letter to Receiving School District**

Academics:

1.   Frank likes pictures of the teacher's family. Pictures of the teacher's family and his can be used for discussion and perhaps short sentence writing.

2.   He likes to listen to music on the cassette player. However, **do not allow him to do this activity with earphones plugged into the cassette player.**

3.   He does well with money tasks that are presented in the TEACCH format. We have used real money because we don't think that he can generalize or understand play money.

4.   Menus from local restaurants have been the basis of an interesting task for Frank. He selects his menu and then uses the calculator to determine how much his meal will cost. Ask his mother which restaurants they go to and get some menus from those locations. He loves tacos. Here, they often frequented Taco Bell.

5.   He likes to work with attribute shapes.

6.   His reading is about first grade level, but his comprehension and understanding are about the fourth grade level.

7.   In science, the teacher reads the main points in the chapter one or two times. Together, they summarize it on the computer, and Frank reads the simplified summary.

8.   Spelling. He is given a paper with three words. There will be seven or eight words at the bottom. He must circle his three spelling words. At other times, he copies his spelling words by typing them on the computer.

9.   Literature. Use second or third grade level books. The teacher reads them once. Then Frank reads or retells the story.

10.   He must have easy tasks interspersed with difficult work. For example, multiplication followed by some addition.

11.   He is working on telling time, but tends to stem on the hand of the clock.

12.   Science. The content of book is covered with Frank. He does one project per six weeks with the assistance of his teacher.

13.   He loves maps. His teacher got one of his town with a picture street map similar to some seen in textbooks. Frank quickly learned the location of local landmarks by using a map.

Figure 11.2 *Continued*   **Letter to Receiving School District**

Other Behavior Management Techniques:

A detailed behavior management plan is included as part of his IEP.

1. Tell Frank, "No, I will not tolerate that." Support your command with a visual cue by crossing your hands and then moving the hands to your side to give emphasis to the verbal instruction.

2. Tell him what to do two times and then make him do it. You may have to use physical prompts.

3. Frank has memorized the code of conduct and appears to relate his misbehavior with the code of conduct. This is being used as a reading lesson. When he misbehaves, he will sometimes repeat the parts of the code of conduct that are relevant to his misconduct.

4. If he begins to regurgitate, tell him to "swallow." That usually stops the behavior. If it does not, he must clean it up. If you tell him to swallow and he doesn't, he has immediate time-out for five minutes.

Things you should have available when Frank comes:

Kelli Vest (Large with extra set of 3/4 pound weights.)

Weighted Quilt (Moderate—use two weights or consult with OT

Bazooka gum

Chewing tubes (available from Preston or PDP Products. Check with your OT.)

Bean bag chair, large pillow, exercise bicycle, exercise trampoline

Swing on the playground

I hope that this information will be helpful to you. Please feel free to call me if you have additional questions.

Sincerely,

Beth Fouse, Ph.D.

Chapter Twelve
Common Mistakes Parents Make

Dragging Old Luggage

One of the most frequent mistakes parents make is not being able to forget previous incidents that have impacted them and their child. It is like heavy luggage they have to drag with them everywhere they go. Although their feelings may be justified, "old luggage" is not helpful in developing appropriate educational programs for the future.

CASE EXAMPLE

An example of "old luggage" occurred when I attended an IEP meeting at the request of a parent. Before we met at the school with the rest of the IEP team, the parent asked that I meet her at a small deli across from the school. When we met, she showed me papers from a previous teacher in a different school. She kept telling me how bad the teacher was with her child. Although I agreed that the comments on the papers were not appropriate, it was not relevant to the current situation because she was in a different school district and working with different people.

On arriving at the meeting, I found three other parent advocates attending at the request of the parent. The parent kept rehashing incidents that had occurred in another time and place. Finally, her advocates had to talk with her. Although affirming the impact of the previous situation on her feelings about schools and school personnel, the advocates emphasized it was not productive or relevant to continue to discuss the past. The purpose of the meeting was to discuss the future and develop an appropriate educational program for her daughter.

So, as hard as it is sometimes, parents should leave their "old luggage" behind. This is very difficult when past experiences have eroded any feelings of trust that may have existed. For the sake of the child, however, it is better if parents can leave their past experiences at home when they attend the IEP meeting.

Anger and Hostility

Another mistake frequently made by parents is attending the IEP meeting with anger and hostility. It is difficult to be rational and clear-thinking when energy is directed through a mist of anger. In one situation, when acting as mediator, the parent was so angry that she started yelling at the special education director about her child. I stopped her, and as calmly as I could, stated that we would not be able to continue the meeting if she could not calm down. She responded, "If she can talk about my child, I can talk about hers." Her anger was so great, she had forgotten that the purpose of the meeting was to discuss her child and the type of educational program development that was needed to best meet his needs.

Because of the parent's intense anger, mediation did not help, and the placement decision was referred to a hearing officer. This particular case was unusual because the school district requested residential placement and the parent requested a placement with more opportunities for social interaction between her child with autism and age-appropriate peers. By requesting residential placement, the school district admitted that their program could not appropriately meet the needs of this student. The hearing officer ruled in favor of the school district request for residential placement because it appeared there was no way for the school and parent to collaborate and cooperate to provide a structured, consistent program for school and home.

Signing Yes When You Really Mean No

Because parents are frequently anxious about the IEP meeting and sometimes intimidated or overwhelmed by the number of people attending the meeting, they are sometimes afraid to ask questions about the proposed program. They may also sign the document even though they really don't agree with some of the provisions listed within it. This is a major mistake. **Never** sign a document without reading it and agreeing with it.

Sometimes school districts ask parents to allow them to send a copy later instead of providing the parent with the written document at the meeting. I am aware of some circumstances where pertinent information was left off of the document. This occurred because the parent trusted the school staff to include everything that was discussed at the meeting. However, he did not read the IEP document, he just signed it.

As with any legal document, it is best to read it before you sign it. In one specific instance, the parent thought the child was going to be moved to another setting. When he received the actual document, the IEP stated that the school would *consider* another setting. When he asked about the proposed transition, he was told that the IEP committee only agreed to consider and discuss the change in placement. Another meeting would have to take place before

214

a move could be made. The moral of this IEP story is, *"Get it in writing before you read and sign the IEP document."*

Some of the wiser or less trusting parents that I work with insist that everything be completed before they sign the IEP. Last spring, one parent insisted on getting confirmation about special transportation from the school superintendent before she would sign the document. In other situations, additional information was added to the IEP in an effort to "clean it up" prior to sending a copy to the parent. Since the IEP document drives the educational program and is what the school is accountable for, parents must be sure they agree with what is written before signing it. If you don't agree, state your disagreement and discuss other available options with members of the IEP team.

A Baker's Dozen: Suggestions for Parents

1. **Set realistic expectations.** Don't expect to solve all of your child's problems at once. Target the most important areas and take a short list of desirable outcomes that can be accomplished. Make your list by writing down your child's accomplishments during the previous year. Make a list of your child's strengths. Be prepared to say some good things about your child.

2. **Act like the IEP meeting is a business meeting.** Communicate with school officials in writing and make a copy of everything that is submitted to the school. Use certified mail or hand-deliver important documents. I prefer certified mail with a return receipt because it provides you with written documentation of receipt of the article sent. It is recommended that the return receipt be attached to the copy of the letter which was sent. Request that you receive copies of assessments and the proposed IEP several days before the meeting so you will have time to review and analyze them prior to the meeting. Take the whole day off of work, if possible.

3. **Get some training. Know your rights.** The IEP process is a complicated task. Get some specific training in IEP planning. Learn the terminology. Learn appropriate methods and techniques for students with autism. Learn to distinguish between what is desirable and what is required by law. Hearing officers base decisions on what is legally mandated, not what is desired. Technical knowledge can make you feel more comfortable in the IEP meeting. When you know your rights, you can feel confident your requests are appropriate. Go to conferences and workshops. Read books and journals. Learn

everything you can about autism and the educational process.

4. **Be prepared. Do your homework.** Keep a notebook of all information related to your child. This will assist in remembering when certain things were requested, provided, or discussed. Keep copies of all assessments and IEPs in this notebook. This is your personal record of information about your child. It is helpful to compare last year's IEP with progress on goals for this year's IEP. Make copies of documents that you want to share with the committee.

5. **Take your notebook with you to the IEP meeting.** Most of the professionals in the room come in with their own stack of papers. Take your own "stack of stuff." It alerts the IEP team that you are knowledgeable about the IEP process. One school principal related a story about a new parent to the district meeting with the IEP team for the first time. He said she started with, "I hope you'll help me, I don't know much about this process." However, he told me, he immediately knew that she was much more knowledgeable than she admitted; she had brought a full, three-inch notebook of previous IEPs and assessments with her to the meeting.

    If you are not provided with a copy of an agenda or the proposed IEP, it is helpful to have the previous IEP to use as a guide for the discussion. Take a note pad with you for taking notes. Remember, that you can tape record the meeting if you wish. Some states require notice if you plan to tape record the meeting. Taking your own notebook and copies gives the impression that you are very well prepared for the meeting and plan to be an equal participant in the process.

6. **Document your perception of unaddressed needs; be prepared to discuss them** at the meeting. Be specific in your discussion of needs. Be prepared to present any evaluations from other professionals to the IEP team. Request in-home and parent training.

7. **Take someone with you to the IEP meeting.** You will not feel so outnumbered if you take someone with you. Be sure to discuss the meeting in advance so that you both have a clear understanding of your objectives. It should be noted, however, that the *IDEA Amendments* do address inviting other persons to the IEP meeting. Previously, parents or agencies could have other individuals as members of the IEP team at the discretion of the parents or agency. Under the new final regulations, "the IEP team may, at the discretion

of the parent or the agency, include 'other individuals who have knowledge or special expertise regarding the child (*Federal Register*, p. 12478).'" The final regulations go on to add that the determination as to whether an individual has knowledge or special expertise, within the meaning of the law, shall be made by the parent or public agency who has invited the person to be a member of the IEP team. Therefore, persons who attend with parents must now have knowledge of the child or special expertise regarding the child to become a part of the IEP team.

8. **Don't be intimidated or afraid to ask questions.** Don't let the educational backgrounds of the professional staff intimidate you. You are the parent and have a "degree" in knowing about your child. You are the expert on your child. If you have questions, ask them! You have a right to know. Express your feelings and communicate.

9. **Establish on-going relationships with school personnel.** You may be working with them for years! As the old saying goes, "You get more flies with honey than with vinegar." Discuss avenues of communication. How are you going to be informed about you child's progress? How should you communicate with your child's teacher(s)?

10. **Deal with feelings. Don't be afraid to show emotions.** It's okay to cry. Learn to deal with natural feelings of bitterness and anger. Recognize your anger and let go of it.

11. **Take care of yourself.** Avoid pity. Be a parent, not a martyr. There are times when you need to concentrate on your child's needs, but there are also times when you need to attend to your own needs.

12. **Remember this is your child.** It is your right to act in the child's best interest.

13. **Recognize that you are not alone.** Take time to nurture your marriage and friendships. Find a support group and become an active member.

**Consider the annual review as one of the most
important tasks you will participate in all year.**

Figure 12.1   Preparation Checklist for the IEP Meeting

___1.   Get and study all relevant information, including:
     ___A.   Assessments for
          ___(1)   Eligibility determination
          ___(2)   Performance levels and progress on goals/objectives
          ___(3)   Related services
     ___B.   Prior IEPs
     ___C.   Teacher progress notes

___2.   Make a list of your child's present levels of functioning in the following areas:
     ___A   Academic skills
     ___B.   Developmental skills
     ___C.   Communication, speech, and language development
     ___D.   Physical and motor skills (fine and gross motor)
     ___E.   Emotional/behavioral skills
     ___F.   Social skills/social interaction in school and home environment
     ___G.   Self-help/activities of daily living
     ___H.   Vocational or prevocational skills

___3.   Make a list of positive outcomes you would like to see for your child.
     ___A.   Develop annual goals from this list.
     ___B.   Ask yourself: Is each outcome or goal realistic?
     ___C.   Ask yourself: Will the goal help my child become more independent?

___4.   Make a list of special education and related services you believe are necessary for your child to receive educational benefit from special education.

___5.   Prepare your own information for the IEP meeting.
     ___A.   Document unassessed needs.
          ___(1)   Get letters or reports related to these needs from your child's pediatrician, therapists, & other professionals who know your child.
          ___(2)   Be sure that the letter include a description of your child's special need(s), its educational impact, and a "prescription" for needed services.
     ___B.   Develop short-term objectives.

___6.   Review your child's status. Cooperate with the agency's reasonable evaluation process. Find out if additional testing will be needed to discuss additional services.

___7.   Be sure that the IEP committee has accurate reports.

___8.   Work things out before the annual review. The best meeting is a short meeting. If you have questions to be resolved or issues of concern, try to work them out prior to the meeting.

___9.   If your state allows recording at IEP meetings, take your tape recorder to the meeting. Take several high quality tapes and extra batteries with you.

Figure 12. 2   The IEP Checklist

___1. Does the IEP include a review of any formal assessments that have been completed?

___2. Is there a determination of eligibility for special education?

___3. Does the IEP include statements of the child's levels of performance in appropriate areas including how the child's disability affects the child's involvement and progress in the general curriculum?
    ___A. Academic skills
    ___B. Developmental skills
    ___C. Communication, speech, and language development.
    ___D. Physical and motor skills (fine and gross motor)
    ___E. Emotional/behavioral skills.
    ___F. Social skills/social interaction in school and home environment
    ___G. Self-help/activities of daily living
    ___H. Vocational or prevocational skills

___4. For preschool children, as appropriate, does the IEP include a statement of how the disability affects the child's participation in appropriate activities?

___5. Does the IEP include annual goals for each special education instructional area and related service and short-term objectives and/or benchmarks for each goal?

___6. Does the IEP address access to the general education curriculum?

___7. Does the IEP include a statement of the special education and related services and supplementary aids and services to be provided to the child, or on behalf of the child?

___8. Does the IEP include a statement of the program modifications or supports for school personnel that will be provided for the child:
    ___A. To advance appropriately toward attaining the annual goals?
    ___B. To be involved and progress in the general curriculum in accordance with the law?
    ___C. To participate in extracurricular and other nonacademic activities?
    ___D. To be educated and participate with other children with disabilities and nondisabled children in the general curriculum and extracurricular and nonacademic activities?

___9. Does the IEP provide a statement of the extent, if any, to which the child will not participate with nondisabled children in the regular class and in extracurricular and nonacademic activities?

___10. Does the IEP include a statement of any individual modifications in the administration of state or district-wide assessments of student achievement that are needed in order for the child to participate in the assessment?

219

___11. If the IEP team determines that the child will not participate in a particular state or district-wide assessment of student achievement (or part of an assessment), does the IEP include a statement of:
    ___A. why that assessment is not appropriate for the child, and
    ___B. how the child will be assessed (an alternative assessment)?

___12. Does the IEP include the projected date for the beginning of the services and modifications described in the IEP?

___13. Does the IEP include the anticipated frequency, location, and duration of those services and modifications?

___14. Does the IEP include a statement of how the child's progress toward the annual goals specified in the IEP will be measured?

___15. Does the IEP include a statement of how the child's parents will be regularly informed of their child's progress toward annual goals and the extent to which that progress is sufficient to enable the child to achieve the goals by the end of the year?

___16. Does the IEP include a statement of transition service needs that focuses on the student's courses of study for students beginning at age fourteen and updated annually?

___17. Does the IEP include a statement of needed transition services for the student, including, if appropriate, a statement of the interagency responsibilities or any needed linkages?

___18. Does the IEP include a statement that the parents and student have been informed that rights will be transferred to the student on reaching the age of majority? This notification should be given at least one year before the student reaches the age of majority.

___19. If the student is graduating, has notice been provided to the student and parents?

___20. Does the IEP specify any Assistive Technology services or devices to be provided?

___21. Does the IEP include a behavior intervention plan with positive intervention strategies if the child's behavior impedes his or her learning or the learning of others?

___22. Does the IEP specify the position of person(s) responsible for delivery of services (i.e., the speech pathologist, instead of Miss Jones.)

___23. Did a regular education teacher participate in the development of the IEP in the IEP meeting?

___24 Does the IEP include signatures of each IEP team member, with written statements of area(s) of disagreement, if there were any?

Chapter 13
Resolving Differences
Beth Fouse and Jane Ann Morrison

Anytime two or more people interact together, there is a possibility for conflict (Kreidler, 1984, p. 14). Individuals' behaviors and reactions are based on multiple factors. Personal beliefs and values affect perceptions and behaviors (Slavin, 1991, p. 132). The behaviors exhibited by people faced with conflict determines whether the experience is constructive or destructive. Conflict escalates or de-escalates, but rarely remains unchanged. One goal of school personnel and parents at the Individualized Education Program (IEP) meeting should be de-escalation of conflict. Consequently, conflict resolution is a skill frequently needed because parents and school personnel may have differing opinions about what is best for the student.

Factors Impacting Conflict

The IEP meeting is fraught with potential for conflict. The larger the group, the greater the likelihood that different perspectives will be represented. Each person participating in the IEP meeting may have a slightly different perspective about decisions to be made. The behavior of IEP meeting participants reflects their own perceptions and ideas. Parents see the child's situation from their unique perspective and value system, while school staff view the circumstances from the context of the school (Schrumpf, Crawford, & Usadel, 1991).

Even within the school context, there can be disagreements and conflicts among personnel that create tension. Regular and special educators come from different perspectives. The impact of the child's placement on other students and teachers and the benefit of the entire class is often the perspective of regular educators and administrators. Administrators may also be influenced by budgeting constraints. Special educators may look at the child's educational program without considering the impact on others. Each individual has maximum development of the child as the primary goal. We must understand that individuals may differ in their perception of the appropriate or optimal program for the child (Fouse, Beidelman, & Morrison, 1994, 1995).

Controlling Anger

In order to control anger, it is necessary to recognize how individual personality types respond. The "hothead" erupts like a volcano. Here, anger is released and quickly subsides. The "tiger" enjoys anger and uses it as a catalyst for triggering emotions in others. "Tigers" believe that they can say and do anything as long as it is done under the guise of anger. The "smoldering charcoal" type becomes angry slowly. Once angered, these individuals are very slow to forgive and forget. The "acorn picker" goes along picking up acorns and saving them. The anger is stored little-by-little over a long period of time until it is released and all "acorns" are hurled at once. The released anger may have very little to do with what is currently under discussion; the source of the disagreement may be something that happened previously. Regardless of the anger type, each can be destructive to an IEP meeting (Tavris, 1989).

While creating discomfort for IEP team members, anger may justify and support the actions of parents and educators. In some instances, anger is a way for individuals to achieve their objectives. For others, it is seen as a way to gain respect or cause fear. It may even cause the individual to feel empowered or energized. For some, anger restores personal feelings of justice. In other situations, anger protects our beliefs and attitudes. Consequently, venting of anger may provide the release that some individuals need to feel adequate (DeFoore, 1991).

In order to effectively defuse anger in others, individuals must recognize their personal style of dealing with anger, and how others handle anger. It is most important for the effectiveness of the process to control anger. Research shows that the more an individual controls anger, the less angry the person feels (Tavris, 1989).

Conflict between school and home, staff and parents, is detrimental to the child. We must control our anger and not interpret negative comments as a personal affront. We must look at what is right for the individual child, and realize that conflict benefits no one.

Conflict Styles

The *Thomas-Kilmann Conflict Mode Instrument* (Houston Dispute Resolution Center, 1990, p. 82-92) identifies conflict styles that individuals use the majority of the time. The five conflict styles are competing, collaborating, compromising, avoiding, and accommodating. In varying circumstances, different conflict styles apply. In the IEP meeting, the ideal conflict style for all participants is "collaboration." Through collaboration, individuals disclose relevant information about their thoughts, feelings, and interests. They are able to separate people from the problem.

Ineffective Communication

Communication among members of the IEP team is extremely important. Perception of communication is more than "what" is said. Studies have shown that the nonverbal component of communication is more influential than the verbal component (Banbury & Hebert, 1992). Be aware of the messages that you are sending. Vital two-way communication involves active listening, self-expression skills, and joint problem-solving techniques.

Caring Confrontation

When conflicts occur, it is important that principles of caring confrontation be utilized (Fouse, Beidelman, & Morrison, 1994, 1995). Conflict is not necessarily negative (Concerned Teens, Inc., 1988). "Nature uses conflict as a primary motivator for change" (Crum, 1987, p. 31). Schools and parents must work together to provide appropriate education for children with autism throughout their public school experience. School staff might work with parents and children for eighteen years, from three to twenty-one. Therefore, establishing good working relationships that can be maintained even in the face of conflict benefits everyone.

Premises of Caring Confrontation

Caring confrontation requires that both parties make a commitment to nurture a healthy relationship. The premises of caring confrontation are (Veltman, 1980, p. 38):

1. We both have feelings, ideas, and needs that seem to be in conflict.
2. We need to look at this realistically, not with vision clouded by anger.
3. We care enough about preserving our relationship (and what we are working toward) to risk expressing our personal perception of the problem.
4. We have the ability to handle this conflict and reach a good solution.
5. We must be willing to negotiate; not retaliate.

Basic Guidelines for Caring Confrontation

1. Clearly state your needs, desires, and opinions in a nonthreatening manner (Veltman, 1980, p. 39).
2. Express acceptance of others' feelings and viewpoints.

3.   Stick to the issues.

4.   Actively listen to what is being said.

5.   Avoid interrupting others.

6.   If confrontation is inevitable, be sure that your position is legally defensible.

7.   Let go of the past and judge the present situation accurately (Veltman, 1980, p. 39).

8.   Recognize that individuals may be acting out of lack of information rather than a lack of caring.

9.   Treat each participant with respect and courtesy regarding viewpoints expressed.

10.   Use tact, diplomacy, and patience through the use of "I" messages.

11.   Recognize that both parents and school personnel are generally seeking what is best for the child—each from his or her own perspective.

Impasse Techniques

Highlight the investment of all participants. Brainstorm possible solutions. Identify tradeoffs that might be accepted to reach consensus. Ask individuals for specifics and summarize the areas of agreement. Acknowledge impasses by highlighting the alternatives when participants cannot reach agreement.

When extreme anger or emotion is exhibited by parents and/or school staff, it may be necessary to suggest a recess. Reschedule the meeting at a time when participants have "cooled down" and can talk more rationally.

Save the Relationship

There are times when conflict cannot be avoided; concentrate on the child and the issues, not personal relationships. Use caring confrontation techniques to avoid anger and hard feelings. Focus on the child's needs, not the personalities of adults involved. Recognize that differences can and do occur. Learn to move past differences to provide free appropriate educational programs for children with autism. Like a marriage, school and parents are wedded together for the child's school years. Learn the art of reconciliation and negotiation. The lives of all will be enriched.

Chapter Fourteen
Reflections on the Challenge

As stated at the beginning, the IEP process is complicated and technical. Prior to the implementation of *Public Law 94-142*, few students with autism attended public schools. I can remember only two students with disabilities attending high school with me during my own public school education. A very quiet, bright teenager sat in our classes and did whatever the teacher assigned her. She had a severe form of juvenile rheumatoid arthritis. To my knowledge, she had no learning difficulties or behavior problems. The other student had retrolental fibroplasia (RLF) which caused total blindness. This student appeared to be very bright and exhibited no behavior problems. He carried a portable typewriter and braille books from room to room so he could do his lessons.

It appeared that you had to have above-average intellectual ability and exhibit no problems other than physical disabilities to attend neighborhood public schools. All modifications were the parents' responsibility. As difficult as some situations are today, students with autism were generally not included in public schools a mere twenty-five years ago. The students that I taught were all placed in self-contained special education classes. Other students with special needs were not allowed to attend school at all. My first year in special education (before the implementation of *Public Law 94-142*), a co-teacher and I, sharing one teacher's aide, had twenty-two students with emotional disturbance or autism with three adults in two classrooms. These students taught me a lot in those years in that classroom.

In 1975, IEPs, if you could call them that, were one-half page long. Now, I regularly see IEPs from ten to twenty pages long. One high school student's special education eligibility folder is kept in four boxes!

We have come a long way since the time of limited services and student rights. The journey, although bumpy at times, seems to be heading in the right direction. Students with autism have a right to be in public schools, developing their talents in many ways. Some schools have wonderful, quality educational programs; others do not. If your child attends a program meeting minimum standards, you may have a struggle getting improvements in the school's program. Improvements will not happen if parents and special educators do not take the lead and push the doors open for children with autism now and children in the future.

It will be up to parents and professionals to see that we do not lose ground. We must actively support our children. Congress reauthorized *IDEA* by passing the *IDEA Amendments.* The final regulations for the amendments came out March 12, 1999. We must now wait and watch as we see how each state interprets the final regulations. Even with final regulations now available, several areas of the law and the regulations are still unclear. There will be court cases that will define more clearly certain areas of the law.

There continue to be threats in Congress to amend certain portions (behavior and discipline sections) of *IDEA* because of current concerns about school violence and safety in the nation. Many of the proposed amendments could result in students being denied an opportunity to a free appropriate public education. Most of these amendments have been defeated because of ever vigilant advocate groups that have mounted telephone and letter writing campaigns to defeat any amendments that endangered FAPE. We must be knowledgeable and aware of legislation and educational methodology related to students with autism

Be actively involved in your child's educational program. Be assertive in the quest for appropriate programs. The IEP is the vehicle for accountability in the education of students with autism. Learn the process. Ensure that your child receives needed educational services. If you feel overwhelmed, join a support group. Read a book. Be creative in getting the support that you and your family need. Just do not fail to be actively involved in your child's educational program.

Remember, the best educational programs are based upon individual needs. Appropriate assessments, well-developed goals, objectives, benchmarks, and necessary special and related services allow you to reach that star guiding you to a free appropriate public education.

A final review of the book's major points for empowering parents to be active, informed participants facilitating their child's educational program is provided on the last two pages. Both parents and educators must be team players collaborating for optimal student success.

Figure 14.1   **Educator's ABCs for IEPs**

A   Accept parents as they are.

B   Build relationships with parents.

C   Consider assistive technology needs.

D   Designate a rapport builder for the IEP meeting.

E   Encourage parents to actively participate in the development of the IEP.

F   Familiarize yourself with the needs of the student and his or her family.

G   Give parents opportunities to express opinions about their child.

H   Help parents understand the information presented.

I   Invite parents to be part of the IEP team.

J   Judge not, for you have not walked in their steps.

K   Know what educational options are available.

L   Listen to others' perspectives.

M   Make appropriate modifications and accommodations for the student.

N   Never say it can not be done.

O   Offer opportunities for parents to visit suggested programs.

P   Plan goals, objectives, and benchmarks from accurate assessment data.

Q   Question parents about their concerns and issues.

R   Remember, you may be working with this family for several years.

S   Show that you are a professional—control your anger.

T   Treat parents with respect.

U   Use understandable language—not educational jargon.

V   Validate parental involvement and input.

W   Win-win situations are best.

X   X-ray your own position.

Y   You must look at students' strengths and weaknesses.

Z   Zealously guard against win-lose or lose-lose situations.

> Parents need professionals,
>
> professionals need parents,
>
> and the children need us all.

Figure 14.2   **ABCs of Parent Empowerment for IEP Meetings**

A   Advocate for yourself and your child.

B   Bring your own "stack of stuff."

C   Control your anger; anger begets anger.

D   Develop long-range plans for your child.

E   Educate yourself about autism and your legal rights.

F   Find supports for you and your child.

G   Get involved in your child's educational program.

H   Help other parents to cope with the stresses of autism.

I   Initiate IEP meetings or discussions when you have concerns.

J   Jump into the discussion; don't be intimidated by professionals.

K   Know what you want for your child—work toward those goals.

L   Leave old luggage behind—what happened before should not impact the future.

M   Make lists of concerns, issues, and questions and take the lists with you.

N   Negotiate—don't form battle lines.

O   Open up and listen to other perspectives.

P   Plan longitudinally for your child.

Q   Question what you do not understand; do not be afraid to speak up.

R   Recognize the realities of the situation.

S   Summarize and restate major decisions of the IEP team.

T   Treat all parties with respect.

U   Understand that you have a right to express yourself.

V   Visualize your dreams for your child and work toward those dreams.

W   Welcome opportunities for interactions with the school.

X   eXpect the best.

Y   You are the key to a good program.

Z   Zeal can be an asset. Be zealous in your pursuit of a good program.

Parents need professionals,

professionals need parents,

and the children need us all.

References

ADDA (1996). The top 15 mistakes school districts make doing IEPs. *ADDA Newsletter.* 9 (1), 16.

Advocacy, Inc. (1991). New Hampshire federal court awards attorney's fees despite limited recovery. *Special EDition.* _6_ (4), 8-9.

Advocacy, Inc. (1993). OSEP "Clarifies" Medical v. school health services. *Special EDition.* _8_ (1), 14. (Coleman v. Hudson School District, 17 EHLR 889 [D.N.H., 1991])

American Psychiatric Association (1994). *Diagnostic and statistical manual of mental disorders. Fourth edition.* Washington, D. C.: APA.

Ahston-Shaeffer, C. (1996). The ART of leisure. *Disability Solutions.* 1 (1), 6-7.

Autism Society of America. (1994). Two recent decisions involving autism and individualized education plans. *The Advocate.* _26_ (3), 10-11.

Autism Society of America. (1995). What do I ask for? *The Advocate.* _27_ (4), 7.

Autism Society of America. (1998). What is autism? *The Advocate.* _31_ (4), 3

Banbury, M. M., & Hebert, C. R. (1992). Do you see what I mean? Body language in classroom interactions. *Teaching Exceptional Children,* _24_ (2), 34-38.

Bettleheim, B. (1967). *The empty fortress.* New York: Free Press.

Board of Educ. v. Rowley. 45 U. S. 176 (1982).

Boomer, L. W., & Garrison-Harrell, L. (1995). Legal issues concerning children with autism and pervasive developmental disabilities. *Behavioral Disorders.* 21 (1), 53-61.

Bossey, C. P. (1994). *A Review of the Texas Education Agency's Impartial Hearing Officer's Decisions in Autistic Cases form 1983 to 1994 and their Relevance to Public School Administrators.* Unpublished doctoral dissertation.

Carl, D., & Zabala, J. (Speakers). (1994). *What's the big idea? Legal and practical aspects of assistive technology in the IEP.* Handout from The 1994 TCEC Conference, March 4. Houston, Texas.

CEC (1990). *Fact sheet on ADA.* Reston, VA: CEC.

Clark, G. F. (1995). Special needs in the lunchroom. *Exceptional Parent.* March, p. 45-46.

Concerned Teens, Inc. (1988). *Conflict management training guide.* Houston: Concerned Teens, Inc.

Conderman, G., & Katsiyannis, A. (1996). State practices in serving individuals with autism. *Focus on Autism and Other Developmental Disabilities.* 11 (1), 29-36.

Crum, T. F. (1987). *The magic of conflict.* New York: A Touchstone Book, Simon & Schuster Inc.

Deling, E. M. & Nastaszczuk, M. (1996). Use of music to increase language/social skills with children with autism. *The 1996 Autism Society National Conference Proceedings.* Madison, WI: Omnipress, 284-286.

Diesback, S., & Jester, D. (1994). High functioning children with autism: Structuring for success in general education classrooms. *A New Dawn Awakening. 1994 Autism Society of America Conference.* Arlington, TX: Future Education, Inc.

Dixon, B. (1991). My dream IEP meeting. *Special EDition.* 6, (4), 19.

Donnelly, J., Grandin, T., Bovee, J., Miller, & McKean, T. (1996a). With a little help from my friends: People who have opened doors for me. *The 1996 Autism Society National Conference Proceedings.* Madison, WI: Omnipress, 7-14.

Donnelly, J., Grandin, T., Bovee, J., Miller, & McKean, T. (Speakers). (1996b). With a little help from my friends: People who have opened doors for me. (Cassette Recording No. ASA-601-96) EARS, P. O. Box 2200, Athens, TX, 75751; 1-800-782-7961.

Durkel, J. (1994). Related services: Direct versus consult. *P.S. News!!!* 6 (1), 15 - 16.

Edge, D. *The Exceptional Parent Blues.* Cassette Recording No. 050. Louisville, KY: The Learning House.

Family Education Rights and Privacy; Final Regulations FERPA. *Federal Register.* Monday, April 11, 1988. Part II. 34 CFR Part 99. V. 53. No. 60 p. 11942 - 11958.

Fouse, B., Beidelman, V., & Morrison, J. A. (1994). Conflict resolution for parents and teachers of gifted and talented students. *Gifted Child Today Magazine, 17* (6), 39-41.

Fouse, B., Beidelman, V., & Morrison, J. A. (1995). Keeping the peace with parents of the gifted. *The Education Digest.* 60(5), 37-40.

Fullerton, A.. (1996). Who are higher functioning young adults with autism? In Fullerton, A., Stratton, J., Coyne, P. & Gray, C., in *Higher functioning adolescents and young adults with autism.* (pp. 1-19). Austin, TX: Pro-Ed.

Gense, M., & Gense, D. J. (1995). Identifying autism in children with blindness and vision impairments. *The Advocate*. <u>27</u> (4), 7.

Graham, S. B. (1996). Related Services: Enabling students with disabilities to benefit from special education. *Texas School Administrators' Legal Digest,* 12, (2), 1-6.

Grandin, T. (1995). *Thinking in pictures*. New York: Doubleday.

Grandin, T., & Hart, C. (1993). Autism and personality: A review of the literature on subtypes. *1993 International Conference Proceedings (ASA)*. Arlington, TX: Future Education, Inc.

Grandin, T., & Scariano, M. M. (1986). *Emergence labeled Autistic*. Novato, CA: Arena Press.

Granite School District v. Shannon M. 18 IDELR 772 (D. UT 1992). reported in Advocacy, Inc. (1992). Federal district court rules that constant nursing care is not a related service. *Special EDition,* <u>7</u> (3), 8-9.

Gray, C. (1994) *The Social Story Book.* Arlington, TX: Future Education, Inc.

Hammill,D. D., Ammer, J. J., Cronin, M. E., Mandlebaum, L. H., & Quinby, S. S. (1987). *Quick-Score Achievement Test (Q-SAT)*. Austin, TX: Pro-Ed.

Hane, R. E. (Speaker). (1996). <u>On a clear day</u> (Cassette Recording No. ASA-667-96). EARS, P. O. Box 2200, Athens, TX, 75751; 1-800-782-7961.

Houston Dispute Resolution Center. *Mediation training.* Houston, TX: Houston Dispute Resolution Center.

Hutchison, K. (1995). Interview with Lorna Jean King. *The Advocate*. <u>27</u> (5), 18-19. (Interview conducted on April 2, 1995).

<u>Individuals with Disabilities Education Act of 1990.</u> *Federal Register*, <u>57</u>, (189), Sept. 29, 1992.

<u>Individuals with Disabilities Education Act of 1997.</u> *Federal Register*, <u>64</u>, (48), March 12, 1999.

Irving Independent School District V. Tatro. EHLR 555:551 (1984). 468 U.S. 883 (1994).

Johnson, (1994). Interview with Ivar Lovaas continued. *The Advocate*. 26 (6), 19-23.

Johnson, L. A. (1999). N. J. town might have unique cluster of autism. *USA Today,* Jan. 22, p. 10.

Kanner, L. (1943). Autistic disturbances of affective contact. *Nervous Child*, 2, 217-250.

Kreidler, W. J. (1984). *Creative conflict resolution.* Glenview, IL: Scott, Foresman and Co.

LDA (1995). A guide to Section 504: How it applies to students with learning disabilities and ADHD. *LDA Newsbriefs.* 313 (2), 14-15.

Lowe,S. (1994). *The IEP, residential placement and reimbursement for the student with autism..* Handout from The Texas Conference on Autism, July 15, 1994, Austin, Texas.

LRP Publications. (1992). Assistive technology devices may be required for home use. *Individuals with Disabilities Education Law Report. Highlights.* 18 (12), XIV-234. (Schrag, 18 IDELR 627 [OSEP 1991])

LRP Publications. (1994a). Annual review of IEP can be conducted at any time within the year. *Individuals with Disabilities Education Law Report. Highlights.* 20 (15), XIV-158.

LRP Publications. (1994b). Behavior disorders classroom was appropriate for child with autism. *Individuals with Disabilities Education Law Report. Highlights.* 20 (13), XIV-140. March 24. Baldwin County Bd. of Education, Muscogee County Bd. of Education., 20 IDELR 1020 (SEA GA 1994).

LRP Publications. (1994c). Notice/consent not required for tests measuring IEP progress. *Individuals with Disabilities Education Law Report. Highlights.* School Admin. Unit No. 29 [NH], 20 IDELR 1011, 1993.

LRP Publications. (1994d). Reimbursement awarded for private school/psychotherapy. *Individuals with Disabilities Education Law Report. Highlights.* 21 (4), XIV-35 - XIV-36. (21 IDELR 333 [SEA TX 1994])

LRP Publications. (1995a). Daily allotments of services in IEP not required, but preferred. *Individuals with Disabilities Education Law Report. Highlights.* 21 (16), XIV-147. Letter to Copenhaver, 21 IDELR 1183 OSEP 1994).

LRP Publications. (1995b) District was authorized to conduct occupations therapy assessment. *Individuals with Disabilities Education Law Report. Highlights.* 22 (4), XIV-41. Capistrano Unified School District, 22 IDELR377 (SEA CA 1994).

LRP Publications. (1995c). Improperly constituted IEP committee was not a denial of FAPE. *Individuals with Disabilities Education Law Report. Highlights.* 23 (2) Nov. 2, XIV-22.

LRP Publications. (1995d). IEP not required to include 5-day teacher training course. *Individuals with Disabilities Education Law Report. Highlights.* 22 (1) March 23, XIV-6.

LRP Publications. (1995e). Students missed full school day due to long bus rides. *Individuals with Disabilities Education Law Report. Highlights.* 22 (3) April 20., XIV-   128.

LRP Publications. (1995f). Supreme Court denies cert in two special education cases. *Individuals with Disabilities Education Law Report. Highlights.* 22 (9) July 27, XIV-105.

LRP Publications. (1996a) Regular education teachers must be informed about IEP content. *Individuals with Disabilities Education Law Report. Highlights.* 24 (2) , XIV-25, July 27. [Letter to Ellis, 24 IDELR 176 {OSEP 1996}. - p. XIV-25]).

LRP Publications. (1996b). Reimbursement awarded for costs of in-home, behavior therapy due to improper placement for child with autism. *Individuals with Disabilities Education Law Report. Highlights.* 23 (14) , XIV-174, May 30. (Capistrano Unified School District, 23 IDELR 1209 [SEA CA 1995]).

LRP Publications. (1996c). Use of "blanket wrapping" technique not a due process violation. *Individuals with Disabilities Education Law Report. Highlights.* 24 (2) , XIV-17 -XIV-18,July 27.

Lynch, E. W., & Hanson, M. J. (1992). Developing cross-cultural competence. A guide for working with young children and their families. Baltimore, MD: Paul H. Brookes Publishing Co.

McKean, T. (1994). *Soon will come the light. A view from inside the autism puzzle.* Arlington, TX: Future Education, Inc.

McKean, T. (1996). *Light on the horizon. "A deeper view from inside the autism puzzle."* Arlington, TX: Future Horizons, Inc.

McLoughlin, J. A. & Lewis, R. B. (1994). *Assessing special students. Fourth edition.* New York: Merrill.

McMahon, A. (1991). Is help on the horizon? *LDA Newsbriefs.* 26, (3), 5.

Martin, R. (1994). What the courts have said about inclusion. *LDA Newsbriefs.* 29 (3), 22-25.

Matthews, N. C. (1996). When must transportation be provided as a related service? *Texas School Administrators' Legal Digest.* 12 (2), 6-9.

Miller, S. R. S. (1993). Some insights into autism. *The Advocate.* 25 (4), 7-8.

Miller, S. (1996). Interpreting behaviors: An autistic review of the movies. *The 1996 Autism Society National Conference Proceedings.* Madison, WI: Omnipress, 303-306.

Moss, K. & Blaha, R. (1993). Looking at self-stimulation in the pursuit of leisure or I'm okay, you have a mannerism. *P. S. News!!!* 5 (3), 10-14.

NASDSE. (1999*). IDEA-Part B Final Regulations. Provisions of Special Interest to Parents.* March. (NASDSE Internet Site).

NICHCY. (1991). *The education of children and youth with special needs: What do the laws say?* 1 (1), 1-15. Reprinted as a special section in *LDA Newsbriefs*, Sept./Oct., 1991.

Nowak, M. Poster session. The effects of music on learning of children with autism. *The 1996 Autism Society National Conference Proceedings.* Madison, WI: Omnipress, 308-309.

Palomo, K. What is "in-home and parent training." *Autism Advocacy.* July, 4-5.

Parker, R. (1996). How can I help my son or daughter get that job? The job interview, the ADA, and the Rehabilitation Act. *Pacesetter*, June.

Partners Resource Network. (1996). Sensory integration therapy brings more OT requests to schools. *Pathways.* 9 (2), 2.

Patrick, (1996). An interview with Michael d. Powers, Psy. D. *The Advocate.* 28 (3),11-15.

Pratt, C. (1995). Book Review s *(Movement differences and diversity in autism/mental retardation: Appreciating and accommodating people with communication and behavior challenges* by Donnellan, A.m., & Leary, M.R. [1995]. Madison, WI: DRI Press). *The Advocate.* 27 (4), 25-26. the ADA, and the Rehabilitation Act. Pacesetter, June, 19.

Pratt, C. & Poro (1994). *Autism Matters,* Nov-Dec, p. 7.

Public Law 99-457. (99th Congress of the USA, S.2294; NICHCY, 1991, p. 9)

Public Law 99-457. Part II. Department of Education. Early Intervention Program for Infants and Toddlers with Handicaps: Final regulations. *Federal Register*, June 22, 1989, 54 (119), 26306 - 26346.

Schopler, E., & Mesibov, G. B. (1994). *Behavioral issues in autism.* New York: Plenum Press.

Schrumpf, F., Crawford, D., & Usadel H. C. (1991). *Peer mediation. Conflict resolution in schools.* Champaign, IL: Research Press Co.

Section 504. Rehabilitation Act of 1973. *Federal Register.* Friday, May 9, 1980. Part II. Department of Education. Establishment of Title 34. 45 (92). 30938-30955.

Siegel, B. (1996). *The world of the autistic child. Understanding and treating autistic spectrum disorders.* New York: Oxford University Press.

Slavin, R. E. (1991). *Educational psychology. Theory into practice.* Englewood Cliffs, NJ.

Smith, S. W. (1990). Comparison of individualized education programs (IEPs) of students with behavioral disorders and learning disabilities. *The Jl of Special Education*, <u>24</u>, 85-100.

Smith, S. W., Slattery, W. J. & Knopp, T. Y. (1993). Beyond the mandate: Developing individualized education programs that work for students with autism. *Focus on Autistic Behavior.* <u>8</u> (3), 1-15.

Stehli, A. (1991). *The sound of a miracle.* New York: Avon Books.

Stewart, R. (1995). A sensory Perspective on self-injurious behavior. *Autism Matters.* Summer, 9. (Reprinted from the Winter 95 issue of the *Indiana Resource Center for Autism Newsletter).*

Tavris, C. (1989). *Controlling anger.* An Audiocassette Seminar. Boulder, CO: Career Track Publications.

T-CASE. (1998). You can't know how far you've gone if you don't know where you started. *Special Report. Newsletter of the Texas Council of Administrators of Special Education.* p. 1,3-4. (Reprinted with permission from LRP publications, *The Special Educator.*)

Tsai, L. (1995). New diagnostic classification of autism and other pervasive developmental disorders. *Autism Matters.* Summer, 5. (Reprinted from the Winter 95 issue of the *Indiana Resource Center for Autism Newsletter).*

Twachtman, D. D. (1996). *Blinded by their strengths: The Topsy-turvy world of Asperger Syndrome.* The 1996 Autism Society National Conference Proceedings. Madison, WI: 182-184.

Veltman, J. (1980, February). In and out of anger - constructively. *Texas Outlook,* 38-39.

Volkmar, F. R., & Klin, A. (1994). Autism and Asperger Syndrome. *LDA Newsbriefs.* <u>29</u> (4), 8.

Walsh, J. (1988, January). *Ten rules for the ARD meeting.* Paper presented at the annual mid-winter conference of the Texas Council of Administrators in Special Education, Austin, TX.

Walsh, J. (1992, March). *Diagnosticians and the law.* Paper presented at the annual meeting of the Texas Educational Diagnosticians, San Antonio, TX.

Walsh, J. (1993a). So What Can the Regular Ed Teacher Do? *This just in. Developments in Special Education Law.* No. 45, December, p. 2.

Walsh, J. (1993b). Stop the presses!!! Regular ed teacher held liable for damages!!! *This just in.Developments in Special Education Law.* No. 45, December. 1-2.

Walsh, J. (1994a). I suppose you're wondering why I called this meeting. *This just in. . Developments in Special Education Law.* No. 53, August.

Walsh, J. (1994b). LRE case goes to parents: Residential placement denied. *This just in. . Developments in Special Education Law.* No. 47, February.

Walsh, J. (1994c). Parents have "Meaningful Input" but not veto power. *This just in. . Developments in Special Education Law.* No. 46, January.

Walsh, J. (1994d). Please Make my Home Accessible. *This just in. Developments in Special Education Law* No. 53, August.

Walsh, J. (1994e). School Wins Reimbursement case: It can be done. *This just in. . Developments in Special Education Law.* No. 46, January.

Wilbarger, P., & Wilbarger, J. L. (1991). *Sensory defensiveness in children, age two to twelve: An intervention guide for parents and other caretakers.* Santa Barbara, CA: Avanti Educational Programs.

Williams, D. (1992). *Nobody nowhere. The extraordinary autobiography of an autistic.* New York: Times Books.

Williams, D. (1994). *Somebody somewhere. Breaking free from the world of autism.* New York: Times Books.

Williams, D. (1996). Autism. *An inside-out approach.* Bristol, PA: Jessica Kingsley Publishers.

Williams, K. (1995). Understanding the student with Asperger Syndrome: Guidelines for teachers. *Focus on Autistic Behavior. 10,* (2), 9-16.

Wolfe, P. S., & Harriott, W. A. (1998). The reauthorization of the Individuals with Disabilities Education Act (IDEA): What educators and parents should know. *Focus on Autism and Developmental Disabilities. 13,* (2), 88-93.

Appendix A

Dictionary of Acronyms Used in Special Education

AACD	American Association for Counseling and Development
AACH	Association for the Care of Children's Health
AAFA	Asthmas and Allergy Foundation of America
AAMD	American Association on Mental Deficiency
AAMR	American Association of Mental Retardation
AAHPERD	American Alliance for Health, Physical Education, Recreation and Dance
AB	Adaptive Behavior
ABA	Applied Behavior Analysis
ACB	American Foundation for the Blind
AD	Asperger's Disorder
ADA	Americans with Disabilities Act
ADD	Attention Deficit Disorder
ADDA	Attention Deficit Disorders Association
ADHD	Attention Deficit Hyperactivity Disorder
ADL	Activities of Daily Living
AE	Age Equivalent
AEA	Area Education Agency
AEP	Alternative Educational Program
AFB	American Foundation for the Blind
AFT	American Federation of Teachers
	AFT Teachers' Network for Education of the Handicapped
AIT	Auditory Integration Training
ALA	American Lung Association
AMA	American Medical Association
ANI	Autism International Network
AOI	Accent on Information (on products and assistive technology devices)
AOTA	American Occupational Therapy Association
APA	American Psychological Association

APE	Adapted Physical Education
ARC	Association for Retarded Citizens of the United States, now renamed The Arc.
ARC	Admission and Release Committee
ARD	Admission, Review, and Dismissal (Texas terminology for the IEP team)
ARRI	Autism Research Review International
AS	Asperger's Syndrome
ASA	Autism Society of America
ASE	Alternative Sheltered Employment
ASHA	American Speech, Language and Hearing Association
AT	Assistive Technology
AU	Autistic/Autism
AUD	Audiologist
Aud Dis	Auditory Discrimination
BD	Behavior Disorders
BESB	Board of Education and Services for the Blind
BIP	Behavior Intervention Plan
BMP	Behavior Management Plan
BRS	Bureau of Rehabilitation Services
CA	Chronological Age
CBA	Curriculum Based Assessment
CCBD	Council for Children with Behavior Disorders (A Division of CEC)
CCP	Comprehensive Care Program
CD	Communication Disorders
CEC	Council for Exceptional Children
CF	Cystic Fibrosis
CFR	Code of Federal Regulations
CHADD	Children and Adults with Attention Deficit Disorders
CIA	Comprehensive Individual Assessment
CIDC	Chronically Ill and Dependent Children
CIE	Community Integrated Employment
CLASS	Community Living Assistance and Support Services

CLD	Council for Learning Disabilities
COP	Change of Placement
COSAC	Center for Outreach and Services for the Autism Community
CP	Cerebral Palsy
CPI	Crisis Prevention Institute
CRC	Curriculum Resource Consultant
CSE	Committee on Special Education
CST	Child Study Team
CTRS	Certified Therapeutic Recreation Specialists
DAHS	Day and Activity Health Services
DAP	Draw a Person Test
Db	Decibel (a hearing measurement)
D-B	Deaf-Blind
DCCD	Division for Children with Communication Disorders (A Division of CEC)
DCDT	Division on Career Development and Transition (A Division of CEC)
DCF	Department of Children and Families
DCLD	Division for Children and Adults with Learning Disablities (A Division of CEC)
DD	Developmental Disability
DEC	Division for Early Childhood (A Division of CEC)
DIS	Designated Instruction and Services (California)
DHH	Department of Health and Hospitals (Louisiana)
DMH	Department of Mental Health
DMR	Department of Mental Retardation
DPHAS	Department of Public Health and Addiction Services
DPRS	Department of Protective and Regulatory Services
DRI	Differential Reinforcement of Incompatible Behaviors
DRO	Differential Reinforcement of Other Behaviors
DSM-IV	Diagnostic and Statistical Manual of Mental Disorders, Fourth Edition
DTF	Discrete Trial Format
DVH	Division for Visually Handicapped (DVH)
ECH	Early Childhood for the Handicapped

ECI	Early Childhood Intervention
ECN	Early Childhood Network
ECSE	Early Childhood Special Education
ED	Emotional Disturbance
ED	Education Department (Federal)
Ed. Diag.	Educational Diagnostician (a person who assesses students in some states)
EEG	Electroencephalogram
EH	Educationally Handicapped
EHA-B	Education of the Handicapped Act - Part B
EI	Emotionally Impaired
EIP	Early Intervention Project
EMI	Educable Mentally Impaired
EMR	Educable Mentally Retarded
EPSDT	Early and Periodic Screening, Diagnosis, and Treatment
ERIC	Education Resources Information Center
ERS	Extended Rehabilitation Services
ESC	Education Service Center - an intermediate education agency
ESY	Extended School Year
EYS	Extended Year Services
EYSE	Extended Year Special Education
FAB	Functional Analysis of Behavior
FAE	Fetal Alcohol Effects
FAPE	Free Appropriate Education
FAS	Fetal Alcohol Syndrome
FBA	Functional Behavioral Analysis
FC	Facilitated Communication
FERPA	Family Educational Rights and Privacy Act (or the Buckley Amendment)
FISH	Foundation for Science and the Handicapped, Inc.
fq	Frequency range (used in hearing exams)
FY	Fiscal Year
GT	Gifted and Talented

HCS	Home and Community-Based Services Program
HHSC	Health and Human Services Commission
HI	Hearing Impairment
HRC	Human Rights Committee
Hz	Hertz (refers to measurement used in hearing exams)
IAES	Interim Alternative Educational Setting
ICFMR	Intermediate Care Facility for the Mentally Retarded
ICFMR/RC	Intermediate Care Facility for Individuals with a Related Condition
IDEA	Individuals with Disabilities Education Act
IEE	Independent Educational Evaluation
IEP	Individual Educational Program or Individual Educational Plan
IEPC	Individual Educational Planning Committee
IEU	Intermediate Educational Unit
IFSP	Individual Family Service Plan
IHFS	In-Home and Family Support Plan
IHO	Impartial Hearing Officer
IHP	Individualized Habilitation Plan
ILRU	Independent Living Research Utilization Project (ILRU)
IQ	Intelligence Quotient
ITP	Individual Transition Plan
KABC	Kaufman Assessment Battery for Children
KAIT	Kaufman Adolescent and Adult Intelligence Test
K-BIT	Kaufman Brief Intelligence Tests
LA	Learning Aptitude
LAC	Local Advisory Committee
LD	Learning Disability
LDA	Learning Disabilities Association
LEA	Local Education Agency (i.e., the local school district)
LEP	Limited English Proficiency
LPR	Local Percentile Rank
LRE	Least Restrictive Environment

MA	Mental Age
MAAP	More Advanced Autistic People
MD	Manifestation Determination
MD	Muscular Dystrophy
MDA	Muscular Dystrophy Association
MDCP	Medically Dependent Children's Program
MDT	Multidisciplinary Team
MET	Multidisciplinary Evaluation Team
MHA	Mental Health Authority
MH	Multiple Handicaps
MHMR	Mental Health and Mental Retardation
MOD	March of Dimes Birth Defects Foundation
MR	Mental Retardation
MRA	Mental Retardation Authority
MRDD	Mental Retardation and Developmental Disablities
MRDD	Division of Mental Retardation and Developmental Disabilities (A Division of CEC)
MRI	Magnetic Resonance Imaging
MS	Multiple Sclerosis
MSW	Master Social Worker (indicates a master's degree)
MT	Music Therapy
NAHSA	National Council on Stuttering
NARIC	National Rehabilitation Information Center
NASB	National Association of School Boards
NASDSE	National Association of State Directors of Special Education
NASPAS	National Association of Protection and Advocacy Systems
NASSP	National Association of Secondary School Principals
NAVH	National Association for visually Handicapped
NBD	Neurobiological Disorders
NCEMMH	National Center on Educational Media and Materials for the Handicapped
NCLD	National Center for Learning Disabilities

NCOS	National Council on Stuttering
NDIC	National Diabetes Information Clearinghouse
NDSC	National Down Syndrome Congress
NDSS	National Down Syndrome Society
NEA	National Education Association
NFB	National Federation of the Blind
NICD	National Iinformation Center on Deafness
NICHCY	National Information Center for Children and Youth with Disabilities
NICODARD	National Information Center for Orphan Drugs and RareDiseases
NIMH	National Institute of Mental Health
NHIC	National Health Information Clearinghouse
NLS	National Library Service for the Blind and Physically Handicapped
NMHA	National Mental Health Association
NORD	National Organization for Rare Disorders
NPR	National Percentile Rank
NPRM	Notice of Proposed Rulemaking
O & M	Orientation and Mobility Specialist
OBRA	Omnibus Budget Reconciliation Act of 1987
OCD	Obsessive Compulsive Disorder
OCR	Office of Civil Rights
ODD	Oppositional Defiant Disorder
ODS	Orton Dyslexia Society
OH	Orthopedic Handicap
OHI	Other Health Impaired
OSEP	Office of Special Education Programs
OSERS	Office of Special Education Rehabilitative Services
OT	Occupational Therapist
OTR	Occupational Therapist, Registered
OTR/L	Occupational Therapists, Registered, Licensed
P & A	Protection and Advocacy
PAC	Parent Advisory Committee

PACE	Program of All-inclusive Care for the Elderly
PACER	Parent Advocacy Colatition for Educational Rights
PARC	Pennsylvania Association for Retarded Citizens
Part B	Refers to regulations for school-age students in IDEA
Part H	Refers to the Early Childhood portion of IDEA
PASSAR	Pre-Admission Screening and Annual Resident Review
PBA	Performance Based Assessment
PDD	Pervasive Developmental Disorder
PDD-NOS	Pervasive Developmental Disorder - Not Otherwise Specified
PDP	Procedural Due Process
PEP	Psychoeducational Profile
PET	Pupil Evaluation Team
PH	Physically Impaired
PHC	Pupils with Handicapping Conditions
PINS	Persons in Need of Supervision
PL	Public Law
PLEP	Present Levels of Educational Performance
PLOP	Present Levels of Performance
PMAB	Prevention and Management of Aggressive Behaviors
POHI	Physically or Otherwise Health Impaired
PPCD	Preschool Program for Children with Disabilities (replaces ECH)
PPI	Preprimary Impaired
PPT	Pupil Personnel Team
PPT	Planning and Placement Team
PPVD	Peabody Picture Vocabulary Test-Revised
PQ	Perceptual Quotient
PR	Percentile Rank
PRC	Peer Review Committee
PR/HRC	Peer Review/Human Rights Committee
PS	Partially Sighted
PSEN	Pupils with Special Educational Needs

Psych	Psychologist
Psy Assoc	Psychological Associate (a psychologist with a master's degree)
PT	Physical Therapist/Physical Therapy
PTA	Pure Tone Average (used with hearing exams)
PTA	Parent Teacher Association
RD	Rett's Disorder
PTI	Parent Training Information Center
RESC	Regional Education Service Center
RFSCC	Regional Family Service Coordination Center
RID	Registry of Interpreters for the Deaf, Inc.
RLA	Responsible Local Agency
RMT-BC	Registered Music Therapist - Board Certified
SAIT	Society for Auditory Integration Training
SAT	Student Assistance Team
S-B, IV	Stanford-Binet Intelligence Test, Fourth Edition
SBAA	Spina Bifida Association of America
SBOE	State Board of Education
SCANS	U. S. Secretary's Commissionon Achieving Necessary Skills
SDP	Substantive Due Process
SDS	Special Day Class
SEA	State Education Agency (i.e, Texas Education Agency)
§ 504	Section 504 (This is part of the Rehabilitation Act of 1973, civil rights
(Sec. 504)	legislation which prohibits discrimination because of age, gender or disability)
SED	Serious Emotional Disturbance
SEDC	Special Education Dissemination Center
SELPA	Special Education Local Plan Area
SEM	Socially and Emotionally Maladjusted
SERC	Special Education resource Center
SH	Speech Handicap
SI	Sensory Integration
SI	Speech Impairment

SIB	Self-injurious Behavior
SII	Sensory Integration International
SIT-R	Slosson Intelligence Test-Revised
SKIP	Sick Kids (Need) Involved People, Inc.
SLI	Speech and Language Impaired
SLP	Speech, Language Pathologist (formerly called a speech therapist)
SMI	Severely Mentally Impaired
SPH	Severe/Profound Handicaps
SRT	Speech Reception Threshold
SSDI	Social Security Disability Income
SSI	Supplemental Security Income
SSW	School Social Worker
STC	School to Career
STWP	School-to-Work Opportunities Act
STOMP	Specialized Training of Military Parents
SXI	Severely Multiply Impaired
TAPP	Technical Assistance for Parent Programs
TASH	Association for Persons with Severe Handicaps
TBI	Traumatic Brain Injury
TC	Teacher Consultant
TEACCH	Treatment and Education of Autistic and Communicatively Handicapped Children (The North Carolina Model)
TDD/TTY	Teletypewriting Device for the Deaf/Teletypewriter
TMI	Trainable Mentally Impaired
TMR	Trainable Mentally Retarded
TS	Tuberous Sclerosis
TS	Tourette Syndrome
TSA	Tourette Syndrome Association
TSLI	Teacher of Speech and Language Impaired
The Arc	Formerly The Association for Retarded Citizens (ARC)
UT	United Together

VATK	Visual-Auditory-Tactile-Kinesthetic
VI	Visual Impairment
Vis Dis	Visual Discrimination
Voc Ed	Vocational Education
WIAT	Wechsler Individual Achievement Test
WID	World Institute on Disability
WISC-III	Wechsler Intelligence Scales for Children, 3rd ed.
W-J	Woodcock Johnson (Psychoeducational Battery)
WRAT-R	Wide Range Achievement Test-Revised

Appendix B

Person First Language

When *Public Law 94-142* was reauthorized in 1990, the name was changed from *Education of the Handicapped Act* to *Individuals with Disabilities Education Act*. This change reflected the trend toward person first language which puts the person first and the disability last reflecting the opinion of many individuals that they are persons first. Their disability does not define them as a person. It is also recommended that you do not use initials such as MR or LD in your speech or your writing. This implies that the individual can be reduced to a set of initials. The use of "is" in "he is handicapped" connotes that the "handicap" is equal to the person just as "is" in mathematical equations indicates equality ($2 + 3 = $ [is] 5). Use emotional neutral language; avoid using language that elicits pity such as "suffering from" or "victim of." Use of person first language reduces your chances of offending people. Use the following suggestions to make person first language a habit in your daily speech.

Do . . .

emphasize individuals by saying
    "individuals with" or
    "children with"

emphasize the person rather
    than the disability

Say. . .

child, children, students, or
    individuals with . . .
        disabilities
        autism
        mental retardation
        a hearing impairment
        a visual impairment
        mental illness
        an emotional disturbance
        a seizure disorder
        learning disabilities
        cerebral palsy
child who
        uses a wheelchair
        walks with crutches/braces

Don't say . . .

He is autistic
the disabled man or autistic child
John is retarded. Joey is a retardate
Susan is deaf or the deaf girl
the mentally ill man
the epileptic woman
Becky is a slow learner. She is LD
She is MR
Doug is cerebral palsied
Look at that CP child
Bob is crippled
He is afflicted with autism
Sam is blind or the blind man
Josh is wheelchair bound
Jerry is one of my cases
He suffers from autism

Remember. . .

Children may have labels for student eligibility purposes, but don't let the labels define the person.

If you can use the person's name without a label, **just use his or her name.**

Appendix C

Sample Letters

Letter Requesting Initial Comprehensive Individual Assessment

(Date)

Special Education Director or Principal
Position of Person Named on Previous Line
Name of School
Address of School

Re: Request for Comprehensive Assessment for (name of student)

Dear Mr(s) (Name of Principal/Sp. Ed. Director):

I am writing to officially request a comprehensive individual assessment for my child. (Name of student) is three-years-old. I am concerned about his developmental progress. His language is limited to some sounds and a few words. He is not toilet-trained, and he withdraws from other children when they visit. I suspect that he/she may have a disability. Therefore, would you please inform me as to the appropriate procedures for requesting a comprehensive individual assessment to determine the presence or absence of a disability? I understand that there is a timeline of ____ days from your receipt my letter for the assessment to be completed.

Sincerely,

Your name
Your address
Your telephone number

Send all correspondence by certified mail with a return receipt for your personal documentation. You may wish to send a copy by certified mail, return receipt, to the superintendent of your school district.

Letter Requesting Records from School

(Date)

Principal or Special Education Director
Position of Person Named on Previous Line
Name of School
Address of School

Re: Request for School Records

Dear Mr(s) (Name of Principal/Sp. Ed. Director):

I am (student's name)'s (mother/father). He has been a special education student at (name of school) for the past two years. He is in Mr(s) (teacher's name)'s class. Would you please send me a written list of the types and locations of all education records that are collected, maintained, or used for my child, (student's name)? Please include the location of his permanent school file and special education eligibility records. Please describe the school district procedures for examining his/her records. I understand, according to the *Family Education Rights and Privacy Act,* that I may obtain a copy of any of his or her records..

Thank you for your assistance. I look forward to hearing from you soon. If there is anything that I can do to facilitate this request for records, please contact me.

Sincerely,

Your name
Your address
Your telephone number

Send all correspondence by certified mail with a return receipt for your personal documentation. You may wish to send a copy by certified mail, return receipt, to the superintendent of your school district.

Letter Requesting a Change in Your Child's Records

(Date)

Principal/Special Education Director
Position of Person Named on Previous Line
Name of School
Address of School

Re: Request for a Change in my Child's School Records

Dear Mr(s) (Name of Principal/Sp. Ed. Director):

I am (student's name)'s (mother/father). S/he is currently placed in (teacher's name)'s special education class for half of the day. I just reviewed the written report of assessment completed by (assessment personnel/related services personnel). As you may remember, I requested an occupational therapy evaluation at his last IEP meeting. I believe that his sensory dysfunctions impede his educational progress to such an extent that he would benefit from the provision of occupational therapy.

After reviewing this report, I am concerned about some of the statements made by (occupational therapist). Her interpretation of some of his behaviors indicates a lack of understanding of autism. I request that you change my child's occupational therapy records so that they will no longer be inaccurate.

If you have further questions about my concerns, I will be glad to discuss these concerns with you. I do appreciate your assistance in this matter. You have always been very helpful. I look forward to hearing from you soon.

Sincerely ,

Your name
Your address
Your telephone number

Send all correspondence by certified mail with a return receipt for your personal documentation. You may wish to send a copy by certified mail, return receipt, to the superintendent of your school district.

Letter Requesting Additional Testing

(Date)

Principal/Special Education Director
Position of Person Named on Previous Line
Name of School
Address of School

Re: Request for Additional Testing

Dear Mr(s) (Name of Principal/Sp. Ed. Director):

I am (student's name)'s (mother/father). S/he is currently placed in Mr(s). (teacher's name)'s classroom. I have just reviewed the written report of the comprehensive individual assessment completed by multidisciplinary assessment team last week. I have studied this assessment report and feel that it is incomplete. The current assessment of performance levels do not address his/her needs. A grade level score does not tell me what s/he can and cannot do. Some major areas of assessment were not addressed at all. One of my child's major areas of difficulty, social interaction with others, was not addressed at all. Language was only addressed in the setting of a test situation. I believe that communication is a most important skill for my child to learn, and current functioning levels should be assessed in natural environments, such as the community, home, and classroom.

I would like to have these remaining assessments completed before we meet for her IEP meeting because I believe that they are critical to the appropriate development of goals and objectives. Please notify me as to the school's plans for further assessment. I understand that I should receive formal, written notice if the school district chooses to refuse my request for further assessment. If you have further questions about my concerns, I will be glad to discuss these concerns with you. I look forward to hearing from you when the assessment information is complete so we can schedule the annual review of his/her IEP.

Sincerely ,

Your name
Your address
Your telephone number

Send all correspondence by certified mail with a return receipt for your personal documentation. You may wish to send a copy by certified mail, return receipt, to the superintendent of your school district.

Letter Requesting an Independent Evaluation

(Date)

Principal/Special Education Director
Position of Person Named on Previous Line
Name of School
Address of School

Re: Request for an Independent Educational Evaluation

Dear Mr(s) (Name of Principal/Sp. Ed. Director):

I have just reviewed the recently completed comprehensive individual assessment for my child, (student's name) After studying this assessment report, I have major concerns about the interpretations and recommendations. Therefore, I am requesting an independent educational evaluation.

Please inform me in writing about necessary criteria under which the independent assessment must be conducted. Include the criteria the school uses in its assessment. Also, please provide information as to where I may obtain an independent educational evaluation for my child.

I understand that independent educational evaluations are provided at public expense unless the school district requests a hearing to prove that the district assessment is appropriate. I will send you the results of the independent educational evaluation so that it may be considered in my child's IEP meeting.

Thank you for your help. Please schedule an IEP team meeting as soon as possible to consider this request. I look forward to hearing from you within ____ days as required by state and federal law.

Sincerely ,

Your name
Your address
Your telephone number

Send all correspondence by certified mail with a return receipt for your personal documentation. You may wish to send a copy by certified mail, return receipt, to the superintendent of your school district.

Letter Requesting Review and Revision of the IEP

(Date)

Principal/Special Education Director, Position
Name of School
Address of School

Re: Request for Review and Revision of the IEP.

Dear Mr(s) (Name of Principal/Sp. Ed. Director):

My child, (student's name), is currently placed in Mr(s). (teacher's name)'s classroom. I have just reviewed his/her current IEP. It seems to be inappropriate for her/him. I am concerned about the repetition of so many objectives. My observations of her/him in the home indicate that s/he is capable of doing much more and at higher level skills than has been included in the IEP.

I would also like to see how the school is addressing access to the general education curriculum for my child. It does not appear that the current objectives and/or benchmarks will enable him/her to successfully attain the goals that were developed by the IEP team. Therefore, I request that a new IEP meeting be held to review her/his progress and develop new goals, objectives, and benchmarks. Please contact me so that a mutually agreeable time may be scheduled for the IEP meeting.

I look forward to hearing from you in regard to this matter. Thank you very much for your assistance.

Sincerely ,

Your name
Your address
Your telephone number

Send all correspondence by certified mail with a return receipt for your personal documentation. You may wish to send a copy by certified mail, return receipt, to the superintendent of your school district.

Letter Requesting Mediation

(Date)

State Education Agency
Complaints Resolution
SEA Address

Re: Request for Mediation

Dear (Head of SEA or Director of Special Education Program or Complaints):

I am writing this letter to request that the SEA furnish a mediator to settle my dispute with the (name of school district) concerning my child's special education program. I am very concerned about this dispute. I believe that my position is right. However, I am willing to negotiate in the hopes that mediation will resolve this disagreement so that I will not have to request a due process hearing.

Sincerely ,

Your name
Your address
Your telephone number

Send all correspondence by certified mail with a return receipt for your personal documentation. You may wish to send a copy by certified mail, return receipt, to the superintendent of your school district.

Letter Requesting an Impartial Due Process Hearing

(Date)

State Education Agency
Complaints Resolution
SEA Address

Re: Request for Impartial Due Process Hearing

Dear (Head of SEA or Director of Special Education Program or Complaints):

I wish to request an impartial due process hearing. I understand that the state education agency appoints the hearing officer. The purpose of this hearing is to challenge the appropriateness of the educational program that the (school district's name) is providing for my son/daughter. My child has been in special education for three years and this year's program is very inappropriate for the needs and present levels of functioning exhibited by my child.

The second paragraph should give specific examples of the inappropriateness of the child's educational program. Briefly describe the facts as specifically as possible. State how and why you disagree with the educational program currently being provided by your school district.

Sincerely ,

Your name
Your address
Your telephone number

Send all correspondence by certified mail with a return receipt for your personal documentation. You may wish to send a copy by certified mail, return receipt, to the superintendent of your school district.

Filing an OCR Complaint

Complaints to the Office of Civil Rights must be written and signed. Include your name, address, and telephone number. The Office of Civil Rights will not take action on oral allegations or anonymous complaints. Questions that seek advice and information are not considered to be complaints. Complaints seek action or intervention. In order for the Office of Civil Rights to assist you, you should provide the following information as you write your letter.

1. A signed, written explanation of what has happened.

2. A way to contact you, the complainant (name, address, and telephone number).

3. Identification of the person or group injured by the alleged discrimination.

4. Identification of the person or institution alleged to have discriminated.

5. Sufficient information to understand the factual bases for your belief that discrimination has occurred and when that discrimination occurred.

Complaints may be filed within 180 days from the date of the alleged discriminatory act.

The web site to get additional information from the internet is:

http://www.ed.gov/offices/OCR/ocregion.html

U. S. Department of Education (Office for Civil Rights)
Regional Enforcement Offices

Eastern Division

Serving: Connecticut, Maine, Massachusetts, New Hampshire, Rhode Island, Vermont
Office for Civil Rights, Boston Office
U. S. Dept. of Education
J. W. McCormack Post Office and Courthouse
Boston, MA 02109-4557
Voice Phone: (617) 223-9662   FAX: (617) 223-9669   TDD: (617) 223-9695
Email: OCR_Boston@ed.gov

Serving: New Jersey, New York, Puerto Rico, Virgin Islands
Office for Civil Rights, New York Office
U. S. Dept. of Education
75 Park Place, 14th Floor
New York, NY 10007-2146
Voice Phone: (212)-637-6466   FAX: (212) 264-3803   TDD: (212) 637-0478
Email: OCR_NewYork@ed.gov

Serving: Delaware, Maryland, Kentucky, Pennsylvania, West Virginia
Office for Civil Rights, Philadelphia Office
U. S. Dept. of Education
Wanamaker Building, Suite 515
100 Penn Square East
Philadelphia, PA 19107
Voice Phone: (215) 656-8541   FAX: (215) 656-8605   TDD: (215) 656-8604
Email: OCR_Philadelphia@ed.gov

Southern Division
Serving: Alabama, Florida, Georgia, South Carolina, Tennesse)
Office for Civil Rights, Atlanta Office
U. S. Dept. of Education
61 Forsyth St. S. W., Suite 19T70
Atlanta, GA 30303-3104
Voice Phone: (404) 562-6350   FAX: (404) 562-6455   TDD   (404) 331-7236
Email: OCR_Atlanta@ed.gov

Serving: Arkansas, Louisiana, New Mississippi, Oklahoma, Texas
Office for Civil Rights, Dallas Office
U. S. Dept. of Education
1999 Bryan Stree, Suite 2600
Dallas, TX 75201
Voice Phone: (214) 880-2459   FAX: (214) 880-3082   TDD: (214)880-2456
Email: OCR_Dallas@ed.gov

Serving: North Carolina, Virginia, Washington, DC
Office for Civil Rights, District of Columbia Office
U. S. Dept. of Education
1100 PA. Ave, N.W., Rm 316
P. O. Box 14620
Washington, D.C. 20044-4620
Email: OCR_DC@ed.gov

Midwestern Division
Serving: Illinois, Indiana, Minnesota, Wisconsin
Office for Civil Rights, Chicago Office
U. S. Dept. of Education
111 N. Canal Street, Suite 1053
Chicago, IL 60606-7204
Voice Phone: (312) 886-8434   FAX: (312) 353-4888   TDD: (312) 353-2540
Email: OCR_Chicago@ed.gov

Serving: Michigan and Ohio
Office for Civil Rights, Cleveland Office
U. S. Dept. of Education
600 Superior Avenue East
Bank One Center, Room 750
Cleveland, OH 44114-2611
Voice Phone: (216) 522-4970   FAX: (216) 522-2573   TDD: (216) 522-4944
Email: OCR_Cleveland@ed.gov

Serving: Iowa, Kansas, Missouri, Nebraska, North Dakota, South Dakota
Office for Civil Rights, Kansas City Office
U. S. Dept. of Education
10220 North Executive Hills Boulevard
8th Floor, 07-6010
Kansas City, MO 64153-1367
Voice Phone: (816) 4880-4200   FAX: (816) 891-0644   TDD: (816)-891-0582
Email: OCR_KansasCity@ed.gov

Western Division
Serving: Arizona, Colorado, Montana, New Mexico, Utah, Wyoming
Office for Civil Rights, Denver Office
U. S. Dept. of Education
Federal Building, Suite 310, 08-7010
1244 Speer Boulevard
Denver, CO 80204-3582
Voice Phone: (303) 884-5695   FAX: (303) 844-4303   TDD: (303) 844-3417
Email: OCR_Denver@ed.gov

Serving: California
Office for Civil Rights, San Francisco Office
U. S. Dept. of Education
Old Federal Building, 09-8010
50 United Nations Plaza, Room 239
San Francisco, CA 94102-4102
Voice Phone: (415) 556-4275   FAX: (415) 437-7783   TDD: (415) 437-7786
Email: OCR_SanFrancisco@ed.gov

*Serving: Alaska, Hawaii, Idaho, Nevada, Oregon, Washington, American Samoa, Guam, Trust
        Territory of the Pacific Islands*
Office for Civil Rights, Seattle Office
915 Second Avenue,
Room 3310, 10-9010
Seattle, WA 98174-1099
Voice Phone: (206) 220-7900   FAX: (206) 220-7887   TDD: (206) 220-7907
Email: OCR_Seattle@ed.gov

Glossary

Activities of daily living: usually include activities typically associated with self-help tasks, such as eating, dressing, and grooming; or domestic activities such as cooking, cleaning, etc.

Adaptive behavior: refers to the individual's ability to adjust to and apply new skills to other situations (i.e., different environments, tasks, objects, and people).

Adaptive functioning: sees how well the individual functions in the home environment and/or community in the areas of personal independence and social responsibility compared to the expectations for his age and cultural group.

Assistive technology device: special items or pieces of equipment that are used to increase, maintain, or improve the functioning abilities of students. The devices may be purchased commercially or developed, modified, or customized for a specific student. Commercially produced devices may include calculators, computers, pencil holders, food utensil holders, etc.

Brushing therapy: a special type of therapy developed by Patricia and Julia Willbarger designed for reducing tactile defensiveness by using a soft surgical brush to brush the arms, back, and legs of individuals who exhibit tactile defensiveness. The stomach should never be brushed, and this therapy should always be supervised by an occupational therapist or physical therapist trained in sensory integration therapy.

Central IEP meeting: an IEP meeting that is typically held after a campus-level meeting has been held and parents have requested a service that campus-level personnel did not have authority to consent to. Generally, a central IEP meeting will include central office administrators who have the authority to commit the resources of the school district.

Comprehensive individual assessment: a complete assessment of the individual's functioning. It should include assessments of all areas relevant to the individual's functioning and educational programming, including academics, related services, and home and school behaviors.

Community-based instruction: instruction that occurs in the community instead of on the school campus. Recreation/leisure, vocational, community, and domestic activities may take place in community settings. The advantage of this instruction is that the student learns skills in the natural context in which they are to be used.

Consultant therapy: a form of delivery of related services in which the related service provider (i.e., speech therapist, occupational therapist, etc.) acts as a consultant to the classroom teacher or other professionals to help meet a student's IEP goals and objectives. Generally, the classroom teacher works directly with the student, using the expertise and recommendations provided by the therapist in the natural context of the classroom.

Criterion-referenced assessments: evaluations that relate to specific criteria or objectives that have been established with specific indications for determination of mastery. The goals and objectives on an IEP can actually become the criteria that are referenced or evaluated. However, there are published assessment instruments that are formatted according to specific criterion or lists of objectives.

Curriculum based assessments: a specific curriculum or bank of objectives used to evaluate the functioning of an individual. Mastery, or lack or mastery, is determined by comparing the individual's functioning to the goals and objectives of a specific curriculum or evaluation instrument based upon a specific curriculum.

Direct therapy: provided when the therapist works directly with the child. It may occur in the classroom or in a pull-out program with the child going to another room for therapy.

Discrepancy analysis: a comparison of the individual's functioning and skills on a specific task to what is necessary to perform the task in a specific environment. The goal of the comparison is to determine the discrepancy between what the individual can do and what the individual needs to be able to do. The skills identified as lacking then become target objectives for the IEP.

Discrete trial format: a specific method of instruction in which a task is isolated and taught to an individual by repeatedly presenting the same task to the person. For example, the individual is given a red and blue block. The instructor will then repeatedly ask the individual to point to or pick up the "red" block. Responses are recorded for each trial (command). The individual generally continues to work on the specific task until mastery is demonstrated.

Domains: general areas of the individual's life. Most life skills programs divide major areas of individual functioning into functional academics, domestic, community, vocational, and recreation/leisure. Most activities, goals, and objectives can be categorized under one of these major life domains.

Due process: legal rights and guarantees that are provided to individuals and their parents. Due process provides recourse to students and parents when there are concerns about the school program provided for the individual.

Ecological analysis: analysis of an environment in which an individual is expected to perform. It involves determining the specific skills and/or tasks that an individual would need to function in the specific environment.

Educational jargon (educationalese): the use of terms that are specific to educational situations, which may not be commonly known, or used, by the lay public.

Expressive language: the language that the individual can use to communicate to others. Generally, when referring to oral expressive language, it indicates the individual's ability to express thoughts, feelings, wants, and desires through oral speech. Expressive language may also refer to gestures, signing, communicating through pictures and objects, and writing.

Free appropriate public education (FAPE): was first guaranteed to all students with a disability by Public Law 94-142. *IDEA* now ensures that students with a disability are provided an appropriate education at no cost to the student or parent through the provision of all educational services needed by the individual to benefit from the individualized educational program.

Formative procedure: a developing process that involves appropriate planning for future events.

Functional academics: academic skills that the individual needs to function as a contributing member of the community. Skills include such things as telling time, measurement, and basic money management.

Functional analysis (assessment) of behavior: a method of evaluating behaviors exhibited by an individual by carefully observing what happens before and after the behavior occurs. Specific behaviors are looked at in terms of the purposes of the behavior and what functions the behaviors are serving for the individual exhibiting the behavior.

Hypersensitivities: characteristics generally exhibited by individuals in relation to sensory input. Hypersensitivity to sound may indicate painful hearing at certain frequencies. Hypersensitivity to touch may result in the individual exhibiting tactile defensiveness because certain forms of touch are uncomfortable. Hypersensitivity to smell generally indicates more acute reactions to certain smells. In most cases, persons with hypersensitivities of the various senses exhibit more acute reactions to input from the sense involved.

Independent educational evaluation: an evaluation conducted by a professional not employed by the school district. Parents may pay for the evaluation or may request that the school district pay for the evaluation if the parents disagree with the school's evaluation.

Individualized instruction: instruction designed to meet the individual needs of the student. It does not necessarily mean one-on-one instruction. Individualized instruction may be provided in a one-on-one situation, a small group, or the complete class as long as the instruction is designed to meet the specific needs of the individual student.

Initial placement: the first time that a student is placed in a special education program in the public schools. This initial placement requires parental consent. Once consent is given, it is not required for continued placements in special education programs.

Integrated systems delivery: the delivery of services by a collaborative team that works together to meet the total needs of the student. This is opposed to a delivery of isolated services by various service providers where each is concerned only with their own specialty. Services are provided through a coordinated and integrated plan.

Joint compression: a technique used by occupational therapists in which various joints are "pushed together" to meet the need for deep pressure exhibited by many individuals with autism. Joint compression should only be used when carefully supervised by an occupational therapist.

Labeling: the procedure in which students are referred, evaluated, and identified as having a disability. The school must "label" or identify the student as having one of the disabilities specified in federal law in order for the individual to receive special education services.

Longitudinal planning: looks not only at the current needs of the individual, but also at the future needs of the individual as he or she moves into adulthood. Therefore, goals and objectives that the individual will need over time are prioritized and worked on.

Lovaas Method: an intensive behavioral therapy that requires a minimum of forty hours per week in one-on-one therapy. A discrete trial format is one technique used to provide the intensive behavioral therapy.

Methodology: refers to how goals and objectives are taught. Different methods may be used to teach an objective. Only goals and objectives are specified in the IEP, not the methods for teaching the goals and objectives. For example, language may be taught in discrete trial formats, other intensive behavioral methods, or in natural contexts, such as at snack time.

Minimum standards: standards specified by law as the basic levels of educational services. School programs must meet these "minimum standards." Although some schools may provide more than minimum standards, appropriateness of a program is evaluated according to minimum requirements specified in law.

Multidisciplinary team: an assessment team that has professional members from various disciplines (education, speech pathology, psychology, medicine, etc.) to evaluate the total child.

Neurobiological disorder: a disorder that has its origin in the neurological or biological functioning of the body.

Neuropsychological evaluation: an evaluation usually performed by a psychologist or psychiatrist that uses specific tests to evaluate neurological functioning known to be associated with various parts of the brain. The *Halstead Reitan* is one instrument commonly used in this type of evaluation.

Present levels of performance: the current level of functioning for the student in the areas of academic achievement; behavioral performance; social interaction and adaptation; prevocational and vocational skills; sensory and motor skills; self-help skills; and speech, language, and communication skills. Essentially, present levels of performance indicate the person's strengths and weaknesses or what the individual can and cannot do.

Proprioception: provides individuals with input that tells the brain when and how the muscles are contracting or stretching, and where each part of the body is and how it is moving.

Receptive language: the ability to understand what is being said, signed, or read.

Regression information: data gathered to determine the need or lack thereof for extended year services. The data is collected to determine how much regression or loss of skills the student exhibits over the course of the summer or other school vacation. This loss of skills is then considered in terms of how long the student takes to regain or "recoup" the lost skills.

Sensory defensiveness: a group of symptoms that are indicative of over reactions of our normal protective senses across sensory modalities. Individuals may exhibit patterns of avoidance, sensory seeking, fear, anxiety, and even aggression in reaction to certain sensory stimuli.

Sensory defensiveness therapy: therapy usually provided and supervised by occupational therapists designed to reduce sensory defensiveness in individuals.

Sensory diet: according to Patricia and Julia Willbarger, "an activity plan that includes specific activities designed to decrease sensory defensiveness. Timing, intensity, and sensory qualities of these activities are highlighted." Jumping on a trampoline or swinging are examples of activities that might be part of a sensory diet.

Sensory integration: the organization of sensory input for use by the individual. Parts of the nervous system work together through sensory integration so that an individual can effectively interact with the environment.

Sensory integrative dysfunctions (disorders): irregularities in brain functioning that make it difficult for the individual to integrate sensory input. Sensory integrative dysfunctions or disorders may be the basis for difficulties experienced by individuals with autism as they interpret the world around them.

Social skills: positive, appropriate, social behaviors that are generally considered as skills to be taught.

Standard scores: a generalized term used to refer to scores that have been transformed from raw scores and can be used to compare an individual's performance to that of a norm group. Grade level scores and percentiles are two forms of standard scores.

Surrogate parent: one is assigned to a student when the student's parent cannot be located. A surrogate parent acts in place of the parent by attending IEP meetings and acting as a representative for the student.

Tactile defensiveness: a sensory integrative dysfunction in which tactile sensations create discomfort for the individual with autism. Lightly touching the individual with autism may cause excessive emotional reactions or other behavior problems because of tactile defensiveness.

Task analysis: the process of breaking down learning tasks into small steps or individual skills so that each step or necessary skill of the task may be taught independently. The individual skills are then sequenced together so that the individual eventually learns to perform the complete task.

TEACCH: a structured teaching intervention developed by Division TEACCH of The University of North Carolina at Chapel Hill. The components of the program include: physical structure, schedules, individual work systems, visual structure, and routines.

Transitions: changes from one environment to another such as an early childhood program to a kindergarten or first grade class or a secondary program to the world of work. Transitions may also refer to changes from one activity to another. Transitions are typically very difficult for individuals with autism.

Transition to the world of work: a transition for which *IDEA 97* requires a special plan. According to federal law, an Individual Transition Plan (ITP) must be developed at the age of sixteen. The purpose is to prepare the student for the transition from school to the world or work at an early age so that the student acquires the skills necessary to successfully function in community environments. The individual and the parent are also introduced to adult service agencies that may be needed by the person.

Vestibular stimulation: used to stimulate the vestibular system, which provides us with our sense of movement and gravity. It tells us whether or not we are moving, how quickly we are moving, and in what direction we are moving. Swinging, spinning, and rocking provide the individual with vestibular stimulation.